Silence
and
Silences

Silence

and

Silences

Wallis
Wilde-Menozzi

FARRAR, STRAUS AND GIROUX

NEW YORK

Farrar, Straus and Giroux
120 Broadway, New York 10271

Grateful acknowledgement is made for permission to reprint
the following previously published material:
"As if the Sea should part" from *The Poems of Emily Dickinson: Reading Edition*,
edited by Ralph W. Franklin, Cambridge, Mass.: The Belknap Press of Harvard
University Press, Copyright © 1998, 1999 by the President and Fellows of Harvard
College. Copyright © 1951, 1955 by the President and Fellows of Harvard College.
Copyright © renewed 1979, 1983 by the President and Fellows of Harvard College.
Copyright © 1914, 1918, 1919, 1924, 1929, 1930, 1932, 1935, 1937, 1942 by Martha
Dickinson Bianchi. Copyright © 1952, 1957, 1958, 1963, 1965 by Mary L. Hampson.
Excerpt from "The Ship of Death" from *The Complete Poems of D. H. Lawrence* by
D. H. Lawrence, edited by Vivian de Sola Pinto and F. Warren Roberts, copyright
© 1964, 1971 by Angelo Ravagli and C. M. Weekley, Executors of the Estate of Frieda
Lawrence Ravagli. Used by permission of Viking Books, an imprint of Penguin
Publishing Group, a division of Penguin Random House LLC. All rights reserved.

Library of Congress Cataloging-in-Publication Data
Names: Wilde-Menozzi, Wallis, author.
Title: Silence and Silences / Wallis Wilde-Menozzi.
Description: First edition. | New York : Farrar, Straus and Giroux, 2021.
    Summary: "A meditation on the infinite search for meanings in silence
    from Wallis Wilde-Menozzi, the author of *The Other Side of the Tiber* and
    Mother Tongue" —Provided by publisher.
Identifiers: LCCN 2021032240 | ISBN 9780374226299 (hardcover)
Subjects: LCSH: Wilde-Menozzi, Wallis. | Silence. | Noise—Psychological
    aspects. | LCGFT: Memoirs.
Classification: LCC PS3563.E54 Z46 2021 | DDC 811/.54 [B]—dc23
LC record available at https://lccn.loc.gov/2021032240

Designed by Gretchen Achilles

Our books may be purchased in bulk for promotional,
educational, or business use. Please contact your local bookseller
or the Macmillan Corporate and Premium Sales Department
at 1-800-221-7945, extension 5442, or by email at
MacmillanSpecialMarkets@macmillan.com.

www.fsgbooks.com
www.twitter.com/fsgbooks • www.facebook.com/fsgbooks

1 3 5 7 9 10 8 6 4 2

For Lucia, whose blazing spirit showed us a new world in silence

I think we are blind, Blind but seeing, Blind people who can see, but do not see.

—JOSÉ SARAMAGO, *Blindness*

As if the Sea should part
And show a further sea—
And that—a further—and the Three
But a presumption be—

Of periods of Seas—
Unvisited of Shores—
Themselves the Verge of Seas to be—
Eternity—is Those—

—**EMILY DICKINSON**

There, near the reeds, it is possible to hear a flap displacing air, to feel the lift from personal self to bird to sky, from inside to outside, drawn to an instant of accelerating wings, where duality and words are pushed out.

—WWM

Silence
and
Silences

The Bronx River in Yonkers is a silt-brown color that rarely reflects the sky. The changes in its industrial tone appear when the surface is glassy, or when currents capture the surroundings, or when it is striped by lights falling from the hospital windows toward evening and dragged into waving orange ribbons. Today it is still, with pewter collars of ice along the edges. The man-made waterfall near the bike bridge is foaming with pollutants, gluey white, that attenuate as they bubble and break up downstream. It is dusk, but the sun is not visible. The few runners are mimetically absorbed in the gray ending to this January day. No birds are on the water.

I find myself here, not to do the lake, even by walking slowly. I want to look up. With runners checking their watches and wearing black gauges on their ankles, I see robots, in woolen hats. The fixed eyes of the joggers get on my nerves. We have become anxious people measuring ourselves.

I am here because I wanted to get out of our steam-heated apartment, to feel the wind, and, I admit, to look out of the corner of my eye for the white heron I saw late last summer on the day before I returned to Italy, where our house and work patiently wait.

Since Paolo, my Italian husband, and I returned to Bronxville for the holidays, the bird has been nowhere to be seen. Tonight, again, the elusive solitary is missing. It's almost my last chance, since in another week we turn back to our life in Italy.

Nothing in particular seems in touch with me, unless it is my wistful mood. The cars from the Bronx River Parkway are at my back, their lights on high beam. The sludge of commuter traffic has started. The petulant geese are gone for the night. Some evenings last summer as they spread out on the grass in the park and dozed, they reminded me of cows I'd come across in Italian villages. They'd faded into the dark, but their smell, their rustle, made them suddenly emerge as a phantom herd, all heads pointedly turning.

There is definite silence in this falling darkness. It is an atmosphere rather than an objective lack of sound. It is a withdrawal, while at the same time the cover is getting closer, far closer than the day ever seems. The closing-with-us-inside nudges nature's great loom. Silence rides not on the withdrawal of light but on its infiltration of the dark. Night is the tide, with darkness coming farther and farther in. When I manage to experience its approach, not from the tight frame of an apartment window or car, its shawl casts itself over my body. It holds me in peace, in spite of shifting movements in the dark.

Along the east bank of the river is a relic of a stone mill. Now it is little more than a ghostly suggestion of window frames in a wall. The plash of the river and then the whine of the water-driven engines were two different pitches defining this place. The sound of the metal blades hitting stone must have been deafening. The barely legible historical marker is a camouflaged whisper, while the signs for the police call boxes are large enough to convey menace. If they were of equal size, would we see past and present differently?

A melancholy question sits in my head, perhaps because I have not seen the heron and the crack in consciousness that I like to believe its appearance brings, perhaps because I am returning to Italy, perhaps because recent U.S. politics have been a reversal and deterioration of many patterns I like to count on as true. My question seems to be—where are we going?

Why I don't ask the question directly about myself is strange. It would be appropriate. But I seem to need to make some distinction and at the same time to claim a collectivity. I am part of this land, these woods, this destruction, and this system of government. We have gotten used to ignoble numbers; our scales for value, our measures for time are weirdly banal. We add numbers up and most often they lead us to money. Many calculations are too small, too self-interested, too shortsighted. Numbers are grocery bills, stock earnings, the surreal dollars and cents of guns. Bargains and good deals. Test scores. Costs from one side only. Numbers are "likes" and immigrants massing at borders. Just standing here, my idea of a few minutes of silence has been taken over.

I always had an inner life: after I moved to Parma forty years ago, the intensity of the unspoken changed dimensions, as if a new, broader, steeper slope leading underground was now part of my everyday identity and awareness. The eleventh-century duomo in Parma, constructed of stone, held the center of the life I crossed every day, majestic and unchanging. My U.S. roots: the red roofs of Stanford University in California, the pea-green soup of Lake Wissota in Wisconsin, the turquoise night sky of Grand Central Terminal in New York City churned, unanchored. In the early Parma years, I was a married tree, a rooted transplant, with disturbed underground systems spreading out to make connections wherever I could. Feeling invisible, I drew surprising conclusions from the effort to define roots of any significance. Women and time, science and religion stirred questions and comparisons arising from my new situation and the old assumptions.

I hear that silence and noise over and over in others. The resistance to telling stories that come from another place is palpable in the Nigerian women with eyes that dart and slide away like stones skipping across water, when they wind their way to a dusty room where I am holding a class for them as refugees in Parma, where they are safe to talk and write about what their names mean to them. The silence chokes them, it wells up and almost presses tears from their eyes while their lips stay closed. The intensity of the unspoken is down deep. They insist that they have no memories; they know nothing except that living on the streets in Nigeria was very hard.

My awareness of silence changed with my experience of changing languages and country, but this book will not linger on that development. Awareness of silence has grown far beyond words or myself. It is all around me and us. The spiritual dimension of silence can be like a shocking plunge into a glacial lake. If it continues, its enveloping presence makes us grow silent in fear and trembling. Sometimes I am a presence in it within myself. Putting that dimension of silence into words is a contradiction: it is the silence beyond all silences, the dark and light of transcendence. It is a search that began in the earliest rituals of human beings and continues: Stonehenge; Job; Saint Augustine; Joan of Arc; Ibn Arabi; Etty Hillesum; the mysteries of universes; the mysteries of love.

Instead, what drew me into imagining a book on silence, one in which I would use the first person in order to make it intimate enough to be believable, was a feeling that silence is a fear and a gift experienced by everyone alive. Mine is not a single point or point of view, nor an admonition that our world of cell phones and computers does not allow us to perceive or pursue it. Rather I wanted to make a tapestry of silences from the middle world: stories about how we think and how we think we know and how we continuously discover that we don't know.

I wanted to suggest silence as a life-force underlying our sense of freedom and extending to all of evolution—a space inside a plum pit, an ocean covering volcanos. I wanted women's silences, wordlessness through centuries and millennia, to appear in minute and exquisite detail. Their viewpoints, each voice, each story touching new ideas about what is real. Women's versions of things often start from omissions, events covered by shadows. But they more often signal silences about priorities, complexities, intimacy, and healing that will change what is ahead.

Reading a book is a way of withdrawing into silence. It is a way of seeing and listening, of pulling back from what is happening at that very moment. For me, the pause is a space where awareness finds silence. In the pause, silence may appear as a new color, or as a tiny seed, or as a revelation.

Recently reading Alberto Moravia's troubling novel *Agostino*, set in 1940s Italy, I sympathized with the American translator's dilemma about a character who was referred to stereotypically throughout the novel in Italian. The terms *moro* and *negro* were interchangeable with his name, Homs. In Italian, *moro* is a color, for hair brunet, for skin brown. It was also once used for a familiar figure, an Arab peddler. It would be highly unlikely that Homs was a young man with black skin, that is, an African American.

Using this as an example of the complex and significant choices to be made, if the term is translated as a Black man or African American, it is historically inaccurate and alters the book. Yet it makes the character seemingly more familiar to an American English reader, who imagines a different history. The terrain in the English edition modifies and dominates not only what might have been intended but will be overlooked because it is not recognized as valuable. Losses and gains are a challenge and a dilemma for anyone who enters words to find their equivalents in another place and time, with different social consciousness.

I learned, living in Parma, that in the twentieth century, most Italians had never seen a Black man in a village until African American soldiers, in nonintegrated units, appeared as U.S.

troops battled up the western coast of Italy in World War II. When Black Americans entered Italian village communities, the perception of African Americans as different was amplified because they were segregated in the U.S. military. Meanwhile, in the Apennines, Brazilians of all colors battled shoulder to shoulder in the same unit. Integrated Black Brazilians, from the first night their battalion swept through cramped streets among curious and frightened Italian villagers, were more apt to be accepted because the soldiers were seen as equally hungry, equally exhausted men, each of whom was offered a place at the table. Given human nature, separate but equal appears as a flawed legal concept before even speaking to its moral limits. Two different stories emerge from the silent shadows of that divide.

A closer translation of *Moro* might be imagined as a man physically like Meursault, a North African Arab, whom Albert Camus invented in *The Stranger*. Camus's North African also is touched in English by associations with Shakespeare's Moor in *Othello*. Making the choice is apparently not an earthshaking decision, especially now, most readers today would say. Much prose, even literary prose, has favored contemporary recognition over irreducible, historical textures. Yet small decisions in using languages add up to different impressions, destinations, and accumulated effects. Novels are intricate compositions that can be shredded and blurred.

In the Italian novel presenting the boy of color on the beach, whatever shade of skin we give him, as a literary character in 1940s Italy, he carries the burden of negative Western stereotypes and the negative implications of darkness. Rooted in the prejudices of a place and time, no translation can erase these shadows, nor take back the effects of those words. They loom, painful and ominous. However, not long ago, consciously or unconsciously, they were not spoken about. Now that implicit silence is challenged and filled with resistant and audible speech. The text remains, but the society reading the text can challenge it in new light.

There is such a thing as the right to remain silent. This refers not only to the legal protection not to incriminate yourself, but to a more personal need. Putting experience into words is to make something of it—and that means to let go of many of its subtle layers and complicated aspects. It means telling a story.

There are many motives for remaining silent.

The right to remain silent, in the way I intend it now, does not even vaguely refer to self-incrimination or story-making. It refers to feelings that are real. "The right to silence" in these instances is not a tactical defense, but a personal need to use silence as a treasured space to preserve something, absorb it, sort it through, offering speech only when the receiver has been identified as worthy of trust. The right to silence can be, in many instances, a cherishing. When I first started to write, it was a private thing. Written words were like breathing on a glass in an unheated room. Seeing the circle condense was a miracle that I would then smear and erase.

The decision not to let the world touch a precious essence, fearing or knowing that when it is passed on its intense wordless significance will be dissolved or distorted, holds important freedom. The decision to cherish was a common experience for me, in spite of the pull to tell, to share something good or something that shone on me. The desire to keep silent because there was no one to receive it without altering it was deep. I knew that my words rarely touched all the light that I often felt. I also knew that my mother might take what I said and, like a string of pearls, snatch it and watch it break.

As a kid during the Cold War in the late 1940s, keeping silent under torture was a narrative in our games. We twisted each other's arms to see if we were capable of resisting Communism. In our forts behind the garage, a few more years were needed to abandon such piety, learning that not only Communists tortured. "Keeping silent" gives various shadings to the word "nerve." "Nerve" means courage, pluck, temerity, transgression. "Nerves" can also mean anxiety. Making such distinctions were often pastimes on long summer days in the Midwest, when Scrabble might be the evening entertainment for an adolescent girl and her two brothers often cut off from their peers and hoping to reach, with an obscure word, a space with triple points.

The Sunday walk along the river in Parma has been skipped for a week. I have been in Geneva, teaching. I am curious to see what has changed. Rains have been heavy, thus instead of the dry June gravel bed with festoons of water here and there, the aquamarine flow of water is still abundantly powerful.

A friend has mentioned she is having dreams that are all about water. She sees waves, not terrifying, but strong, and there are large expanses, even water colored red. Dreams about water have been conventionally interpreted as a symbol of the unconscious. To borrow a thought from Virginia Woolf, dreams are a resource of "blue-gray silence." Without any limits, dreams appear and take over a waking state, revealing slits in what is in front of our eyes. Certain dreams give the sensation of a portent. Such singular dreams arrive with the same force as a sudden kiss in life or the pained look on an oncologist's face as she accepts telling the truth to a patient. In a powerful dream something is announced; often the information is already in motion, half present, declaring that something needs to be seen.

Two weeks ago, the grass along the riverbanks was cut. It had wrapped the pheasants in protection while the females were nesting. How rapidly it has grown back. The male pheasants are still here, red crests, white collars, spaced in the grass one hundred feet apart.

The new appearances are herons. White herons. Two in the water, with their distinctive way of pulling back their heads and, almost like a hinge, resting their trapezoid skulls on their necks. Another is fishing in white gravel. Going along the path, another heron, like a balloon losing air, hunches precariously in a tree. At first, I thought it was a torn plastic bag. Once Paolo identified it, the heron transformed in my mind into a slightly magical oddity, a benevolent, beady-eyed creature in a Bruegel painting.

Another two herons, like elegant vases, their necks extended, stand in the churning water, and water birds circle from river water to tree, while javelin swifts dip down and flip away. Suddenly a pheasant flies straight close to the ground, as if it were a flat Frisbee traveling at great speed. A hare leaps through the grass running as fast as the pheasant flew. The herons rise. A romping, unleashed dog explains the panic. Until it was let loose, all the river life was going on in its own way.

We've been back in Parma for a few months, unable to decide when to turn around to New York. I don't teach there until the spring. The Alps in the distance, the wide bowl of sky, the church bells banging in unison, with different iron and recorded clangs, make the moment seem coherent—a scene, something captured in pleasant bucolic engravings hundreds of years ago and now sold as inexpensive mantel-sized reproductions to tourists here. Only the most superficial glance would say the panorama hasn't changed from when the engravings were conceived. But the mind is satisfied by the outlines of the river and the buildings following its curves; it can say of the fairy-tale city in the print, I've been there. Memory erases and without any particular reason embraces what pleases it.

Every form of art gives space to silence.

Painting describes it.

Music uses it for what precedes the first note and follows the last. Notes mark what would otherwise be silence.

It is the primary material required for concentration.

Silences hold the most obvious places to look for hypotheses in science.

Silence echoes everywhere on the longest, most worn paths to God.

P*ling. Pling.*
        Pling.
        Paolo forgot his smartphone, leaving it on my desk. The clever engineers who designed the sound for alerting users about the arrival of emails made the note an eyelash longer than a single beat. The sound he elected is not alarming, not hectoring. It plays into my attention.

Soft single sound.

Each *pling* enlarges a sense of curiosity—of wanting to know what's been left on the phone.

Pendulous sliding drop.

The depth of the word "unknown," which was beginning to unfold in relation to silence on the preceding page, is dissolving in the fusillade of unread messages.

Making a list of silences is not how I want to make vivid what I wish to convey. A list moves too fast, it compacts too many generalizations. Any person could make such a list.

I don't want to suggest to a reader that she can master silence or sort through its contents and move on, as if silence were a logical argument or a prescription that in five steps will change your life.

Silence takes time to notice. I want to create the sense of

pling myself, to offer small alerts or awakenings. I want to develop, in stories and non-stories, the missing, the assumed, the forgotten and unremarkable, the world with its infinite trapdoors covering the hidden. What follows then might become an entirely different dimension.

When my neighbor in Parma began losing her ten-year fight with breast cancer, I volunteered to be part of the group helping her to die at home. Every morning as the doctor and nurses came, crowding in the hall, cramming into the bathroom to wash their hands before measuring her temperature, blood pressure, before giving the morphine and washing her, I came to massage her feet. No matter how long I pressed the skin and gently moved her toes, added cream and ran my thumbs under her arches, it was never long enough. She often slept through the massage, but when I stopped, her eyes opened instantly. She always said the same thing: So soon? Are you stopping so soon?

The day that was her last, the phone calls increased between those of us who were helping. Her Jewish landlady said that we needed to prepare a linen shroud. Although she'd asked to be cremated, and the Jewish rabbi did not want to perform the burial ceremony because cremation was against Hebrew law, we were to find the linen sheet. That was the rule and practice. One woman would do the washing of our dear neighbor and she would then anoint the body with precious oils. My neighbor's finely shaped bald head would be covered, her body wrapped like a swaddled baby. Her bed would be moved to the center of the living room, where she would be laid out. The night before, the friend who had stayed with her had opened the window to let in the light of the full moon. The light on the bed was nearly blinding, the helper said. It was not soft, bathing light. It was like a spotlight on her alone.

My neighbor wanted me to have a red pashmina scarf. It was so intensely red that I could not put it on without feeling I was burning. My neighbor did not want to die. She was in her fifties. She organized a party about six weeks before her death. She hired musicians. We all linked arms, dancing, faster and faster, as the musicians played "Hava Nagila," Hebrew for "Let us rejoice," until we were panting and dizzy. Even in her last days she continued her Hebrew lessons. She wanted to know the language God spoke. She would get angry if her teacher could not make the words clear. I've lost my sight, she told him, you must read it for me. I don't have much more time to learn.

I gave the scarf away. The decision haunts me. I could not bear the feeling of flames on my neck. I want to say it was sadness that made me do it. She wanted to live and the intensity of her desire was feverish, fierce; the red was as bright as spurting blood whose life-giving power was escaping. But it's self-protecting to say I gave it away because it made me sad.

The scarf frightened me and now I miss it. Now I think I could bear the wild intensity of that color, which was part of the energy she possessed and didn't want to relinquish. The scarf was pure passion.

I don't know what she meant by her gift. Its memory keeps reappearing. Maybe she wanted to remind me to use that intensity in my writing. Maybe she wanted me to remember the dance going faster and faster and to rejoice. Maybe she wanted me to recognize my timidity.

On our smartphones, we read short pieces accompanied by more and more pictures and animated additions. The invention of the printing press six hundred years ago demolished some ideas about authority and who could disseminate knowledge and how. There are no statistics that can measure the pathways and number of effects that flowed from Gutenberg's trays of lead or typographers' fonts of gold and silver. N+1+N+1+N+1.

Our determined, skilled thumbs get us to information hour by hour. Our opinions and a sense of joining a crowd make us find words to send around. Words ping in on our message list, emails fly with their blind copies, events and stories whirl with calls for action, we raise our voices, utterly outside the scope of a literary text. Words are no longer static and fixed. They travel at high speeds and long distances, moving in new ways. They play out differently what and how we learn from a page.

Schoolchildren, when I was young, learned how to open a new book first by reverently pressing its front cover and then back cover until the book's cloth-bound casings touched the desk. The pages then were carefully separated, turned one by one, starting from the middle. Thus, we stretched the book's spine, an exercise that reminded us that books belonged to others. *Little Women* had to survive, but more than that remain pristine not just through a single school year, but for years to come for other students. Once opened, it was a companion.

The highly anticipated experience was one of withdrawing into silence, exchanging one world for another, riding on words: line by line, consenting, objecting, skipping pages, and at the end, making a judgment. The long journey taken on a couch or in bed or under a tree—effort or passion in exchange for attention and time—was known as reading a book for pleasure. The time frame might be all night or all week. It was an encounter with silence, a space reserved for personal experience without hearing a sound from boredom or duty.

The opening of a book and the finishing of it are mini births and deaths. A life hatches, the nest holds the creature until it flies off and we are left to remember it, perhaps even mourn its departure. Turning pages, the inhalation, exhalation, become a kind of breathing. Sometimes a yawn, sometimes panting. Books have a physiological function. They are lungs keeping us alive.

At a minimum, books are a pound of paper, ink, glue, and letters, in earlier centuries copied by hand. In recent times these physical objects, machine-made for centuries, have come under economic scrutiny; uncountable numbers of books are seen as pompous, mold catching, dated, costly to store. Yet the crafts involved in production and the commitment to style, to permanence, to dialogue, and to deep creative motives led to libraries and the opportunity of touching and disseminating knowledge. Libraries and books enforce spaces for silence. There are horrible blemishes, terrible lapses in books; nevertheless, books are one of humanity's greatest efforts. They are the voracious fleets and flotillas, discovering the world, clashing with cultures, dominating them, opening territory, destroying it: the *Niña*s, the *Pinta*s, the *Santa María*s.

Ancients pondered and set the rules of art that made it possible to define art's powers to replicate or invoke reality. The meaning of the emotions that art produced was explored for its relationship to truth. Plato did not consider artists' illusions more than shadows of reality. Aristotle was more technical in trying to establish criteria for an audience to suspend its disbelief. He insisted on the unity of time, sunrise to sunset, as the arc for dramatic action. He also asked for an arc of progression in which the character could reach a climax and reveal new consciousness. In his argument the audience could justify believing in what was an illusion because it had a physical and moral coherence to it.

Paolo told me at breakfast that our brain weighs about three pounds. When we stick our heads forward to look at a screen, gravity makes it seven times heavier for the spine to support it. It's a change in our posture, we who spent millennia to stand upright. Between the screen and the smartphone, we spend much of our waking life in this new position that weighs on our spine.

How could my silences be yours?

They won't be, but I hope silence will become a presence on these pages. My silences won't be yours. Did I already write that? I did it to catch your attention. In books we assume that typos have been caught and facts checked. There are many covenants in books, including ethics of clarity, revision, and artfulness. Because of many considerations of longevity in relation to worthiness of subject and language, the richer the author's use of language, the greater is its contribution to free thought. A well-written book allows us the freedom to use our critical minds to evaluate it.

You will find your own translations of silence. If you are young, you will have your methods for handling silence more sharply defined as the instant. Many of you will seek it at the top of a mountain or behind a telescope. You will have your own ideas about encroachments and false, fast words. If you take a liking to the search and experience silences that are not boring, you may discover that dissatisfaction, restlessness, and speed are addictions. Computers and smartphones are what we know now, and you who are young know them from your first steps. You are often silent in sharing with adults what you find there except for the vote of like or dislike.

An assistant in an elegant clothing store in Parma handed me a coat to try on while she explained how stressed she was. She didn't sleep well. Turning on the computer at night made her even more anxious. I nodded as I buttoned the three buttons on the coat. They were as large as red checkers.

I've discovered knitting, she said. My grandmother taught me. In the dark, just hearing the *click click* of the needles, I find peace seeing the stitches twisting and slipping onto the next stitch, following one by one. That's what I do when I can't sleep.

If I precede the description of the clerk from the previous page with the addition of a few lines of simultaneous facts about the actual store, the effect of the clerk's final words changes. Like the store itself, the narrative contains less silence and room for peace.

An assistant in an elegant clothing store in Parma handed me a coat to try on. Behind us loomed an enormous full-color screen with models marching toward us like implacable soldiers. They came down fast, the supply of them never stopping. Ominously swerving at the last minute when it seemed they would knock us down, they never paused. The loop kept proposing them, impassive, short-haired. They marched. Repeat. The message was vaguely menacing. They swerved before reaching the edge. Their eyes fixed beyond. They set our pace. Dead-eyed and militant. Repeat.

If I introduce the clerk's comments about knitting after this description, the reader can no longer feel the dark or the silence in which stitches slide and the needles can be heard clicking. Our attention has been disturbed by the runway glare and slightly fascistic image of the fashion models. The written page loses its peace.

I don't want to belabor the point that we are under the continuous influence of these images and that they create a sense of speed and slickness we can't tune out. But the fact is I decided to leave the models out of my piece because they distract from the quiet that I want to create and offer. Writing and its relationship to truth is a complex one. Facts are not always the closest way to re-create the truth. They are building blocks of different structural significance in arguments and atmospheres.

The writer's power resides in choosing what to put in and what to leave out in order to create a truth she is after. We often read material with a single idea driving its animation—a message worked and reworked. The more the construction is simplified to a perceptible message, the less freedom there is in its truth. Edgy is a style: a push to twist language not necessarily from the experience or feeling, but for the artifice of impact. It is a narration, which, like advertising, pinpoints an atmosphere that make us confirm it even though it's a deliberate invention. It is a closed loop, a tautology, contributing to how we see the world.

Agnes Martin, a painter born in Macklin, Saskatchewan, in 1912, was sent alone by her mother to have her tonsils removed. My sister and I discussed this as we wound up the spiral at the Guggenheim Museum, moving in and out of the indented passages, starting with some of Martin's white works with striped gradations that were immediate calls to snow, infinity, silence, and the changes that occur because of the ways light falls on her painted surfaces. The subtle interactions present as brushstrokes also make her presence known.

Martin's mother put the five-year-old on a streetcar (they were living in Lumsden by then), gave her her fare, and told her to get off at the hospital. She was instructed to stay overnight once the infected tonsils were removed and to return home on the same streetcar the following morning. Who thought about her fears or her pain? Martin's mother's harsh expectations as well as the flat, isolated landscape Martin grew up in suggested a deceptively easy way to enter her work. Early on, she learned solitude and to absent herself from what must be endured by using her own intelligence.

As I followed the light vertical and horizontal lines ordering her snow/cloud paintings, I recognized childhood memories of breathing through a woolen scarf with my mouth open, moist air rubbing against my face with the sound of air puffing in and out of my ears. The temperatures in Wisconsin winters were well below zero for weeks and the damp warmth between the scarf and my face chapped my cheeks, turning them bright red. You could not force me to be driven to school when I had a chance to run free in a world thrilling for its crackling ice and gleaming daggers. Boys, the bigger ones, often gave chase, armed with icy snowballs. Martin's work summoned up the infinite horizon in snow, often its exhilaration.

The movements of colors on the painted surfaces of Martin's canvases were invitations into states of being in moving light, everything in minute gradations of inwardness and silence.

Translating an Italian word into English for a written purpose, I may well spot five or six different meanings, moving like iridescent fish inside a single bowl. I know I can't catch them all. I will craft a sentence using a part of the word's reality and letting the rest go. Only in my head, nearly beyond words, is there space for all meanings because they are half-formed, superimposed, felt.

This is not true if I am writing a poem. There, words carry images that from the beginning carry all meanings possible. I process an image as feelings, an integral part of a puzzle created with more than logic. The image is a messenger carrying treasure without a code.

This ineffability was at work in Martin's vision. She summoned images that represented subtle feelings freed from ideas. The level of identification I felt made me grope toward a sense that I was seeing a woman's work. Her work had put aside public definitions and reflected the identity of an artist who had surpassed those structures. She was painting how she observed the world: "The truth is that it's not in the lines but the emotions."

I will call her representations of feelings as minute gradations a woman's capacity to simultaneously perceive self and non-self and to remain empty enough to receive what enters in that space. Martin observed that the scale of her compositions expressing feelings was what gave them their truth. There's "no hint of the material world in my painting." Why, in the end, was Virginia Woolf's first volume of essays, entitled *A Woman's Essays,* if not to underline the fact that her interest in intensity, variations, excursions originated from "her own point of view." "What is my own position toward the inner and the outer? I think a kind of ease and dash are good; . . . some combination of them ought to be possible."

Martin drew from various schools of work and specific artists—Mark Rothko and Cy Twombly—but she expressed her own way of showing what had not been previously seen. Her vision was about expressing a deep otherness, "known forever in the mind." The general premise of art, making it new, is just that. What had been missing in terms of recognizing changes in subject matter and points of view up until the 1970s in the United States was that we had not yet seen many, or in any fair proportion, major exhibitions of women making art new, bringing their sense of otherness into what exists.

I felt at home in Martin's spiritual renderings. I recognized their tranquil beauty. I needed her journey, but so did the world. Her paintings were pulsing like a rarely sighted species of butterfly, just unfolded, wet, on a black branch in the sun, then another and another, each resting its wide-open wings, allowing itself to be contemplated. The subtle movements, the single and unified strokes, reinforced Martin's mysterious observations. "I was thinking of the innocence of trees," she wrote. "I thought it was quite easy to be innocent if you're a tree," thus claiming the animistic depths of her understanding of the connections among living organisms.

The sensation of my having an affinity with Martin's work hovered between excitement and joy. It arose from recognition that we spoke the same language, the way the Nigerian women in Parma, from different villages, speak similar dialects, different, but close enough to understand one another. It was joy, and a perception of change. In these years of visiting New York City, I had seen exhibitions by Doris Salcedo, Louise Bourgeois, Marisa Merz, Tarsila do Aramal Alma Thomas, Kiki Smith, Hilma af Klint, Vija Celmins, Betye Saar, room after room, saturated with subject matter that was galvanizing because it was so familiar and yet so unknown. A deliberate silence, an invisible set of judgments defining worthiness, talent, originality, was being amended.

I had never been taught by a single woman professor during my years at the University of Michigan. The narrative of women's inadequacies as well as those of minority voices was nearly unquestioned then. The relativity of how reality is told was just barely inching into consciousness. Perhaps if I had not changed cultures, I would have seen this narration of progress for women differently. Changing countries, as I did when I was nearly forty, feels to me as if many previous memories, from the years I lived in the United States, are frozen in time. It is a special kind of arrested development.

I had never seen a woman violin soloist until I attended a concert in Turin, where Viktoria Mullova, a musician who left Russia with the fall of the Soviet Union, swayed as if the Brahms concerto was wind moving around and through a tree's branches. She took up the stage in a way that seemed to me radical and new. Yet to many people by then, her presence as a woman soloist seemed unremarkable. She was not making a feminist statement, but rather expressing her being.

I was in Turin to follow the steps taken by Natalia Ginzburg in the city. The editor of the *Kenyon Review*, who was pursuing essays on women's work, had asked me to write about her life and writing.

I was given a copy of a conversation between Natalia Ginzburg and one of the festival organizers of Poetry International in Rotterdam when I was a participant there. In it Ginzburg said: "Maternity is beautiful, happy, traumatizing . . . strange . . . Maternity is a theme in my work. It can be out of hand, too much love, too much fear—fear of losing something—losing the child, losing self." That voice was startling and powerfully balanced. It had always fascinated me. I liked the way Ginzburg was reticent while being frank.

Ginzburg was raised in Turin and forced to return to it after her husband was tortured and killed by the Germans in the Regina Coeli prison in Rome. Left alone to support three children, she returned to Turin to work as an editor for the publisher Einaudi, and to live with her parents, whom she loved and who loved her, and who would help with her children. But after remarrying, longing for her independence, she left her parents and moved back to Rome. Later she moved with her second husband to London, but returned to Italy because she did not feel at home outside of her language and customs. She claimed that writing outside of her country was too difficult for her. I often heard her voice as I wrote in her country, outside of my own. I remembered her honesty about writing and having children. She had two more with her second husband, neither of whom she brought into her writing (one died in his first year, the daughter was severely disabled), and one foster child. Her unmeasured constancy, so unapologetic about contradictions, gave me strength. "No substitute exists for family. Nothing can take its place. You can try to make relationships better, closer, freer, but not substitute the family."

Ginzburg resisted victimization of any sort. She distinguished between women of privilege and women who lived in poverty and subjection. She did not believe they could be compared under the same cry for women's rights. Rather she preferred a different point of view. "At the center of a fair vision of the world, love and hate are at the center, and false and true."

Agnes Martin's paintings showed silences where the spirit does not deceive. She painted emptiness filled by consciousness. Her solitude, her silence, was so different from Ginzburg's engagement, and yet both had codes of ethics, both limits of personal reticence. Martin, as a painter, didn't have to deal with the silences of omission. Her journey was to give space to inspiration and to keep sweeping the surface clear and clean of ideas. She wished to give light and feeling infinite play: the world in a grain of sand. Her imagination painted this: waking up to energies: the life we are living.

The tonsil story from Martin's childhood was one of many my sister brought up. We nodded over it. My sister and I had so many mother stories that we competed over versions of the variations. With more than twelve years' difference in age between us, it was inevitable that we felt we had lived starkly different lives, because of the time/space reality and the different roles created by that gap. I being the older girl and she being the baby in our family of four kids determined different ways our mother managed to affect us before and after our father died, when I was nineteen and she was seven. My experience of wanting communication from a mother who didn't give it made it inevitable that I protected my sister as a mother would.

The list of crimes easily unwinds when we are together. A slight comment and events from years past, as if kept on a very large ball of yarn from which we could both knit a year's worth of hair shirts, crop up. If we tugged or pushed, forgetting that we were touching events that were long past, it would be difficult to stop its momentum. Even in the museum, if it escaped from our understanding, a worn thread of scratchy, knotted pieces could roll out. Sisterly love, cross-stitched by responsibility, makes a fierce, proud, odd garment. It felt good to me to touch my sister's cotton sleeve.

People poured into the Guggenheim's open entrance space. The day was dark and rainy. Wet and shiny black coats, black umbrellas abounded. The vision from above was of hunched, brooding crows. Cézanne said colors were where the brain met the universe. What did that say about the urban brains below? I stepped back into the painting in front of us. Agnes Martin had a definite view of black. She let it speak as thin lines, often graphite ones, as fine as hair, drawn by hand and eye.

It was ridiculous to let the past take up any of our time while my sister and I had the chance to enter a niche holding a painting called *Untitled #15*. Martin's paintings said, You decide. This is infinite and now. Stop and look. Are they there, those pale black lines? Are we leaning on one another's arms? Are we connected? Is white snow structural silence? Is anything more real than intuition and its reception?

One day, historians may draw a line that marks how the world understood and managed itself once computers were the vehicles for information. BC, "before Christ," and AD, "in the year of our Lord," started to migrate toward BCE and CE centuries before we thought we were being politically correct. Johannes Kepler in the seventeenth century and Jewish scholars in the eighteenth century began using more culturally neutral and inclusive abbreviations for keeping track of years in the Gregorian calendar. Yet the way that Christians' "before Christ" and "after Christ" marked the whole narration and meaning of time by portioning it as a universal revolution suggests that sometime in the future, the world will eventually add another starting point or ending point to the vast arc of the past two thousand years. It may be identified as AAI, after artificial intelligence.

The world that existed and was created and assumed by human thought and writing, on clay, parchment, and paper, led to perceiving other worlds. Paper once stored, defused, and defined vast limits and possibilities of what we could know by turning pages. How much time it took to convert a story, an oral transmission told and retold for eons, into a written text and then condensing those texts into an authoritative single version is relevant to understanding those narrations. The Gospels took shape nearly fifty years after the events described. They chronicled the same story with different emphasis.

Now we inhabit another world where in seconds our minds are told what is happening around the globe and how to believe what we see. Everything is a heartbeat away. The eyes and reading were not involved in either personal or official exchanges on the telephone. Now using eyes to read words has become the way we understand simple conversations. We receive much through written forms, both text messages and emails, that aspire to the niche of speech. In rapid writing, we invest ourselves, not with the deliberateness of written thought, but as if we were saying something to someone. We imagine our subjects listening as our fingers tap. We are that close in time. Once we might have interpreted expressions on faces; thus, our eyes played a part in dialogue, as did our ears and other senses. We read conflicts and fleeting intimations by seeing pauses, silences, masked expressions. Now, if not in texts, a conversation on a screen introduces a framed filter, the sensation of being onstage, of speaking as the equivalent of broadcasting.

Dialogue in novels is a written approximation of speech. It is a creation. Hemingway's brevity and rhythms are models of how speech can be suggested in writing. Zora Neale Hurston's writing is a transcription of a personal stylized version of speech. Writers possess and then possibly modify grammatical rules. The primary effect of electronic means for writing short texts may be the perpetuation of the illusion of the authority of the written word previously created by crafted writing. How the text is generated, received, and read has altered without being acknowledged. Accepting the written word as having authority is based on a set of assumptions that are no longer agreed upon. At the same time, the person generating the text possesses a greater sense of empowerment. Language has become more populist. In electronic petitions we feel we are part of a group.

Until recently, requests for my signature on a petition for a reasonable cause too often mirrored a disturbing public level of expression. It might have started, "Mr. President, you're stupid." I should have been able to sign for the cause, but I couldn't accept the language. What might be, unfortunately, a silent, half-formed thought became, in a virtual petition, an unacceptable public sentiment, a hyperbolic assault.

Daily, our use of language has been redirected. What we read and sign is electronic language that often aggravates a sense of impossible differences. Sometimes, I add my signature anyway, because I belong to this age. When I do sign one that approaches rabble-rousing, I feel the precarious cliff I am standing on. Or if I step back, it seems obvious that the words are a script: Hey, Mr. President, I demand that you . . . Would I ever use those words speaking to someone face-to-face, much less the head of our government? Would I write them, except in a novel?

Tatiana, who left Ukraine, has cleaned our house for ten years. She is a stacker, makes piles of things, and we struggle still over simple ideas of what works or how to do it. But she is determined, good-hearted, open to admitting a pessimism that she would like to shed. Today she has a terrible toothache, but in spite of that, wants to sit for a cup of coffee and a chat. Her story is about walnuts. Someone brought her fifteen pounds of nuts picked from his family's trees in Sicily. They needed to be dried because they were still a bit green and would taste acidic. She spread them on her balcony and left in the dark for her early-morning job of cleaning offices. She imagined that the warm sunlight that had scorched the balcony all summer long, when it arrived, would be ideal for calling up the oils in the nuts and pulling them toward ripeness. It was a satisfying vision of abundance.

Fifteen pounds, one tan shell next to the other. Like a hemp carpet. She laughed, even though half her face was swollen in pain.

She said: When I got back after five hours, they had vanished. The balcony was empty. Nothing remained. Well, seven or eight nuts still rolled around.

Perplexed, she checked with her neighbor below.

Had there been a wind? Hundreds had disappeared.

Her neighbor frowned at the sky.

I didn't know you had nuts. I heard bickering and screaming up there. Magpies were flying in all directions. They were fighting and dropping nuts like bombs.

The people Tatiana works for in private houses worry about thieves. She dislikes them for their prejudices. They don't answer their doors, they peep through keyholes. They worry about dust. They worry about having their treasures stolen by immigrants.

I've seen *gazze* on my balcony before, she said to me. I've shooed them away. I've never believed people who said, Watch out for magpies, they're smart. *They are smart.* The birds figured out that you can't eat gold.

Her story made us laugh. She would never have written it down in an email. It was only face-to-face, drinking a coffee, that the story, as old as the world of fairy tales, played out. Small miseries, injustices, worries often drop into silences unless we tell them face-to-face.

From the peace in Agnes Martin's canvases, we could not infer that she built two houses of adobe bricks she fashioned when she had no money. No desolate colors when she lived without heat, running water. No discontinuities caused by medications when her brain would break down, nor evidence of brutal hospitalizations where she received multiple applications of electroshock. Her paintings captured the enormity of consciousness, freed from biography. Her relationship to her canvas was her knowledge of living dialogue within and without in relative freedom from trends and styles and gallery pressure. She observed many times, "Beauty and perfection are the same. They never occur without happiness." Her paintings are of a middle world—abstractions where there is emptiness but always something cosmic to see or hear or feel while she enters in the process of leaving the canvas to silence.

Little explanatory cards flagged passages in her life experience. She was restless, suffered schizophrenia, spent time among a community of New York painters but turned her back on that life when she could not afford it nor count on her mental stability. The cards were beside the point. She did not explain in her art. Her work was the expression of the space and freedom for beauty in a life that had lived solitude, sorrow and depression, love and discovery, rebellion, freedom, alcohol, and even long afternoons betting on horses at the races. She knew being an artist meant to get out of the way, to let her mind be empty, to animate something when it came to her. It was an extraordinary vision of a self, awake beyond torment and appearances.

The chapel effect of the Guggenheim's niches identified her paintings as abstract narrative frescoes in a modern cathedral. They must be visited to be experienced. Martin transformed inwardness into vibrations of silent energies in an eternal present.

I read *The New York Times* online. It is a blessing and an improvement from the decades when, if I ever read an English paper in Parma, *The Herald Tribune* arrived three days after it had been published in Paris. It cost as much as two cappuccinos and two brioches. Often it was torn, or smeared from having been bundled and left in the rain. I wish to make that point before I complain about what I receive now.

To me the new news seems frequently lacking in analysis that would challenge appearances and reveal more disturbing mechanisms and truths in these worrisome times. Every few weeks, I consider canceling my subscription because I think too many of the articles I am reading have been driven by speed or instrumental ways of using sources. I sense vested interests in the caution or rationalized sense of balance, giving equal weight to facts that are not equivalent in weight. Often the stories seem generated by imperfectly described data and its significance or by overly simplified ways of entertaining the reader. Often it feels to me as if journalism has given up on what Natalia Ginzburg called "a fair vision of the world, love and hate are at the center, and false and true."

But when I boil over with disgust at their subtle ways of ignoring the deep challenges of human community, I still don't cancel my subscription. If that day comes, it will be like cutting off a finger. I want to read something coming from a place that I follow as part of my sense of self. But by reading, I also face a mirror, and see ways in which the reflections are shallow.

During the Trump administration, I found it difficult to read about U.S. politics because the administration mocked institutions and basic tenets of social justice in a seemingly new way. A tweet by its very name is a trivializing provocation. Facts need to be assessed and protected from the danger of deliberate lies. The fiery indignity we felt as young people marching for civil rights and protesting against the Vietnam War was possible partly because belief in government institutions was solid enough to be able to survive and even benefit from opposition. We knew that the collective country was still far from equal. We suspected lapses and mendaciousness. However, now words describing the contrasts fail to reach that conclusion—because equality has been captured by a manipulated, cynical sense that all truth is relative, individual, and calculated. Noise and ideology bang unchecked in sentences and a single lie can cast doubt.

Recently, Paolo was operated on for a hernia. It was located below his abdomen on the lower left side of his body. Just before they wheeled him in, the plastic lines from drips swinging above him, while he was still following things through a slowly lowering sense of consciousness, a nurse lifted the sheet and took out a large blue Magic Marker. A colleague made fun of her, but she snapped back that it was protocol. Starting at his left knee, she drew a long blue arrow up his thigh and stopped just short of his groin. It's a way of preventing mistakes, she said to Paolo.

He only remembers waking up. The arrow was still on his leg, bright, blue, something a child could have made. It did its job, because it was clear and didn't aspire to more than that.

It held its own through the silence of his sleep and the changing shift of people working on him. I wish writing had more blue arrows. The arrow was not meant to slay or wound or kill. It was not asking someone else to load a bow. It was a simple direction, able to be interpreted because the rules and the context were understood. It showed where the work needed to be done. It couldn't be missed in a blur of rationalization or covering one's trail. There was no tattling, or moralizing, in that blue arrow: no gain except to hold an instructive place without pointing fingers. It admitted, without blame, the fact that we as human beings make mistakes and need solid information.

An idea that started in Wisconsin more than ten years ago has cropped up here, in Parma: a Little Free Library house fastened to a tree. It has two shelves, the lower being designated for children's books, and the upper, with a higher space before it reaches the slanted roof, is for adult ones. The zinc latch is simple and can be dialed up or down.

Often on my way to a meeting, I take a detour to see its state of being; is it empty, full, have the contents changed since last week? Its size reminds me of a little playhouse I used to visit as a child, walking two streets from ours and boldly knocking on the door of the real house. I simply asked if I might play for a while inside the miniature house with curtains over its windows, a stove, and a sink, something that seemed just like a house found in "Goldilocks and the Three Bears" or "Little Red Riding Hood." I never told my parents. The people who let me play never asked me questions, nor explained where the children were who used it. We kids in the neighborhood were not hovered over or checked. Nor did we think it unusual that we could knock on doors and ask for magical things.

Yet I sensed lots of missing elements, in the hilly landscape with large houses. Just knowing the Black maid, Josephine, who worked for our childless neighbors, I discovered eyes that cried when they smiled. Her laugh, when it bubbled up, wrapped her like a robe that once was new. It was good like her patience and tarts covered in sparkling sugar. She wore time like an apron with pockets and welcomed me to the back door and let me stay close as she cooked or cleaned the canaries' cages. Yet her whole body sighed. She expressed feelings in silence and that drew me to her. I didn't know the word for poverty, but I don't think that was her sadness. It was other things: Bill who drank, and a mother who was sick. I knew hard times felt like her sighs.

The little free house holding books changes from day to day. People pass and choose and although I have never seen anyone near it, either to borrow or to give or to clean its rectangular window, I so appreciate its existence, silently being used, an exchange, a destination that is not virtual but a hot spot, not for a computer but for trust, free choice, curiosities. I like its lighthouse aspiration and how it dares to exist without locks, without limiting its message by defensive warnings, codes to open the door and join only the privileged. It reminds me of times when we could knock on doors and ask for magical things.

S ometimes I get together with a neighbor who is a journalist in Parma. We lose track of one another for years and then we cross paths again, like deer who freeze, caught in the high beams. Recently while I was waiting at a bus stop, he hopped out of his car to tell me that an essay of his that I had translated in the early 1990s for *Granta* had been turned into a play in Sweden. We promised to celebrate.

Once he settles in his chair, after having offered an espresso on a tray and cracking open the window onto the terrace (asking if I mind if he smokes, assuming that if I say that I do, he has permission for tolerance), he drifts through time, with some nostalgia, about how it once was for journalists. A natural storyteller, fascinated by people and their individual paths in a world where stories help others to understand, he looks back with an intense sense that he did important work by analyzing experience using human sources. He nearly died in several violent encounters, lost his hearing in one ear because of a blow to the head. He has met guerrillas in the jungle; ridden on public buses as the future Pope Francis guided him through the streets of Buenos Aires; interviewed the man who flew the mission with the *Enola Gay*, heard his tormenting anguish about the deed two days before he died by suicide. He was the first European journalist to interview Arafat, in an underground hideout in the middle of the night.

In general, his newspaper encouraged him to write about the background underlying the context of his reporting, which assumed an analysis. His point of view, while it used the persona of himself, was not an advertisement: I did this, I was there, I met this challenge. Its purpose was to illuminate human conditions, alliances, and moves where he was present and a witness. He was to suggest the significance of his experience, using knowledge, analysis, as much as his humanity.

One morning he explained that he had been sent regularly as a correspondent to Latin America for stays of three or four months. His eyes brightened and he paused. He said: We developed networks, got close to sources, but also deepened our understanding of the politics. We correspondents from all the foreign papers used to travel on the same planes and share sources and tips. We met each other often during our stays. A secret meeting with someone high up in ISIS would be shared. After an encounter with an Iraqi—near the border with Iran, incidentally—a French reporter and I were ambushed and beaten. I was hospitalized in various places for three months.

He said: Any trip now to a war zone creates exorbitant costs. The newspaper correspondent in these times is heavily insured and the insurance is measured by the minute. No one can stay for months. Too expensive. A weekend, generally, counted to the minute: the insurance kicks in when the plane takes off and expires when it touches down on the same runway. Getting there first, and getting that lead back to the paper so it can be rushed out, means no one tips a hand. What constitutes a story has changed. It's a happening, not an analysis anymore. Journalists themselves can't feel the proportions of most stories. They just describe a surface. If there is violence, something exciting, that is what all the newspapers will be reporting. Often, they are paid to draw an ideological line or not to offend corporate interests.

Along the Parma River again, after a hiatus, not seeing a single rust-colored pheasant for the long walk above the banks for nearly a kilometer, I concluded that the large elegant birds had migrated. Gone until spring. My mind worked on that idea of nature, autumn, disappearance, and went home.

The next day as I walked the river, I didn't turn left toward the Cinema Astra, which I normally do so that I can see if the film has changed. They have extended cycles of African, Indian, Arab films. Yet many are projected for two or three days only.

Instead, I went straight, for no particular reason, deciding to reach the traffic circle and then to turn left for home from there. I changed routes and moved farther ahead, tracing the river, which edges south.

The sun was golden that afternoon and spread, at that hour, all over the grass. The light was autumnal, slightly misted, like the opaque dusty film on Moscato grapes. Instantly, my eyes fixed on a pair of pheasants: the bright-colored male, the green dash, the red collar, the female looking not all dull but with dappled browns and tans and rusts. They were grazing, actively, head up, head down, in the grasses. From the meadow, they appeared like enameled jewels, luscious colors, but from there my mind kept panning the scene, opening, changing where my eyes rested. Red, green, plump, long spotted tail feathers, in twos, pheasants abounded. The large birds were under trees, near the wall, across the slash of grass, on the edge leading to the river. I didn't break my pace, and never stopped, so it is likely that I missed many in my count. I saw forty-two pairs before reaching the traffic circle. Eighty-four pheasants, and I probably missed many. If I had written my piece the day before, if my figurative insurance had run out and my story was due, I would have said the pheasants had gone. Even if I had had doubts, I probably wouldn't have admitted them. If I had written that I saw none, I was reporting the fact. It was true. But as an observation, it had little truth in it. It was only a story told by me.

Once I saw the tapestry of birds as a significant number, the embroidered order and purpose of the birds feeding and sharing territory along the *torrente* changed. I couldn't answer if the pheasants had been in that place the day before. Perhaps they had been. If I hadn't changed my path, however, my yearlong habit would have insulated me from such a question. I would not have known that I didn't know. In a year of observations, my highest total was ten sightings in one day.

The discovery of eighty-four pheasants in plain sight stopped a running assumption. After a year of uninterrupted repetitions, my mental frame broke. The unknown was the sidewalk I had walked in a certain way, so that I believed I knew it nearly step by step. Two steps beyond where I turned, the pheasants lived in a universe. They were alive beyond my words. They were not ornaments decorating my narration but mighty birds living and organizing their lives.

John Cage, when he wrote his piece "4'33"," composed silence beat by beat by measuring that amount of quiet. Four minutes and thirty-three seconds. When he first performed it, expectations led listeners to believe that there was something to hear. Instead he meant the piece to be a new way of listening. The frame he gave "4'33"" on paper, three movements, meant that it had a shape that could be performed. The early audiences, particularly, filled the performances with sounds of objection. Getting attention by challenging complacency was not a wholly unknown strategy among artists. Cage thought that prior expectations for the meanings of sound cut off most of experience. Many in the early audiences sat through the piece. Some reacted by leaving. A few heard a world they hadn't imagined.

Years after its world debut, the surprise no longer exists. The ego has been tamed. But the illusion of silence is penetrated anyway: chairs still scrape, coughs escape, programs dryly brush the air. The contradiction of musicians holding instruments on their laps and pages being turned can be refused or experienced. You can listen or you can think about farce. Each performance frames differently the dimensions and variations of silence and music's relationship to measured time. On YouTube there are various versions of how the directors signal stop and start. Cage's instruction is to lift and drop the piano keyboard cover to indicate beginnings and endings of movements. Some perform the drop by making a noise, some do it silently. John Cage and Agnes Martin were friends.

In the Quiet Car on Metro-North, holding my smartphone, in the same way I can hear Aretha Franklin as long as I have earbuds, I can click on a website and hear a sound that has been captured in space. With a click, I can hear different iterations of data that lasts 0.004 of a second: a whoop, a blip. They are versions of the sound of a binary black hole merger emitting a gravitational wave that was registered for 0.02 of a second. The brief frequencies are the very first sound to be detected that reveal the presence of gravitational waves occurring within the current universe. The event, and the sound, GW150914, were named using the initials of gravitational waves and the date it was heard: September 15, 2014. If I were reading an e-book, the URL site of the sound could be embedded in the text—and I could listen to it between the lines. The sound was recovered more than a billion light-years from the earth.

I can't put it in any context. I know that's true. I can't do the first equations supporting the theory for gravitational waves. Nor do I understand them even verbally as predictions in Albert Einstein's general theory of relativity.

Holding the smartphone in my hand, hearing the whoop lasting no longer than reading the word in the Quiet Car on Metro-North, there is no way I can feel reverence, or appreciate the knowledge needed and the vision and persistence, as well as the monetary cost of the twenty-year Laser Interferometer Gravitational-Wave Observatory (LIGO) project, and the theories in physics that it took to obtain it, and the research facilities, and the thousands of secondary researchers, and the distance between that sound and my banal acceptance of it. I can click the link and consume it as the beginning discovery that may eventually fit into other captured sounds in celestial spaces we have never heard. But my mind might as well imagine it as a harbinger of a space symphony. As it is, the man next to me, drinking coffee from his brown thermos, and the woman next to him, painting her fingernails, are utterly unaware that I am a billion miles away. Her brick-red fingernails are almost finished. She snaps the bottle shut and holds her nails out to dry.

The sound is free. The sound is here to be accessed by me, my pleasure, without work, without knowing. I don't have to pay a cent. I have no gap in my perception. I'm listening to outer space as I head to New York City. How cool is that? In the dark bowels of the station, on the tracks leading in, I am numb to it. What I mean is I have no idea of the enormity of what I have just heard.

A few days before seeing the Agnes Martin exhibit, another museum in New York, the Morgan Library, lured me into exploring objects from the Brontë family, with a specific focus on Charlotte Brontë and her manuscript *Jane Eyre*. The objects exhibited middle-class demands for status and mastery.

Charlotte, within a family arrangement, was the flowering rose. Her tenacious break out of social conventions neatly joined a twenty-first-century consensus. Her famous declaration in *Jane Eyre*—"I am no bird; and no net ensnares me; I am a free human being with an independent will"—was fiercely satisfying, but its boldness had altered in the present day. Her statement now fit in a wholly audible, more general, expanding chorus of women's voices, past, present, and from around the world.

A theme one could see nearly everywhere in New York City's store windows, images of elated and charged women, behind desks, running in sports gear, the word "POWER" larger than any of the figures, was subliminally at work in our perception of Charlotte Brontë's statement. We read Charlotte's words as bold. From all we see of the family's purposeful activities in the exhibit, she claimed her share of power aspired to by the middle class. What we were unable to perceive as the overwhelming war in the Brontës' lives was disease, where powerlessness and terror were real.

Charlotte's sister Emily's early poems describe the consequences of her disembodied state as a girl: "The heart is dead in infancy / Unwept-for, let the body go." Emily's book, *Wuthering Heights*, characterized by Dante Gabriel Rossetti as "a fiend of a book, puzzling for its interest in cruelty, inhumanity, diabolical hate and vengeance," was a creation of an author who also declared her independence as well as her rage. She wrote in another poem attributed to her, "I'll walk where my own nature would be leading: it vexes me to choose another guide." The violence and absurdity of existence was Emily's narrative. She had stepped a bit further away from the identity society expected her to perform. Her work was not on display.

The exhibit's underlying theme was triumph or purposefulness in the face of bitter odds. Built from objects in the Brontë home, the domesticity of a family parlor put the viewer at ease. Here, brother Branwell also participated in all the pastimes of proficiency—painting, music, composing plays. The lighting, the sheen of tattered wear on the fading objects, indeed called up a domestic household with its cherished memories and its suffocating ones.

The exhibit, by stressing the importance of individual striving, led viewers to feel that we were closer to identifying with the Brontës' frustrations and solutions than not. The collective elements that explained and complicated the focus were missing. That allowed us to celebrate the formula for success and industriousness, like the apps that link one site to the next, the clicks leading us away from what advertisers had not programmed for us.

There were inferred messages: Charlotte's gown. She was as

tall as a girl (if boosted by Nike sneakers) might be at age ten today. Her dress, rigid with a hoop, showed social and territorial aspirations. Its similarity to a birdcage was hard to overlook. Her size evidenced scarcity about what was eaten winter and summer in northwest England two centuries ago. People were short and small. The exhibit was topical in its translation of a particularly current American narrative. Not a poem, it was rather a display offering selected information, realism in things and objects, without filling out the definition to lift us beyond ourselves.

As I zipped my coat before exiting onto a dark, rainy Madison Avenue, I wondered how a different context might have helped me to learn more. If a few of Charlotte's other texts (viewpoints less tumultuous than Emily's) had been enlarged and hung as banners, might we have understood the desperation in the discipline driving the Brontë siblings to invent exits from their circumscribed and bleakly pitiless world? Would we have felt silences gnawing and whispering as terrors?

I always had found more to contemplate in Charlotte's quieter observations. "The soul, fortunately, has an interpreter—often unconscious, but still a truthful interpreter—in the eye," Charlotte wrote, directly referring to silence as thought. The eye perceives silences that are powerful elements for the soul. It discerns grief and secret pleasure. The soul can sometimes be read in a person's eyes. The power we hear Charlotte give to the eye is the task of "truthful interpretation." That phrase would have been useful in changing the tone of the exhibit. It might have clarified a reality that we can't absorb, striking a note of a different focus. The perceptions we brought to the rooms, the present positions about the connections between determination and success and power, might have changed shadings if truthful interpretation made us feel some of the inescapable desolation and determinism in the lives of that small family.

These thoughts swirled like the small perplexing clouds in front of the moon as I left the library.

When Natalia Ginzburg wrote the book that caught the world's attention, *Lessico famigliare* or *Family Sayings*, in 1963, she completed it in less than a month. She never asked herself if it was intellectual enough, or Communist enough, or if her way of expressing herself was too feminine when for years she had been trying to write like a man in blunt, hard sentences. She stopped judging herself, overcoming her fear of the Italian taboo of writing about personal things. She wrote as herself. She drew pictures of family members, telling stories about her father, who was a towering figure, morally and intellectually, a Jew who resisted Fascism, a professor who produced two students who became Nobel Prize winners. Ginzburg showed him in the family, a benevolent dictator, choleric and impatient, holding high standards that forced his children into high standards, often conflicting ones. It was a bold and endearing viewpoint. The more personal side of public figures interested her. Ginzburg went on to fill out a picture of Alessandro Manzoni, the most celebrated and frequently taught nineteenth-century Italian writer, exposing him as a human being with contradictions, who expounded charity and religion and failed to meet the requests of family members who asked for his presence and love. By taking up the subject of the family as memoir, she entered the realm of women's lives and view-points, which had been largely unwritten and untold.

Her artfulness was a position of humility but ironically real confidence. "When I write something, usually I think that it's very important and that I'm a serious writer. I think that happens to everyone. But there is a corner of my soul where I know perfectly well and at all times what I am—which is a small, small writer. I swear that I know it. But it doesn't matter much to me. Only I don't want to think about names: I've noticed if I ask myself 'a little writer like whom' I grow sad thinking of other little writers. I prefer believing that no one has ever been like me, however small, however much of a flea or mosquito of a writer I may be."

When I was no more than three, I used to go down our street to visit my friend, Patty Cake, who was two years older and lived at the bottom of our hill, one house from the corner. When I came home with stories, my father would say, You are not to talk about our family. You are telling family secrets. Don't be fooled. They don't like you, they just invite you in to pump you for stories. I was off at an early age, resisting lines being drawn, looking for alternatives for behavior, for mirth, for lapses like mine. It took me until middle age to realize that my resistance, my determination to make my own mistakes, was often an unexamined response, a defense reflex that didn't admit what was there to be seen and chosen, or what I really felt.

By using the internet, we gradually acquire an easy belief that we are free to express ourselves. This practice gradually assumes a forced attitude of entitlement to see and to expose, to take grievances out into the public without irony or knowledge or proportion. There is a herd reaction, as if it were really true that we all understand the same thing, the same words, the same way. There is the power of numbers—so many thousands or millions like or dislike this. It didn't take long, either, before companies began selling ways to buy "likes" on sites to create the appearance of approval, popularity, common agreement about the flaws or virtues of the person or piece of work. Non-existent herds were created—mobs, masses of empty false noise.

We need quiet to feel nothing, to hear silence that brings back proportion and the beauty of not knowing except for the outlines of what we live every day. Something inner settles. The right to silence unmediated by social judgment. Sitting at a table in an empty kitchen, peeling an apple, I wait for its next transformation. The red, mottled, dangling skin slowly unwinds what happened to it on earth.

I think of my father and his sudden death at age fifty-one usually as a story that I grasped as well as anyone could. My narrative, until quite recently, was that he was an artist and by abandoning that life, he died young of a heart attack. I have only a few factual images. It was as if he wore a light shroud of distance around his personal self. He maintained it by condemning most conversation as small talk. The daily toll of six to eight cigars literally kept his mouth closed, unless feelings were broached. Then his wet, chronic cough erupted and his large body convulsed with asthmatic choking.

When I compare him with the journalist who was struck in the head and kicked by ISIS fighters, who expressed his disdain to powerful figures offering him bribes, I see how unfair such comparisons are. My father and the journalist had completely different versions of life and what they wanted to learn from it. They came from different cultures and absorbed differently what a performed identity meant. It would be a feat to find commonalities where their experiences overlapped.

My father passed on to me his draining and stoic acceptance of duty, along with many other attitudes that were never given real shape. I see some of them now, among roots that still nourish me in surprising ways. A few of them are certainties, their intentions invaluable. I cannot judge them. They are part of my inheritance, like a Chesterfield sofa, willed with great love, and for that simple reason there is no issue about giving it away. It has always been a question of how it fits into the rest of the room.

1. My father, in Milwaukee, Wisconsin, who was not an immigrant or the son of immigrants, started a dowry chest for me. He started buying linens. My mother, after his sudden death, gave away my little inheritance to the Goodwill without ever asking me. For years at Christmas he had made certain I received embroidery hoops and cross-stitching patterns. I used to cry every year when they tumbled out of the wrapping paper. My brothers received Erector sets, and both got new bikes while I was given a used one, because girls don't ride bikes as often. Yet I regret not ever having had the chance to use the embroidered tablecloths and placemats he assembled as an assumption of what girls needed to bring to a marriage. One set of linens, in my memory decorated with green pineapples and passion fruits with black knots, remain a unique deviation. They were not kitsch, one of his most frequent judgments for people, ideas, and taste. Instead they were joyous, oddly proclaiming something exotic and missing. They were out of character, as was the lapse of a diamond ring he had had made for himself, with four large diamonds, each representing one of us children.

2. My father taught us that people of the nouveau riche were bad. For him, a third-generation Wisconsinite, that meant all the people who lived in California. Immorality all started, he would say, with gold diggers. We were taught that public schools were good and the basis for sustaining democracy. In fact, we went through the public system and benefited from

it. He preached that graduated income taxes, no matter how painful, were the way to ensure chances for others who were less fortunate. The week prior to April 15, he was usually locked in his study after dinner. In rare piques of cholera, before shutting himself in, he would rage against a few acquaintances who evaded their public obligations with offshore accounts. Patriotism equaled duty.

3. We were reminded, usually in the context of a shortcut we were taking in our homework, that Picasso didn't make his scribbles without first knowing how to draw. We were informed that because Eleanor Roosevelt was homely and had buckteeth, she worked. We were told that labor unions were about having five men to change a single light bulb when one would have sufficed.

4. Nearly every day, we were reminded we must not cheat or copy. We saw my father once challenge the Milwaukee Bar Association by protesting and then insisting that a Jew be allowed to take the qualifying exam. We heard one story from his last job about how he, as the company's director of public relations and its treasurer, protested a man being fired after having worked for the company for thirty years. My father told us he threatened to quit if they fired the man, who was sick. He insisted the company had an ethical obligation once the disabled man had given them the best and most productive years of his life.

5. The day that the company put my father on half pay, after he had suffered a stroke six months earlier, he died in the afternoon of a heart attack. He had no pension from the company and had been denied life insurance because of his asthma and a previous gallbladder operation. No doctor checked on him in the six weeks after leaving the hospital before he died. He had

been brought home because my mother thought he needed to come home. The doctors told her that if he left the hospital, they would take no responsibility for his life. There was silence around his diagnosis and condition since no one in our family had medical knowledge or connections. He never asked to see a doctor once he came home. We were all passively ignorant. None of us said that or even considered our inadequacies.

6. We knew that my father did not let my mother sing in the church choir or go out at night alone. Once (a rare occasion, because she loved to drive), she went downtown on a bus because she was meeting my father. For some reason, she forgot her purse. An African American man, seeing her distress and embarrassment, paid her fare. His gesture thrilled her. She excitedly told my father about the man as soon as she got off the bus. My father sulked silently through their dinner. Finally, he made his pronouncement. Didn't she realize that he provided for her? He gave her everything she needed (although as a wife she didn't have a signature on their checking account). Never, he said, as long as he was alive, was she to accept money from another stranger.

7. My father, during their marriage, never attended a single concert with my mother. Classical music, he declared, held no interest for him. What he meant was he didn't know anything about it. He never went to museums either, and that was his supposed passion. Didn't we have portfolios of his paintings in the basement? Wasn't his degree in fine arts? How deep did he bury his conflict? On our only family visit to New York City, neither alone nor with us in tow did he visit the Met or the Museum of Modern Art. He took us to Radio City Music Hall to watch the Rockettes.

Father didn't want our friends or my mother's in the house

if he was home because he could not tolerate spending the little time he had outside of work with others. His house was his castle and his place for privacy. He often called himself the king. One of his rationalizations was he deserved the privilege of being free to walk around the house in his underwear.

On our stairs there was a print by John Steuart Curry of a man holding a lamp and descending the stairs in his long johns. I always found it disturbing and tried to focus on the lamp and its light. It seemed odd to me as a subject and made me feel strange in the same way my father did by refusing to wear a robe over his boxer shorts. Dad, I would prod, I thought kings loved robes.

When the journalist sits in his chair, his eyes light up with amusement and his thought process runs across his face like a ticker tape. His eyes sift information, what to tell and how to tell it from all he knows about what is so fascinating about life and the experience he has had access to. Words for my father were paid work. He was in public relations. He sold ideas by using phrases. When he came home at night, he went to bed for a nap. When he got up for dinner, after eating, he turned the television on. Sitting in his chair, he would fall asleep. He was full of unstated regrets and could not rearrange or shed his responsibilities for four children, his wife, a dog, a swimming pool, two cars. The pool, incidentally, in order to save money was dug by prisoners from the county jail. They arrived and left in shackles.

I remember being told I was not to speak to the men, but I could not resist. I worried about their thirst. Each day, I filled up two half-gallon milk bottles with water and took a stack of paper cups, hoping I could get in and out of the backyard before my mother looked out one of our windows.

Willy Loman, Arthur Miller's American character, a salesman, lives a sense of self from the point of view of a man who must sell things. The self-loathing Willy speaks for a deep element in American capitalism, where people silence their opinions for fear of losing a job. They take up scripts they only partially believe, knowing that the task is to sell illusions of goodwill.

My father felt that even buying stocks was immoral because one had not worked for the windfalls that might come. Working in public relations, it is unlikely that he did not feel the burdensome toll of selling ideas that were manipulative.

He did not lament. He did not really complain. He was passively silent about his feelings. His criticisms were moralistic, and often, fatalistic predictions. When I was nineteen and leaving to get on a Greyhound bus to work in the inner core of Pittsburgh, living in the basement of a church and working in the African American community with other college students, he reached out, now from his bed at home, the latest of various beds in which he had lain paralyzed for more than six months after suffering his stroke. His idea of himself as the provider had collapsed. No one had a measure of his despair or his fear. We were ignorant, oblivious, and silent about those feelings. Our view was focused on the future and his getting better. He cried and held my arm. Don't go. Stay here. You understand me so much better than your mother.

The silence broken free in his words startled me. Stunned by his tears, I panicked. You have both boys staying at home, and the joy of our little sister, I said. There will be other times for me to stay. I reverted to our public family language. Our country is in shreds. Civil rights are important. I knew my positions and actions deeply frightened him. Three weeks later, he died.

His request made it impossible, I still tell myself, for that young, exposed girl to stay. She would have, Lord knows, because of course she cared, and had tried to come home from university and been rebuffed by her mother. Stay there, it's much easier for us that way.

My father, tugging my arm, expressed a tension that was ongoing in the family—my mother cutting my hair in my sleep, my father rewriting my essays—the back and forth over the role of women and who wore the pants. His eyes signaled how much was buried and how I had been used silently as a hostage in their relationship to themselves and to each other. His last words to me were, Take care of yourself. Because I left that morning, even now it is difficult for me to hear his last wish.

Sometimes, he's right there in my ear with one of his corny jokes—what did the Greek tailor tell his client? You rip-a-des, you men-a-des. It is only right that the pun I best remember remains a joke about responsibility and a garbled sense of culture. It reflected his Germanic humor, which was always quite kitsch. Euripides. *Eumenides.* An author and a play. But he was making a point about life, not art. You ripped these. You mend these. I wish I knew if he ever saw the joke as on himself, a mirthless standard for choices he never allowed himself to revisit.

The Nigerian women I teach, hoping to encourage them to write about their experiences, often shrug their shoulders and say they have nothing to write. Sometimes, I hand them colored markers and say don't bother with the words. Words are so hard to get right. Words to get them so that they feel true, or like truth, is very hard work. The pens are so much kinder. Pick a color. Pick as many colors as you want. Draw your name. Their eyes question me, and then they bend down over their large A3 sheets of paper. They draw themselves as vases with fine designs. They are trees with multicolored flowers. Ask them to put this into words and answers get dark.

I have no father. My father has four wives.

Those people in my village don't let you go to school. They are Mafia in the schools.

Beautiful, beautiful, the women say.

Did you know that is how you see yourself?

A colored vase.

They listen to that.

Because it is raining outside, one rolls her drawing up and slips it inside her jacket. So it won't get wet. I'll hang it by my bed.

I, too, recognized from early on that I was a beautiful vase, buried, invisible, but I could feel how much the amphora could hold.

Family secrets are a weighty question for anyone who decides to write memoir. Saint Augustine, when daring to make his life the subject of his writing, did so because he could narrate a clear story of transformation. He was someone and then he became himself as he set that earlier life aside. He had no need to reveal weaknesses except his own in telling a story. His identity was at the center of a book addressed to God. The "you" to whom he spoke was silent, but the "you" was a listener to Saint Augustine's reasoning and struggles, doubts and certainties.

Narration is a stunning pathway, full of tragic pitfalls as well as liberating vistas. Especially if it traces long periods of time, it is nearly impossible to decide what is true and what will not be falsified or tinged by putting it in a story with shadings.

One of the first silences that made me open my heart and actually change how I understood silence as reality tugging my whole being, not just someone who had my name, occurred on what would have been the tenth birthday of my son if he had not died. Like Natalia Ginzburg, I probably had held off expressing the occasional psychic side of my experience, fearing it was too female, too irrational, too soft to be admitted to others. I didn't want someone to say of these moments, Oh, these only belong to women. I also had an enormous resistance because of what my Protestant family called bragging and its unattractiveness. Bragging meant calling attention to yourself. Bragging was bad for anyone, but doubly bad if you were a woman. I still appreciate the gentle admonition from Matthew, chapter 6, about not letting your left hand know what the right is doing when giving gifts. Bragging, in our times, has gained acceptance far beyond even the idea of selling yourself. It is a day-to-day experience of drawing blue arrows on the internet that say ME. They are so large and unquestioned other messages are disdained as too quiet, as if they held no conviction.

The butterfly experience was so total I hesitated to talk about it because of my own private nature. I hesitated because I didn't want anyone to think I was looking for proof or comparisons. I didn't want to claim psychic powers—something that cheapened what was very mysterious ground. Yet even if I chose to speak about it, its mystical nature disqualified me, in my mind, from standing on ground that was equal to the language of science or politics. It wasn't embarrassment, but I didn't have a structure that made it possible to speak about the butterfly that settled on my shoulder at the end of our street in Parma on my son's birthday and then followed me into the house and circled my head and passed my eyes and fell to the floor, where I got on my knees and it landed on my open palm and it walked my four fingers and after that I poured my tears on it for nearly an hour, flooding my body with an ever-growing sense of its pinpoint of attention. I talked to it; I flowed from my own deep fountains, and finally, after more than an hour, I knew that it had to go. The event or the connection had to end, to close. I carried the butterfly on my open palm and walked it to the garden. It didn't fly away. I had to break the spell, and it finally flew, leaving me shocked in a strange fold in time. A fellow poet encouraged me to share it. He said: It is the most important thing you will ever write. He was talking about generosity of spirit, of being human. I couldn't do it then. I honored my right to keep silent.

The butterfly experience was such an overwhelming one that I had no interest in sharing it. I didn't want words to cheapen it. I didn't want, long before Facebook even existed, for the story to be snatched and used. For someone to say, I know just what you are talking about. I didn't want someone to touch one breath of the experience and turn it into something in words. Translated into words, the butterfly experience would be forced into meaning, even art, if you will. But I didn't want it reduced in that way. The silence in the butterfly story was an opening too large for fictionalizing with words. Yet it is one of the silences over time that has most deeply challenged me to name it. I decided to write about it, after President George W. Bush bombed Baghdad with an announcement that the firestorms would start at 9:00 p.m. Iraq time. I had been invited to read at a poetry festival in Verona, where a petition from Poets Against the War was being presented. We crowded around a little TV screen in the lounge to watch the sky burst into exploding red crescendos. As the bombs established their relentless rhythm, and the screams of the people shouting in the room in Verona died down, the poetry reading began, an hour late. The speaker refused to make his introductions in English. He gave them in French. Without saying anything, the United States was declared the instigator of war.

After that experience, I touched the butterfly story. I was willing to let it move out of the silent place where it rested. I wrote an essay on its meaning to me, because it seemed like a moment when I needed to reach further into myself, to put down something that was not a moralistic view or a story about myself, but a living piece of writing that favored complexity, exposing me to something I preferred not to share. Thus, I pushed my heart to go forward and to be more generous, with more courage. I claimed some freedom that must become a part of writing if we are to write about what is true and false, good and evil. I used the butterfly story to tell a story of how mysterious life is, how each of us matters, how gifts (however they arrive and are perceived) may change our lives and may crack our rationality for a brief period of time and transport us into another kind of imagination.

E very so often in Bronxville, I watch, at a distance, a white heron, in the middle of the Bronx River that flows past us. He is a clean white bird; his feathers have some fringes that, if there is a breeze, flicker like those on a shawl.

I like stopping and watching. If nothing appears under his purview, often he turns, lifts his sword beak, and faces me. The long-legged creature exits from a peripheral vision then, with no particular meaning, into one of acknowledging my presence. He seems to cross into my world. But the heron always remembers his realm, one of protecting himself. The heron, with his predatory skills and winged contraptions that when opening remind me of the Wright Brothers taking off, usually keeps at least one hundred yards of distance.

There are rapids, boulders, rivulets between us. He often shelters under the stone bridge or away, hunched up in the water plants on the side with the polluted, sudsy waterfall. Sometimes in the day, nonchalantly exposed, he stands rapt on his sand-and-rock dune in the middle of the river. I watch him from a border of respect, fundamental ignorance, and a sense of intruding.

One day (it was Good Friday), I returned from the city after a session with a Jungian analyst, who fell asleep over and over as I talked. This was not his first lapse. He had done it for a few weeks. I asked him directly, as his head bobbed, why this was happening. He replied, It has nothing to do with you. Considering whether it was a test to see if I could explode, react, and reject the intolerable, I nevertheless was uncertain what to do. (Was it me or him?) Mulling as I crossed the river, I would have missed the white heron, except that the nearly four-foot-tall bird almost poked me in the eye. Perched on a fallen tree trunk, inches away from the guard railing, the big bird entered my space. I could see the detail of his hundreds of white pinions, some with insects crawling, a few ripped and torn. They were dry, dullish like bone or soap.

Jesus's words to his disciples—that they would be fishers of men—downloaded into my mind, as close and clear as Heron's eyes. Robert Graves told the myth of the Fisher King. T. S. Eliot refashioned it in *The Waste Land*. H.D.'s bennu bird spoke as the sacred Egyptian symbol of fertility. These texts tumbled on one another. Then the words cleared away a blank slate. Heron and I fixed our gaze in the present. The surroundings broke out of my attitude of holding the bird at a distance and as separate. We were eye to eye at the same level; he on the tree trunk and I on the bridge. We were six inches apart. We were in communication. It was neither good nor bad, but we were in the same realm, without fear, and perhaps with an openness that might be called some form of incipient comprehension.

A pulse of commuters from the next train broke this silence. Checking their phones, few seemed to look up and notice us. They steered past, intent on their destinations. Heron, though, decided to act. He jumped from the branch, shook his wings, and hopped and glided with his long legs extended, down the slope. He waded across the river until he reached the sand dune and climbed on.

I walked the river the next day, leaned over the bridge, and even stretched to see under it, but Heron had vanished. I had been shaken by the long exchange of a gaze that was unflinchingly direct. We had been calmly sharing a kingdom. On Easter morning, I rushed out early, not wanting to explain, and found him, once again on his sand dune, fishing in the middle of the river. My heart, without admitting it, found the sunlit distance painful. I wanted meaning in Heron's reappearance. Could my mind fit it to the story that Christ had risen? The experience, like the Bronx River, mirrored silence. We know a mirror is something we really can't reach, and yet we see ourselves in it.

The transition from Egyptian hieroglyphics and the earlier Phoenician to alphabets with letters, Aramaic, Hebrew, Greek, had always been an interest of mine. The graphic way of using pictures as symbols for concepts and information became absorbed at first as signs and then letters forming words as separate units. I wonder, not just because of the emoji and the RU OK texts, but because of the genuine delight and knowledge we glean from photographs, symbols, and numbers, if we, as readers, are growing more comfortable with language whose symbols will not always be letters. Has written language, unbroken by designs or pictures or formulas, lost authority? The knowledge needed to make written words effective is changing.

Some scholars say that the first Hebrew letters were translations of Egyptian signs. Others that they borrowed from the Phoenicians. There was overlapping and evolution. Over time, the same mark or symbol seemed separate, depending on minor alterations. In the beginning, writing was mostly lists. Writing was useful for commerce and taxes. Writing always had powers to control. For all its beauties, while written language framed definitions of civilization, offering privileges, rights, duties, that same written language was creating for other of its members crushing cruelties and limits. Trends in books veer toward popularizing, simplifying. Are we in touch with "this grand book," as Galileo called "the universe, which stands continuously open to our gaze. But the book cannot be understood unless one first learns to comprehend the language and read the letters in which it is composed." He was referring to philosophy that had to be discerned by using the language of mathematics, "triangles, circles, and other geometric figures" (*The Assayer*, 1623).

My daughter, when she was no more than ten, sitting at a table with a British archaeologist who was visiting, answered his general question about the cause of the conceptual shift from Egyptian hieroglyphics to Hebrew. He was slightly surprised when she explained, with little hesitation, that technology brought about the change. It was the Hittites' use of iron in trade and war that made inroads that contrasted with the Egyptian mind-set. New weapons and means of transport led to the breakdown of a value system supporting an empire and led to a different organization of society. With the need for more abstract concepts, as well as more terms for economic arrangements, the more flexible and precise Hebrew letters evolved. The new logic, the new alphabet, she said, led to new laws, new economic arrangements, new definitions of rationality defined by reason.

He smiled, nodded in awe of her assured answer. He concurred with the ten-year-old, was pleased that she had a fine mind and probably, even as a woman, a fine future. He did say those words and she took no offense. And that was that.

I wrote an email to the Jungian analyst that I'd seen the heron on Good Friday and that he was nowhere to be seen on Saturday. The analyst flashed back: "Having found the tomb empty, men (or angels) asked the women, 'Why do you search for Him among the dead when he is among the living?' Mary Magdalene went looking for Him along the road."

Walter Benjamin, a German Jew who was held an extra night in Port Bou, Spain, in 1940, died by suicide while waiting to immigrate to America. He was a writer whose knowledge of culture and language drew him often to writing about the mysteries of translation and identity. He wrote: "Those who understand a text have largely missed its meaning." He wrote: "Scriptures contain between the lines their virtual translation."

friend sends a photo of the snow-capped Alps as she sees them from a train directed to Zurich. They are her way of sharing beauty.

She wants an opinion on an introduction for a book she has written. The file contains some comments by Jung.

One line is: "I was sitting at my desk once more, thinking over my fear."

Another is from Etty Hillesum, who perished in the death camps. She was twenty-eight when she started a journal. With good reason, as a Jew facing deportation, she called herself a "miserable, frightened creature."

Jung took up an inner dialogue with what he called his soul. She (his soul) was commanded to stir around in his inner possessions and show him what was there. She pulled up old armor, painted stones, images of God, a mixture. She remonstrated with him, saying, "You want to accept everything. You must limit yourself."

The young women from Nigerian villages in the Edo and Rivers States suddenly began speaking over one another in my class. Eyes that were fairly opaque, disinterested, opened wide. They are in different rubber boats, leaving at different times, but the numbers in the groups are always around 160. They had arrived in Libya by different routes, some terrifying—hiding during the day and walking during the night—but all the women spent months in the desert in Libya. One wore the same unwashed shirt for four months. No food, little food. Like a prison. Food like mud, eating horrible roots that tasted like worms.

> *I don't remember anything.*
> *People prayed all night and you couldn't see any land. No trees.*
> *Just horrible black water,*
> *Some was green,*
> *Some was blue,*
> *Dark blue, not like the sky.*
> *It smelled and swayed. Some people died and they threw them over.*
> *That's why the sea smelled so bad.*
> *It was a horrible blue, ugly blue.*
> *They rolled them over the side. Lots of people screamed and cried.*

If I had known I would never have left.
But now where will we go? We will never go home to our villages.
They prayed on the boats.
That's why we're here.
It was so dark on the sea.

Before I organized the class I was told that the young women refused to talk about their journey and I was not to expect to hear anything that was so close to their suffering. Yet in this sun-filled room at the top of a library named for an Italian journalist, Ilaria Alpi, who was murdered in Somalia for her investigative work on recycling that apparently touched Mafia links, the memories spilled out in answer to the question, What is your name? The silence of the space and the question asked worked like yin and yang.

Thich Nhat Hanh, a Buddhist master, imposed silence when we ate during a retreat I attended in Florence years ago. He explained that if we were not caught up in conversation, we could really taste what had been prepared. I remember the not altogether pleasant surprise of chewing and releasing the root taste of carrot, and swallowing cold, wet, unsalted rice. The flavors were so strong they shocked. Waiting until all the strangers at the long table were served before picking up a fork took concentration. Habit, boredom, hunger suggested trying to do something in the endless space. If we couldn't talk, why not get started eating?

Eating in silence revealed a lot of nervousness. By the fifth meal, mental connections with the earlier unremembered, unseen hands that planted seeds, picked, washed, chopped had emerged from the silence. A grain of rice rewarded the tongue with its unsuspected facets. The thought of having to use that same tongue to ask a person nearby, What do you do? became an empty concern. The idea appeared hilarious. We were strangely in touch, with our food, with the desert of quietly shifting space, with each unnamed other, as we were encircled by ancient cypress, a wind rattling the open tent, rain falling softly.

While I picture the boats we in Italy often see on the evening news, thronging masses of refugees and prostrate children being lifted overboard into rafts and carried through the water to shore where many are wrapped in shining gold insulation blankets, some put on stretchers, the rest walking, limping, carrying others who are too weak to walk, I had never imagined what migrants heard and felt listening to the sea and other humans who are falling apart. No one can articulate the truth of those crossings, the whole truth.

What the women in my class articulated is tradition in single words that go back as far as time and sea, used by people who know water as means for crossing distances. The Nigerian women's single adjectives are similar to the way they were used in early Greek writing. Epithets in Homer were a way of fixing reality as specific and traditional. The sea was wine-dark or loud-roaring. Adjectives were used to make the world a story with recognizable parts that could be used over and over. Greeks in Homer's time knew the sea in the way that my Nigerian women in 2018 knew the water. They knew it as a close reality essential to changing borders.

The description of the sea in Ernest Hemingway's classic *The*

Old Man and the Sea proves an interesting contrast. A passage written from the narrator/Santiago's point of view shows us that the sea is a picture of Hemingway's time and Hemingway's mind. "He always thought of the sea as *la mar* which is what people call her in Spanish when they love her. Sometimes those who love her say bad things of her but they are always said as though she were a woman. . . . And if she did wild and wicked things it was because she could not help them. The moon affects her as it does a woman, he thought." Out of context, read now, the sea can barely be felt or imagined. Hemingway, the writer, did not really know the sea as independent of himself or of culture common at the time.

Herman Melville's sea in *Moby-Dick* is rich and detailed: "Consider the subtleness of the sea; how its most dreaded creatures glide under water, unapparent for the most part, and treacherously hidden beneath the loveliest tints of azure." The sea is a subject separate from the writer. His language carries the physical and psychological reality of sails, storms, sailors, charting distances and changes as a way of life determined by the sea. Melville's metaphors are furnished by relearning the ways of water from the sea's point of view. The images plunge him into a relationship with the sea as a character and protagonist. How he writes about it expresses his own deepest, complex, and varied being in relation to the universe.

The Nigerian women, through their use of basic colors, pauses, and silences, brought the Mediterranean Sea to me as the Greeks knew it. The sea was not in their heads, reflecting them. They smelled it and were tossed back and forth in its life-and-death power.

In an indefinable way, their perspective reminded me of one of my favorite books—*The Sea Around Us*, by Rachel Carson. In

1951, as a pioneering woman, she embraced her interest and authority on a topic outside the traditional realms for women writers: fiction, domesticity, or social relationships. A sensitive scientist, she created a role for herself as an amanuensis, clearing space for the sea's life to be recorded. The story she composed is polyphonic, with waves; the subject does not contain one climax, one plot, one point of view. The narrative was written from research by thousands of people who have explored the realities of the sea, hypothesized questions, and contributed discoveries. Carson's book embraces a collective power instead of placing her individual voice at the center of knowledge. Her book overflows with great events. The same holds true for my Nigerian women. Their short, brave tales joined a collective version of sea voyages.

The television accounts of the dramatic landings at Lampedusa do not affect me if compared with the emotion generated by the three Nigerian women speaking of the awful fear they felt on the sea. They roll their eyes and laugh hysterically thinking of how dark night was, how hungry they were in the months of being held in Libya. Yet they do not describe the treeless silence of the nights and the sea as an indifferent universe. The young women accept its menace. When I offer them Shakespeare's twenty-ninth sonnet, in which the poet troubles "deaf heaven" with his "bootless cries," one of the women finds the poem interesting. She understands that Shakespeare, the poet, hears no loving response to his suffering. If God exists, God is deaf. She counters, briskly, perhaps God has better things to do.

Much Gnostic writing holds that no one can articulate the whole truth of God. The number seventy-two circulates as the number of languages feeding into that truth. There is the dark and the light in those languages, the numinous and the problematic. The sea's realities and moods are a reflection of the seventy-two.

The three Nigerian women do not imagine that they could pose a question as large as the one Shakespeare suggested. The sea is green, black, dark blue, and one woman, just one, saw one dolphin.

Deaf?

Not God.

God is too large. The sea is too deep.

We landed. *Thanks be to God.*

After each class, I am sorry to leave the room at the top of the international library, filled with books to be filed and shelved, a room out of circulation, with backlogs, where pigeons nest in the eaves across from the window. The carpet has a humid smell. We are tucked away in a place where this invisible work is happening. Women are writing in response to personal memories. They are bringing them out and telling them on paper, to themselves and each other. They know and are quietly proud.

The room offered by the library allowed me to suggest to the women that answering "What is my name?" might be harder than it seemed. Their lives had changed; they needed space to touch the state of emergency in themselves and in the world. In any hypothetical analysis, the costs-benefits of sharing this silence were paltry, even if I was a volunteer. Six women were the most I ever saw in class. The others in the group of ten had many different excuses for not coming. The few who attended found real words in their blood. The class didn't necessarily stop the rumors that many of the refugees were selling their bodies. Those from the north had fathers with many wives. Those from the south, even though sections 42 and 43 of the Nigerian constitution guaranteed women equal rights and inheritance rights, did not believe that those rights would ever have been enforced. The silences and how to translate them into reality were difficult, and yet many of their everyday stories of village life in Nigeria seemed quite similar to village life in Italy even twenty years ago. Land reform, although it failed in many ways, changed the Italian south. Cars and highways did their part. And women's lives, they began changing, too, when women demanded more for themselves.

My fourth cycle of classes with Nigerian women has been an experience leading to my pulling back from the subliminal attitude of helping. Being with them, listening to their laughter—their voices rising to such intense excitement that they burst from their chairs, clapping their hands, tugging, teasing each other—releases a vitality that astounds me and belies their apparent reserve. Watching them as they bend over their pieces of paper without breaking concentration for twenty minutes at a time, I see that they are fed by the freedom these hours give them. Although they have few ideas of a clear path, they have strength to act without cynicism.

Draw a window, I say. Close your eyes and see if you are looking out, or are you kept in? What would it take to make you open the window? Would that be a good thing? Down their heads go and they nod, trying to answer something that makes no obvious sense. What comes out is the surprise of an answer. They participated fully, instead of copying from the lightning-fast member of the group. Two would like to keep the window shut, to keep out the dust that they must sweep up and to keep out flies that trouble the food. In a few minutes, two of them have turned back to Nigeria, to windows, open or closed, that are fixed in Africa and not in Italy. How much is stopped there, kept inside, without sharing, without processing, as if Nigerian memories amount to a strange sunken trunk, on the bottom of their consciousness with no expectation that someone else, including themselves, can find it?

Many times, one or the other of them told me that she would like to learn to swim, they who crossed the water knowing that they might drown. That journey, which can take a thousand forms, where one might be saved or one might drown, the un-named choice into the unknown and accepting that choice, is a recurrent moment that has sustained more of humanity than we will ever know. Yet after the journey, what happens to the tangle of fears and misunderstandings, longings and loneliness that was carried to the new place?

Unsettled. Unsettling. A boat. A cradle. A chance or drown-ing? Which is it? Can it be two at once, or a cause and an ef-fect? Are we subjects or objects? Not only women, certainly, but women certainly know the duality of crossing. We are aware of passing nearly every day from one world, one problem that is not ours, to another that is, and then that carries us to an-other, whatever choice is made.

W hen Mstislav Rostropovich knocked on the apartment door of my friend James, the cellist was in
his bathrobe, on his way to the sauna in the basement. We were in Lausanne, Switzerland, and he had a question about the temperature controls monitoring some of the
original Shostakovich scores that he housed upstairs in his
apartment.

Rostropovich had not meant to come in. Invited to meet
someone whom my host described as a dear friend, he politely
obliged. He sat down on the wide couch, waited for the maid
to bring tea, tugging his robe tighter while not trying to hide
his bare legs.

Many, including James, observed that Rostropovich liked to
talk. He tended to feel that he towered over those around him,
so he would talk about himself. Like many people of special talent and experience, his monologue was indeed about himself.
The dimensions of his experience meant that he shared angles
on the world that most people never entered nor would dream
of seeing. Many males tell fascinating stories because their lives
have granted them the appealing and authoritative possibility
to acquire and expound upon their experiences in the world.
Many cannot imagine that lesser stories, often women's stories,

might hold the same or a different, more personal, and no less human fascination.

A mother of a friend stuffed hundreds of sheets of poetry and thoughts into a space behind an elaborate picture frame. Her writing voice was discovered after her death. Hidden, with the hope of being found, she silently beseeched her daughter to give voice to her work and to let it receive posthumous praise.

Hidden behind a frame, waiting, the gifts revealed unbearable, fantasized silences. Her poetry was a buried landmine, because in the war that it was destined for, the soldier had been terrified to pull the pin. Inside a family, hidden writing is another attempt at speaking, but often it is a way of crouching to bypass the more difficult and, occasionally, impossible effort of dialogue.

The Nigerians, even those who preferred to stay inside the imaginary window, not opening it and continuing to make good soup, got into real boats, risked real skin, although they knew one in ten drowned making the journey.

It was easy to imagine many of Rostropovich's stories as set pieces. Even if they were, performances are rarely identical. Hearing that I lived in Italy, the white-haired man with rosy cheeks offered a witty story, partly at his expense. His wife accepted all social engagements, he said. After performances, he tried to reach the check first, so that he could direct it to a charity instead of to the family coffers his wife controlled. In Rome (her name was Galina), she rushed backstage to say that they had been invited to the house of a famous actor.

He recalled:

Once we sat down at the table and I looked around, I couldn't recognize anyone who looked famous. I leaned to the man on my right and asked, where is the host sitting? They say he's a very famous Italian.

The man sighed. I suppose they mean me.

You? His face was unremarkable.

I'm probably not very famous, although the French know my films. Maybe they're not shown where you are.

I looked straight at him. I must have still looked skeptical.

Please, he said, offering his hand. Mastroianni. Marcello Mastroianni. And you? Who are you?

We laughed heartily, as Rostropovich knew we would.

The tea came. It was a chance to break in. I asked him something I had always been curious about: Bach's six Cello Suites. Who played them best, in his opinion, and what did he think about playing them?

He said Casals played the Suites well. Then he added, I think that you have to believe in God to play them well. I played them better technically when I was young, but now I believe that I am closer. But I think no one can play them. We are centuries away from knowing how.

Rostropovich told us that afternoon that he had recorded them, recently, in a French church, the Basilique Sainte Madeleine in Vézelay. Its clean geometrical structures fit perfectly with how he interpreted Bach, he said. In the end, he produced the versions himself. He added: Each day, each hour, each minute, you reflect upon these suites, reaching deeper. You think you understand and then the next day, no, there is something new.

I understand from reading critics that his late Bach versions were not considered his best. Claiming no expertise, it's likely that I don't even hear them very well. But silence does seem to enter in: he leaves significant pauses at many points. Occasionally he pushes a phrase in a definite direction and then a microsecond of space follows, so that we might even imagine, for an instant, he lost his place.

The silences, which introduce uncertainty, are palpable around some of the varied colors of musical patterns his cello expresses. The notes strike out and the pauses intimate something unapproached. John Cage's "4'33"" and Rostropovich's conception of space between notes point to different interpretations of silence. The Russian, by opening up instants of silence that illuminate the limits of an individual artist and his interpretation, seems to introduce a higher presence. Cage frames the unknown as a construction. Both delve into the relationship of change to timeless moments.

I am waking up at night. My head flooded with the way the book should go. I am looking back at what I wrote and understanding that many pages have been completely re-arranged. I am full of energy to tear down and let fall. Many have become crumpled pieces of paper. They are obsolete, and the point of view obsolete. They are too timid in stating how hard silences were and are in human lives and, in other parts, they are tossed because they depend on the voice of a girl who always had other voices and is no more. They are trapped and dead ends.

Montaigne says, "I cannot keep my subject still. . . . I do not portray being: I portray passing." I circled and circled an event that troubled me for years, unable to decide what it meant, but I held on to a fixed interpretation for it. Now I believe that I couldn't understand it because I was using the old self as the one who chose its meaning.

The story took place in Florence in the Church of the Annunciation. A priest took me by the hand as I was trying to light some candles.

He said: Candles are nothing. The fire of prayer springs from your heart. He firmly put his hand on my wrist and pulled me, leading me away as if I were Joan of Arc walking to the pyre.

I can still feel the upset for not shaking free of his arm as he pulled me. I accepted his firm grip, curious, embarrassed, caught up in the strangeness.

He went up the steps first, still tugging my arm, and led me to the altar, covered in a white cloth.

Ask Mary. Ask Mary. Put your hands on her and ask.

Put your hands on her.

Mary in blue, chastely bent in a position of receptivity, was to the right, framed behind dusty glass and very large. Gabriel was full of arrow-like beams of light and on one knee. There was gold leaf in golden beams, and silver medals pinned to Mary.

The lights over the altar were bright and blazing: candles, crystals, and electric lights. He continued to command me.

Stand on the altar, he said when I protested, saying I couldn't reach it.

Stand on the altar, he admonished. I climbed two steps and reached from there. Hesitant, I stretched to put my fingers on a dusty piece of glass, wishing I was elsewhere.

There is nothing right or wrong about putting Euros into a metal box to pay for a paraffin candle and to say a prayer. But the priest was right observing that paying for the beauty of a flame will not change the heart. In part, at least, change occurs by facing the gap between doing and actually showing how it is to be human and confused. Maybe the candle is an admission. Change is not all will. It well might include me seeing myself standing on an altar, struggling in resistance to my beliefs, looking exposed, and feeling exposed. But fundamentally unengaged. The glitter of the medals of thanks for prayers answered pinned on Mary in the painting, her deeply receptive bow to the life being entrusted to her, was a tinkling, glittering mass of placed hopes that I was being given a command to touch. The call to join others in belief was an experience I had had more than once and always resisted. He tugged me out of the dark and into a place where I would show myself, accepting the critical glances and stares of people who were trying to pray. What did I want to do? Why did I let him pull me? Why did he choose me in the first place?

P aolo and I were talking this morning about computers and how each new version of a program like Windows leads you deeper and deeper into a language and a logic that is real to those who wrote it, yet probably is not even completely apparent to all working in the same company. Never seeing the whole design described and explained, command by command, it may not even be apparent to those who wrote it. If we on the outside of those languages understand, it is usually a partial grasp of moves that leads us to results we are focused on.

The world that programmers are creating through their designs is tyrannical. We have few means to oppose it. Starting from the basics, we soon are unaware of the structures and the grammar determining where we can and cannot reach. Over and over, we succumb to actions, a click, a check in a box, knowing that there are many levels and layers beyond the click that may not be working in our favor or may not be neutral, but we can't worry or stop for too long. We click, but something somewhere leaves us with a micro-sensation of regret as we join the crowd moving forward.

Many channels, landscapes, and maps are being built from

our moves, our preferences, our links. However, we are unable to know if we are enslaving ourselves and if we will ever have the ability to know where or how to turn as these systems absorb us. We really cannot understand how programs intrude or manipulate, and the depth of influence they have on the present. We know we are being tracked. We cannot possibly understand what it means when we accept that our information is being sold. When we signal that we accept the conditions, we have joined a party, without knowing its political platform.

Today a note on my screen popped up, telling me that I used 33 percent less screen time last week. The figure made me feel watched. In the back room of our house, my study, which is no longer a quiet place since our neighbor took in a blind dog, I feel disturbed by the sensation of a machine tracking my moves. A sense of my privacy has been intruded upon, nudging my sense of self. The machine will notice that my use is still in free fall. I have taken up writing by hand again, at least for first drafts.

It was while writing by hand that I found another page to crumple up. Forgot. I had forgotten that Santissima Annunciata was a stopping point for me because for centuries it had been dedicated to mothers and fertility. Prayers were offered there asking for children to be born. I had lit candles in the church for years, and stood in the piazza before it with hundreds of others, probably also hoping for miracles, during a festival of light, when people put candles in large colored lanterns and stood together and then walked around the piazza. I had forgotten that I discovered I was pregnant after nine childless years soon after that festival of light. That explains to me in part why I let the priest pull me. That is why now I am stunned realizing all those silver medals pinned on Mary were from women who had prayed for children and believed that their prayers were answered. The priest had tugged me up the stairs and asked me to stand on the shrine dedicated to one of the deepest mysteries in the human story: the miracle of birth and gratitude for it.

I explored the idea of nonfiction and persona with a student who had come from Geneva for a face-to-face session. As we went over her current work, we searched for a proxy voice that stands in for the person in the piece who narrates it. Once she found that proxy, I felt she would recognize that the story was not about the subject she had developed in various sections. I believed that finding a proxy would let her open the door to her own story within: she could face the pain, establish a point of view that let readers feel all the chaos. It would change the frame of a story that could be told from many points of view.

The discussion tired both of us. The motive for the story, the ongoing one in real life, was still throbbing. Once the story about the problem shifted from the person who was suffering to the proxy who suddenly needed to turn the story in her direction, the emotional motive was apparent. The back-and-forth between real and simplified, the truth, suddenly turned. The personal assumed another level and direction. Once the persona was established as different from the real person writing the story, the student could see that the writer was present only as the imperative for turning it into a story.

After discussing the manuscript, we resisted the bar's intriguing sweets: the *pasta frolla* with flourishes of bright lemon, raspberries, and zabaglione. Before she caught the train, we visited a few Parma treasures in the city center. The domes of the cathedral, and of San Giovanni directly behind it, were painted by Correggio over a period of ten years, from 1520 to 1530. The aerodynamics of figures who rise or fall are striking in both of them. The energy devoted to these motions, technical achievements, if you will, are announcements of further knowledge of perspective and the impossibility of not expressing that. The central message seems to be that discovery and application of technical knowledge also provided energy for changing belief systems gaining momentum from the discoveries.

In Santa Maria Assunta, Mary is among the crowd of biblical characters generated from the Old Testament figures of Adam and Eve. Mary is reaching toward a descending character who has never been identified in a way that satisfies. His white gown is lifted by a powerful wind as he descends—his legs agape, his genitalia exposed—so that the swing upward of Mary who is reaching, and the motion of the angel or Christ who is descending, suggest a blast of opposing and imaginary forces, rising and falling new messages.

The same dynamism presents itself in San Giovanni. In recent centuries, the central figure of Christ was interpreted as Christ ascending. After the dome was cleaned in the 1990s and the historical documents were revisited, Christ's direction was amended. He was descending to pick up a frightened and ill San Giovanni, who was partially hiding under a rock. The picture was painted with a perspective to be seen by the priests sitting in the choir or refectory seats. They were to be strengthened in their faith by seeing Christ coming to ease San Giovanni through death and to take him back, as promised, to heaven.

Titian observed that if the cathedral dome had been turned

upside down and filled with gold, it still would not approximate the painting's worth. Charles Dickens visiting the cathedral found the swirling clouds of people a "labyrinth of arms and legs." He was repulsed and wrote that "a surgeon in his wildest dreams could not imagine such a thing."

Opposing forces, the technical knowledge that Correggio possessed for depicting motion, led the borders of fixed perspective into mannerism and breaking up static space. The domes are reflections of the artist's need to express knowledge that inherently carried the seeds of opposition. He captured the dynamism of forces in which the directions of up and down, inertia and lift-off, are cosmic. In the third ceiling he painted in Parma, one for the female abbess of a Benedictine order that sanctioned the women to be self-governing since 1054, he ventured once again into opposition. This time the abbess was opposing three successive popes who wished to shut her order down. Correggio painted her above the capacious marble fireplace as Diana. This highly conscious huntress points her finger directly at the horse pulling her cart. It has lifted its tail and we see its anus. A strong message was put forward—a pagan and heretical message—and it belonged to the room commissioned by Giovanna da Piacenza in 1518. Here the forces moving were not winds from the heavens: they were scaled to myth. The opposition was another energy, inside an Arcadian bower painted on the ceiling where mischievous sensuous putti held lifted rocks above their heads and threatened storms and conflicts, alluding to the universe at the time and the authority of the Catholic Church.

The room has still no definitive interpretation or agreed-upon history. Reading the room in part as a political statement, given Giovanna's gender, is not one encouraged by the city. But I showed Diana and her pose to my student, stressing the power of narrative and choosing a proxy to tell a story.

Opposition and new ways of depicting energy were the silent dynamics in all three frescoes. The story of Correggio's work from that viewpoint is nonfiction that still has not been explored. The abbess's room, because of its size, is the most audacious and the most accessible. The Renaissance lives in place there. Classical ideas that had been suppressed by Christianity, nearly destroyed, were on the walls, commissioned by a woman. The room is about belief systems under pressure, censorship, change that should guarantee progress but instead was protesting the repression of freedoms that had already been won.

At the same time, on the same screen that I am vowing to consult less frequently, an email arrives with an hour-long video of a dear friend who, a few months earlier, died too young. It brings her so close that I shed tears many times as I give up my imagined plan for the morning and am drawn hungrily into glimpses of her and sounds of her work. Many of her poems are prophetic in a different way now that they are seen in the light of her courageous struggle against death. In one poem she is in a cemetery in Jerusalem, speaking to a figure who seems to come from the market, who polishes bones and broken bits of lives until they shine. A child of Lamentation and Memory, she lives in a tree and holds a place open for memory, memory being a river that resists history's erasures and fixed views. Torn, but willing to pick up the language of experience between cultures and places and sexes, she finds mud and spittle and a mixture of struggle to include. She manages to speak—without being sucked down or blown up—about moonlight and sun, earth and mud. I weep for the strength of Meena's work, her cries for language and witnessing, and then I weep because I miss her and conversations we used to have flowing from Indian spices to memories of war zones to times of solitude to love.

Avidly watching the video this morning, participating in the commemoration of her life, I felt the power of testimony arrived just when I needed to hear about the cauldron of life and the importance of living while writing. It was as if my friend was in the room, holding my hand even in death, showing borders that can be crossed. For months prior to her death, she felt her strength leaving her, and wondered many mornings if she would ever be visited by more poems. She rose one night and faced Krishna in a poem she titled by the hour on her digital clock, "3:29." She shared it by email days after she wrote it. It is difficult to capture the depth of understanding I felt when she shared work with me. The closeness of a relationship artist to artist, with trust in the giving and taking, the parity, the lack of a competitive border, where respect is a vast land of mutual understanding, is an experience that all artists crave and need. My friend had dialogues with many artists and thinkers. She was quick to listen.

It doesn't fit here, and yet a wave dies if it is interrupted. The video on Meena Alexander's life, sent to me by her husband, David, appeared on YouTube and I watched it this morning. I will let the film push me, or pull me, sincerely, not in the half-hearted way I let the priest pull me to the altar. I will put my thoughts about her thoughts in relation to one aspect of silence.

On the day she died, Paolo found a little ebony elephant she had given me on one of her visits to Parma. It had tiny toothpick-like removable ivory tusks. I had put it in a drawer probably five years before because I feared our first granddaughter visiting might be fascinated and somehow swallow a tusk. On the day Meena died, I noticed the elephant near our fireplace. I hadn't thought about it for years.

Paolo, what's Meena's elephant doing there?

What do you mean?

She gave it to me.

I didn't know what it was, but I thought it was too nice to burn. I meant to put it in a paper bag and move it to my study, where you would never know. I know you often have fits of reducing clutter and throw away great things. It was in the woodpile.

It's so strange. Never would I have thrown out something she gave me.

Smooth ebony in my palm, exotic wood, I rubbed its soft spine. As I put it in the pewter dish my older brother had given me, it felt as if a life had been brought back. Every time I see the little elephant, I remember how its dark round body appeared on the day she died. It was never meant to be burned.

The conversation Meena and I had in the spring, six months before the last one, which took place in the fall, we settled in the usual familiar place, her apartment at the upper tip of Manhattan. That spring, we'd taken the rattling bus together, converging after I finished a class on palliative medicine and she a yoga lesson for cancer patients. The room where we talked was the living room with facing family couches worn by years of conversations, friendships, and children. The March light was fairly wintry, unyielding, and as the hours of our conversation went on, of course, the room grew darker and colder.

My friend was shockingly thin by then, but her voice was her own. We talked basically as if she were not thin, as if this were a state that might well be temporary and, in any case, was not to be put into words, except when she might point out a detail about pain or hunger or how liquid was being drawn from her midsection in order to relieve pain. Her eyes spoke powerfully about the irony of the journey, the strange switch from health and recovery to one of no solution. She put her shoulder against uncertainty, with no reason to pretend. Even writing might not carry her through because she recognized that her creative energy often was elusive. With great courage, even more than the courage she found to continue to teach, to edit two books, to give readings, was the deeper effort to try to keep the door open to possibility and to continue treatments that might or might not rescue her life.

Our spring conversation was about writing. What was unusual was that instead of a mutual sharing of writing, this time she turned the conversation entirely onto me and encouraged me in every possible way to go forward. She knew I had a book to write and she said, This will be the one. She was not referring to sales, but to voice, to freedom and its importance. She knew multiple cultures and that multiple journeys were composed of multiple selves and multiple fractures and that language was both mongrel and composed of the golden eras of classical use of language. She knew women must find voices that carry passions, flesh, spirits, invisible wings and atmospheres of life wanting to be told. What are we waiting for? she asked, opening her large, dark eyes wide and raising her hands.

She was thrilled that I was working with Nigerian women, thrilled I was working with nuns and priests in Rome, from all over the world, who were looking for ways to narrate suffering and their own particular stories of setting out in a complicated and needy world. It was as if I was finally connecting in Parma, a place of remarkable uniformity, the voices I had always heard. This book will be it, she said. You are ready to write it. And this time, the world will be ready too. Don't save yourself. Draw from the core of your being. Go beyond style to essence. Your essence, my dear, your essence.

Meena died on the same day as did a very strong feminist poet from Pakistan, Fahmida Riaz. They were friends. Fahmida led a life in which testifying had a high price. It meant that her husband was imprisoned, and she was forced into hiding with her children in India. She herself was imprisoned. She continued to learn languages outside of Urdu and read an Hindi-Urdu-to-English dictionary as if it were the richest book of poetry on earth. "I love words," she wrote. On women's right to freedom, as well as for all the other groups who suffered discrimination, she was an advocate. Yet she still outlined a special feeling for women's struggles to be free: "It's complex, I mean there is the right to walk on the road without being harassed or to be able to swim or write a love poem like a man without being considered immoral."

The deaths of those two women, one my good friend, took place on my birthday: a day that had always marked beginnings and ends. It was difficult not to notice that, particularly because of the appearance of the ebony elephant.

My paternal grandmother died on the day I was born in the very hour I was born. She had a heart attack in the front seat of my grandfather's LaSalle in Milwaukee while he went into his German butcher to pick up some cold cuts and pot roast for the week. I was born in Chippewa Falls, three hundred miles away, where my mother was staying in her parents' home.

A few hours after my birth, my aunt found me covered in blood in my bassinet. For three days, I was given transfusions and then they gave up. It was the small-town doctor who suggested it, having read about the discovery of vitamin K being used in the war to hasten clotting in soldiers with massive wounds. Thus, I was saved in a swirling cloud of drama, blood, and last rites that never stressed the miraculous science but instead picked up a vague, discussable thread of destiny and tugged at the just-out-of-reach opening between life and death.

Being a parent, I can imagine how relieved my parents must have felt over the outcome. I can see the way they told the story was one way of framing it, letting it become like the glittering medals hung on Mary in the painting in Florence, without going any further in their response or search.

The story of that dramatic day followed me every birthday I celebrated in our family. My father, in one of the few letters he ever sent me (I was in my first year of college), made it central. He wrote: I know you and your grandmother crossed and met in that far-off corridor, where life as we know it begins and ends. I know she went along the path we all must follow, serenely happy having met her princess at long last.

In its Disney-like picture of that emotionally draining experience for my parents, I see one of the myths circling my life. When my father died unexpectedly, death stepped into our family again. This time with success. Our politeness and our inability to scream, to cry, to be sincere about conflict, left us ghostly prisoners who resisted at all costs any signs of breaking. We swallowed our grief, shallow silence covered over by the positive notes of American life where one goes on. This attitude was encouraged by my mother. As the Lutheran minister said at my father's funeral, "O death, where is thy sting? O grave, where is thy victory?"

Only this time, death broke the locks in our suburban banality. As if death were a god swinging our entire family on its little finger, we were centrifugated by it, spinning out without knowing how to catch on and stay still and talk to one another and cry.

Our fireplace was fitted two years ago with an insert that recycles the heat. After long years of debate, Paolo chopped down a plum tree that had been planted sixty years earlier, when his mother had built the one-story house and taken in boarders and rented the basement, hoping she could pay off the mortgage with their help. She was a widow with three children and the war was still a price being paid in nightmares and shortages.

The plum had split at the trunk and was hollow and as twisted as Donatello's haggard Mary Magdalene. It oozed sap that was dark. Beside the fungi and the green molds, some of the wood underneath the bark was reddish, like its plums. It took half a day to chop down the tree, but extricating the roots took three. Paolo was determined to dig them all out, and the hole around them grew wider and deeper. They extended more than three feet into the soil.

Now the trunk burns night after night in the fireplace. The roots of so many memories twist in yellow and blue flames. Never having left the land in Reggio Emilia, still living in his childhood home, Paolo feels no in-betweenness, none of the disconnections and fluidity that are what I know. The trunk pieces are dramatic, Rothko-like planes. The hard fruitwood, after so many years of seasoning, is the real thing. The heat radiates from the large stumps of wood, whose rings were figuratively counted, inscribed by his mother and brother and sister, the flour, the rolling pin, the lack of heat, the party line, the lit shrine to Maria, the cats who caught the mice, the walk across town alone to go to middle school, the books with paper covers to save them, the shoes with metal taps to save them, the coats as heavy as blankets, the craziness of his grandmother who was the eldest of seventeen and who carried the landowner's child—the tree lived through it all.

The flames can only burn the tree. The rest remains in memories, so many angles down to the maps of the nine iron wires dangerously bundled in narrow tubes carrying electricity around the house without any grounding. The details are there, in Paolo's mind. How many can he carry on his back, knowing them all so well and believing that they are what made him who he is?

Rachel Carson's book on the sea was read in twenty-five languages. The mixture of scientific knowledge presented in passionate prose brought the powerful subject to a level worthy of the sea's complexity and fascination. "Fury," "battle," "fought," "confused," "tumbling," "bursting," "breaking," "cresting," "rising," "approaching," "rolling," "smoothing": her pages carry the action of water arranging and transitioning and breaking up itself, as she raises subjects involved in understanding the element covering 70 percent of the surface of the earth. The chapter on "Wind and Water" is a favorite of mine.

A wave generally starts from confusion in the middle of the ocean and travels in various forms until it reaches the shore. "How long it will live, how far it will travel, to what manner of end it will come are all determined, in large measure, by the conditions it meets in its progression across the face of the sea. For the one essential quality of a wave is that it moves; anything that retards or stops its motion dooms it to dissolution and death."

The first section in Carson's book is called "Mother Sea." She is not being polemic, I believe, but calling out a truth. The title covers the topic and connects us where life begins. I revisit

Virginia Woolf's novel *The Waves* to see how she eases readers into the water:

> The sun had not yet risen. The sea was indistinguishable from the sky, except that the sea was slightly creased as if a cloth had wrinkles in it. Gradually as the sky whitened a dark line lay on the horizon dividing the sea from the sky and the grey cloth became barred with thick strokes moving, one after another, beneath the surface, following each other, pursuing each other, perpetually.
>
> As they neared the shore each bar rose, heaped itself, broke and swept a thin veil of white water across the sand. The wave paused, and then drew out again, sighing like a sleeper whose breath comes and goes unconsciously.

The pace of her description is a pace that belongs to paper, handwriting, reading for pleasure rather than for information. Words rest on the page. Eyes rest on the page.

The one essential quality of a wave is that it moves; anything that retards or stops its motion dooms it to dissolution and death. Some waves are stopped and thus die.

A few days ago in Parma, I went out in pouring rain to hear and see the presentation at the international library of a photographer who had spent ten years in Africa documenting conflicts. He was remarkable in composure, answering questions carefully, truthfully, with a pace that suggested an emotional cost to speaking about how he positioned himself in such situations. Applause was weird clatter, out of place. He did not feel reluctance about the complications of documenting violence but rather an awareness about how he belonged to the situations, deliberately having chosen to do the work. He trusted the audience to find meanings in his images of violence and kindnesses, censorship and trust. If there was beauty, it was not a deliberate rhetorical point. Indeed, he had humility to be able to find for himself the remarkable resilience of human beings who lived through so many kinds of trials.

He was a man who had been born in a village just outside Parma. He had known before he had finished university that he wanted to photograph lives in Africa.

In the first brief but interminable video, without giving any particular preparation to the few of us who had come in the rain to hear his presentation (there was no warning like those offered to U.S. television viewers that there may be graphic images), the lights went out and immediately screams surrounded us. On a dusty road in a small village in the Congo, women in long dresses were hoisting their skirts and running toward us, coming forward like the models in the publicity loop in the dress shop, except that palpable terror flashed in their eyes, screams flew from their open mouths, and we realized they were running for their real lives. Some were old, some too heavy to run, some younger, but all of them screaming, stumbling, limping as they tried to escape gunfire and men coming after them. The plain huts and houses hemmed them in.

The woman sitting next to me slumped over in a collapse that I could feel in the dark. She put her head between her knees and whispered, I think I am going to faint. She missed the next few frames where one of the women we could recognize by her soft rust-colored dress had already died, smashed by a rifle and left on the road so her head was open and her brain fallen out of her face like a last silent revelation. The size of the screen made our attention more intense.

There were other videos, and many stills. The photographer with a neatly trimmed black beard admitted that he was amazed, as he compiled his book, by how many images showed resilience and beauty. The beauty came on its own terms. It was something that reached out to him and he caught its composition. He had no way to explain its meaning, however. He felt context was crucial to the truth of the beauty. He fastened his images to a facing page documenting background, time, place, conditions. That lent levels of understanding to what the eye was seeing. It removed the images from purely aesthetic considerations and asked for accountability. He was not there for aesthetic reasons but for reasons of telling human stories in which he, too, was making choices in order to live as a witness.

If he was a positivist, historical facts helped to make the images more resonant memories. Facts also fastened the images to lives so that they could not become stories, cleaned up, edited, cropped of suffering and gazed on as objects or works of art.

B ecause of its solid gesturality, one of his images, drawn from a war where the government military soldiers patrolled villages, reminded me of scenes from paintings done by Masaccio. The photo's central focus was a young man, who, the facts explained, had stolen a piece of a computer phone and been publicly apprehended. The soldiers stripped him naked. While he was beaten, the frightened and approving and/or disapproving population looked on.

The reality of the event shared in the village, where each person saw it happen, reminded me of Italian villages where buildings are so close together the possibility to observe one's neighbor is ever present. In the turbulent decade immediately after the Second World War, many witnessed retributive acts of violence. Yet, the possibilities to deviate from ideological and fixed appearances were limited. Opposing views were known and persisted in groups. How can links from art be direct or political in such situations?

Another was a photograph of a young woman with her head down on a desk. We could see exhaustion, discouragement, contrasting with the crisp blue of her dress. A frank image of promises and gaps. Do we know what she feels, do we know? In some way, we do know what we need to know, what the photographer wanted us to understand. Both of those images and most that he showed placed us in front of human beings and human situations that, because of their context, had a capacity to enter our minds and hearts, making connections that were difficult to block. We could not escape empathy. Because he framed moments in which we could concentrate on individuals, he lifted them indirectly from politics and made us imagine ourselves in the same situation. He made us witnesses, letting us understand that the events were real.

He asked us to realize how things are for many people in Africa. While his aim was not to solicit guilt, he hoped we would notice, by ourselves, how little we think about wars and invasions and hunger and our distant connections to their causes and effects. The woman with her head down on the desk, was she an image speaking about the women prisoners in California whose wages are three cents an hour and who are sent to fight fires, then collapse with exhaustion back in their cells?

Yesterday, a dinner guest in Parma brought a pamphlet, *Minerali clandestini*, in lieu of a bottle of wine. We solved the wine problem by offering one made from land taken back from the Mafia. Each Mafia wine has the name of a person martyred by their violence. The table was set for political sensibilities.

The pamphlet would not let us close our eyes to Africa and it used the smartphone as an object we might reframe, realizing that we can't escape from its dark side, starting with the clandestine traffic around minerals. Each of our phones contains 0.317 ounces of copper, 0.009 ounces of silver, 0.0008 ounces of gold, 0.0003 ounces of platinum, 0.123 ounces of cobalt, 0.001 ounces of tantalum, and 0.035 ounces of rare soil. Actually, there was a lot to learn. The little pocket pamphlet had more than one hundred pages.

Having gotten this far, I still need to ask for patience in order to open up thoughts on silence without forcing them and ending up in the wrong place. The connections are there but are not straight lines.

Even if I summarize, I have not even established the description of silence—not its limits or its possibilities or the essence of silence that cannot be named. I have allowed myself some freedom because I am writing a book. Books these days are herded away from complexity. They are rushed into formulas and hard hypotheses to prescribe for the reader why or what she will gain if she thinks about the ideas or plot put forward. That is not unreasonable. However, we must think in terms of discoveries and the psychological costs of not allowing space for unfamiliar perspectives, including the effect of the past on the present or the effect of the present on the present or the past.

I am torn between several directions for the next section. Roots and their meanings are one direction. Death and its obvious and not so obvious considerations are another. Then there is the idea of direction in silence itself. I will take that up, hoping that it will be powerful enough to get beyond the narration I am carrying now.

Theoretically, Freud's ears, his listening ears, must have been among the most highly trained of the late nineteenth and early twentieth centuries. He put forward a term for an analyst's listening called "floating silence." The analyst's attention was to keep moving lightly, stopping to rest on the ceiling and the walls and the patient's face. In order to focus on the patient's words, a partial space of shallow interest in surroundings had to be created so that the psychiatrist would not rush with conclusions and observations to cover over, project, and thus miss what was being said.

R. D. Laing, a British psychiatrist who broke ground in his book *The Divided Self*, put a diagram of Rubin's vase in the opening chapter. The optical illusion is called a bistable because the still figure can be seen in two ways due to the contrasting edges. The eye cannot hold the black-and-white image as a white vase for more than a few seconds. The brain then sees it as two black silhouettes.

Early on in his career, Laing, in dealing with schizophrenic patients at the Tavistock clinic in London, decries physicians who speak in front of them as if they are uncomprehending objects. To Laing, it was intriguingly clear that people with schizophrenia

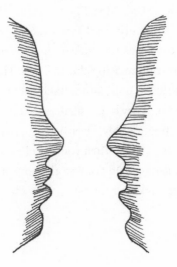

have understood realities oppressive for them. Their sense of identity, their realness, has been shaped by their perceptions that "they cannot take it for granted." Their pathological reactions reflect how others see them as disembodied, incapable of understanding. By using the example of the bistable, he challenges physicians to see the double image that they have in part created. He invites them to discover the other view of Rubin's vase—the schizophrenic seeing himself seen.

W.E.B. Du Bois in the classic *The Souls of Black Folk* articulates the pain of the double self, seeing oneself as Black and an American, and trying to rectify the two images to find a place in the world to be both. James Baldwin passionately re-creates the silences of Blackness, poverty, and being gay.

In *A Room of One's Own*, Virginia Woolf creates a scene in the first pages where women are forbidden free entry into the university library at Oxbridge. She re-creates the feeling of exclusion and all its absurd implications. She sees and explains the position of the Dons but they do not see or imagine hers.

There is a direction to being able to listen. The schizophrenic, R. D. Laing, W.E.B. Du Bois, James Baldwin, and Virginia Woolf ask to be listened to. They break silences that propose that heads turn and minds float openly. Over here, they cry, I'm over here. Don't look straight ahead. Turn your head and listen. Can you hear what I am saying? Do you see the contrasting edges and how they change back and forth?

I was hospitalized at three and one half, with a double pneu-monia and rickets from refusing to eat, and given four strep-tomycin shots daily for the raging infection threatening my life. My mother and my father only visited the hospital on weekends. No one seemed to find it unusual that I passed the week by myself. Lots of children of a certain generation, like Agnes Martin, were expected to be independent. I was too.

I remember climbing over the hospital-bed bars at night, walking down the long corridor in my bare feet in order not to wet my bed. I was afraid of breaking the rule to stay in bed, but more driven by obedience to the other rule of never wet-ting my bed. I made my journeys undetected (as far as memory tells me), and when I left the hospital after four weeks, I was a different child.

I had gained a distinct feeling of isolated independence. This story was not told to me. I told it to myself. I had waited and waited for my parents for long days, when other kids' parents came. My nocturnal visits directed to the lit sign over the bath-room were a strange taste of knowledge and guilt. Scared and cold, I could get up any night and walk on the icy floor, expect-ing with each step to be caught. Even though I broke rules, no one ever called me out or helped me. This sense of worldly power placed in my head an ambivalent sense of freedom and abandonment: Why didn't any adults know of my night journeys?

The events, which occurred frequently (or so says my memory), have a fairy-tale unreality about them. In my daytime experience of being in the hospital for a month, the nurses reminded me every day that I was a good girl who never cried when they gave me shots.

But the story of those interminable weeks is placed here because of the hearing I lost from the massive doses of streptomycin that I received every six hours. Day after day, as the drugs fought off the pneumonia, they deadened nerve endings in my inner ear. By the time my parents took me home, I was partially deaf, having lost bilaterally an important part of my auditory nerve. The nerve died without a peep.

This story is unverified. The hospital records have been burned. This reconstruction may not be completely true. The hearing loss is not fictitious, but perhaps I was deaf even earlier on. I had my first pneumonia when I was less than a month old.

The streptomycin injections saved my life.

The edges of the *t*'s, the *d*'s, the upper ranges, the pitches of women's discourses, the mumbles and shouts of kids were mysteriously gone.

Direction. Throw the ball over here.

Where?

Thud.

A multitude of signals and signs for interpretation dropped, left a lack, a wall, but without ever spelling it out to a three-and-a-half-year-old. Those who understand a text in part have largely missed its meaning.

Until glasses are prescribed, the squint is a solution. Once glasses sharpen the world, the difference is hard to fathom. At that young age, recognizing that my hearing had disappeared would have had to have been an observation made by an adult interpreting lapses.

When my mother frowned and asked, Why are you pulling your shoulders up to your ears, why are you making faces? she didn't know what she was asking. When my father got furious, insisting that I was lying—anyone could hear that shout—I shrugged and simply said that I didn't.

I was over forty when an otolaryngologist in Parma, after removing my headset, broke the news.

Signora, he said, you have the hearing of an eighty-five-year-old woman. You could be one of those ladies who sit at a table without hearing a single syllable, nodding her head. You read lips. Your eyes catch the babble from people's mouths. I can tell you have been doing it for a very long time.

I was strangely captivated.

I had often been struck by women in villages around Parma with swollen knuckles and wide, near-blind eyes, who were often toothless, sometimes playing cards, white-haired old ladies dozing in the sun, their chairs leaning against a wall, and then, surprised by a cat, suddenly shrieking and striking its mangy back while everyone talked over or around them.

Occasionally, they were acknowledged.

The old eyes, white with cataracts, jabbed with wild looks of incomprehension.

"Ahh, our little granny. Our little *nonna*. Be good, granny. Show us your gummy smile."

No one could have been more shocked than me to be told that the dead ends in my ears made me one of them. Yet the knowledge lifted something from my shoulders.

N arrating my loss, which escaped all consciousness when it was lived for forty years on my part and by others near me who, unwillingly, innocently, or ignorantly did not realize it, requires some reckoning for truthful storytelling. What are the particulars that make it worth understanding, that add something not seen or imagined?

The lack of awareness while it was being lived for forty years is central to evaluating some of its effects. I can write about my deafness, even dramatize it, but only as a condition that was unknown—its consequences, its shaping responses, were wholly unrecognized. They were not ever questioned. Deafness was never imagined and therefore the silence it brought about is difficult to recapture or evaluate.

I must imagine a deafness with no moral weight. If my diligence to hear had been a conscious effort, if my parents had deliberately ignored the fact, these positions would be stories with interpretations. If I had known, if my parents had known, undoubtedly I would have understood many things more fully as I grew up. There might be someone to blame. But no one realized it. The level of awareness needs elaboration. Simple revisionism won't work. My deafness was a black hole; it existed, it even possessed gravitational waves, but its effects were not searched for, much less hypothesized. If someone had noticed my deafness, that surely would have changed my sense of self. But the solution would not have been unqualified in freeing me from loss.

In order to bridge that gap of deafness when I was a child, the only means for amplifying such a loss would have meant being hooked to some sort of obvious device. My granddaughter reminded me that Laura's sister in *Little House on the Prairie* was deaf and carried an amplifier in her pocket. Did I have such a device when I was growing up? As an adult, I knew a child of friends who needed a heavy radio-like machine placed on his teacher's desk. I would have been moved to the front row in the class, possibly wearing a pair of microphones. Instead, I went through school always in the last row, where either because of my name's place in the alphabet or my height, I was always far from the blackboard and the teacher. Report cards said that I often talked instead of paying attention.

I would have been keenly aware of being different if I had been identified as having limited hearing. I also would have been protected and given support. The world would have been much clearer and less silent.

Instead, I experienced the gap of missing things without knowing it. I was not one to hold a grudge. Sorry, I'd say to my parents. I didn't hear you. Exasperated nevertheless, it was easy for me to believe that I hadn't been paying attention. My spirit, always one that tugged and was unflagging, lived in part between the lines unspoken. My brain revved up like a speeding engine and strained and soared. I gripped on to life, put thoughts together in my own interpretations. The way I ran clumsily and climbed trees tentatively and sledded prudently,

I never knew for one minute that I could have been tethered to a heavy machine but also would have heard so many more discussions and distinctions that would have added coherence and confidence to spaces I filled in for myself when the world drifted by like clouds.

Underneath, there always is the freedom of human choices, many limited, close to invisible, and often silent except to oneself, even when they have been carried out. Yet they exist and contribute as much as anything else to silent change in consciousness and identity. When I began to write seriously, I was certain they were the silences I most wanted to make visible. I am inside them, I wrote of these words, the way yellow is inside a lemon, black inside an ant.

A friend in Parma phones this morning, her voice excitedly high. She has taken up her paints again. She got up with the sun and moved her easel to the kitchen, of all things. There is pure rebellion in this, a Parma woman painting in the kitchen, the high temple of perfection and skill and social offering. But her rebellion is not what it seems. The squashed tubes, some flat, are nearly all weeping, she says, because they have been so forgotten. The light is splendid in the kitchen. There are some blue tints from the trees just beginning to unfurl. It's not anything, but I'll finish it. I opened crimson first.

Last night, she says, she saw the brightest star she had ever seen in the sky. She had the window open as she lay on her bed. It wrinkled and burned brighter than anything she had ever imagined. She ran upstairs to tell her granddaughter, the one who would understand its beauty. The child told her it was a satellite; the papers had announced it.

She says: I thought maybe it was. Maybe it wasn't. It was the most beautiful light I had ever seen in the sky. What does false mean? she asks me over the phone. What does a star mean, given the distance of light-years?

U ndoubtedly, my unnamed, unperceived deafness made me partial to silence. For example, snow blizzards. They were perfect gradations of quiet building into real silence, the enormous starry sky in December in Wisconsin, the childhood experience when snow was announced and appeared in the deep night sky—first, all around as an exciting possibility, a smell of cold, and then a few flakes, and then white flakes that would not stop all night but would stop the cars, not at first, would slow the cars and stop on the ground, covering colors like brown grass, dusting evergreen branches, covering with a white that always was pristine, where a person's path could be seen, each footstep defined and with the soft flakes falling in at the edges, ruffling and softening the shape of the boots and then gradually filling the tiny ditches in, covering them over, forgetting someone passed. The silence in snow was visible speech, each flake distinct script, bouncing and falling, and sometimes for brief periods of industrious activity at school, cut from construction paper, folding the sheet at least eight times, and with a scissors, careful to leave some contiguous parts, cutting holes and diamonds, and then opening the snowflake and pasting it on a classroom window while real snow kept falling. If the snow fell for days, footsteps were erased, bringing with the storm a marvelous sensation of quiet and disappearance and the delight of new shapes, cars as rounded bunkers, and drifts like sea waves rising, sometimes even to the top of our second-story house, piling up in the corners of the windowsills, turning the roofs to crazy blowing sheets of sparkling powder, joining that pouring from the sky obliterating doghouses, birdbaths, steps, curbs, corners, and signs. Snow or snow as blizzard were events uncovering a world that we could not see until it came, showing itself and dancing over the bland order of the life we were in. The cream in the half-gallon jugs of milk in the milk box always froze and rose like the white buttons on an accordion.

The interiors of our neighbor's houses, never close or easy to see, became more distant. The lights in the windows, mere lines, signaling another household, another inside, warm and set against the whiteness taking over the night. When snow fell for days, it shut down the world, removing it, rendering it unimportant and superseded by the tumbling beauty swirling and spinning and cresting, falling steadily, above all, without interruption, unlike the marked shift of day and night. It just came down, covering us all, taking us outside the normal way days were measured and cut. In those childhood blizzards, silence was peaceful because we were children without adult worries about meetings, or freezing to death, or homelessness. We had no way to make connections even to my father, who was forced more than once to stay downtown at his men's club. Mother always insisted there was no reason to fret even if the wind howled and Daddy didn't come home. All was well and all would be well. We had no weather alerts, we went out as the snow kept falling, and we rolled down hills, with the snow edging down our collars and squeezing into our boots and sticking to our eyelashes. Only when the snow stopped falling did we feel everything glittering. We saw the light of the moon hitting it and making stripes across the cleanly modeled surfaces. The night skies burst with stars but the night became wholly visible in unearthly brightness because of the whiteness of the snow. The night was dazzling, and so quiet that peace was a sensation expanding over the yards and hills. Maybe a dog yelped here or there, mystified and delighted by the snow.

The white snow falling revealed in new proportions what our life was. Whiter and whiter grandeur rolled out. The slowness of the falling was absolute, a wonder, the pace an absolute valuing of beholding, staying still, listening, valuing the hidden, the newly concealed. Snow was extraordinary and as such, because it dominated what was going on before it, unconcealed itself as the hidden truths of grandeur and infinity. Beyond us, snow fell as if silence was a thing, soft snowflakes; falling gave the sensation of exceptional states of mind. Until the first dog left its yellow pee or the branches of a birch snapped by the wind marked it with its black trilling extensions, snow was something to behold in the enchanted vision of a child.

There was no fear of the dark when it was snowing. There was a feeling of benevolence, of generosity, all falling so that streetlights filtered through the steady, feathery falling of flakes of light. It seemed that all the things we didn't know and couldn't understand and didn't see were summed up as a hallelujah in the movement from the sky that became time, and became not knowing, and became what would come and become visible.

There is a smell of snow, just as there is a smell of leaves and a smell of sap. Snow smells like cold waiting, not yet stepping out but identifying scents and erasing them one by one by making the air colder and colder. It's a presence, and the scent is that, just barely felt, but felt as being prepared. When snow appears, the smell is no longer there. The riot of snow fills the air. The air is sharp but not so brutally cold as to make snow impossible.

Snow was a silence that covered and took over. People sheltered in its blanketing, while the snow ran against politics, inequality, plans, and presented the idea of new and getting lost, and making angels appear from the amazing simplicity of lying on your back and moving your arms and legs until they assumed the shape of wings in motion, sweeping snow aside, and leaving suggestions of energy.

I was quite deaf when those blizzards came to our house as a child. But I didn't know it, and the silence, with or without hearing, was real in many dimensions, anyway, mostly because so much human movement stopped. But it was real also because we looked up. Stars were part of the experience once the snow stopped. Freedom was part of it, going out at night, down to the fire at the skating pond, not worrying about being snatched.

Now, even without sliding my hearing aids into my ears, if snow is falling, I hear it as action, words, machines. There were sounds of scraping and scraping walks and driveways when I was growing up, night phone calls to workers to assist my younger brother in making sure, with salt and sand, that the steep driveway would be clean enough for my father to descend in his green Packard while it was still dark the following morning early. Now it's not so common to hear shovels scraping on concrete, but rather machines, whining and blasting snow into the air. Predictions about storms are days ahead of their appearing and the storms are words, numbers, measurements. The smell of snow has been replaced by the anxiety of its approaching. Snowstorms are warnings, interviews, alerts, and updates. They are shots of colored arrows turning into spinning, devouring monsters recorded by weather satellites and threatening the masses. When the snow comes, there is no feeling of obeisance, of being stopped by the movements of vertical and slanted snow. Nearly nothing stops. If I turn on my hearing aids, I hear the snowplows and the salting machines and the wheels spinning in snowbanks, repeating over and over how much they want to get moving. I hear the warnings on TV about stocking up on food and see maps of the electricity outages that cause so much hardship. The feeling stirred up by snow falling is basically one of preparation and anxiety. It is one of action and certainly cannot be linked, as James Joyce did, to movements of the soul across the universe. Snow is an organizational problem, of backup systems, finding places for homeless people to shelter. It is no longer an experience that people accept and navigate often by staying still.

I turn my hearing aids on and I can hear how snow has changed. But even without turning them on, it would be difficult to feel snowfall as a mystical experience in Bronxville. It is difficult even to feel its beauty, or how quiet could lead to a different state of mind.

I take my hearing aids out and turn off the television, shut down the smartphone, and stop worrying about the storm. I regain, in my natural deafness, a way of being shut out. It is not absolute, but the action of retreating, detaching, lets me enter the snow on different terms. But now I immediately sense, in deafness, what is missing, because with a click I can reacquire so much hearing. I can identify deafness now as a wall of sorts, a lack that keeps so much reality outside my range. When I was deaf as a child, snow and not hearing were a continuum of silences. Now that I can hear much more with hearing aids, the silence of snow is much more difficult to find or reach. It has become a matter of searching for silence within.

I turn on my hearing aids and these amazing instruments let me experience so many relationships that would suffer if I did not have them. With or without them, not including a specific reference to their function, silence as a dimension, suddenly assumes a different meaning from sound. Silence is no longer about hearing, but about feeling and receiving, where any ripples of mysticism are about listening and openly stopping and waiting. Silence and soul and snow are synonyms when detached from hearing snowplows or spinning wheels. Separated only by "the cold pane of the window"—that now nonexistent glass replaced by insulated solutions for ecological savings, where now the word "pane" sounds of defenselessness, along with "cold," a measure for the vulnerability of a human being—James Joyce, in *Dubliners*, narrated snow as his own soul falling through the universe. Silence was a state of mind spreading west and snow was falling on all "the living and the dead." One hundred years later, depicting this silence, a state of mind where the variety of snow crystals probably exceeds the number of atoms known in the universe, is no longer a given, because it is very hard to find silence. Especially a metaphorical one like his that included the migration of souls in a city.

The silence of deafness, the deadened nerve, before I knew I was missing anything led me in a different direction because of where I lived, who my parents were, and what I knew at the time. So many elements meant I was far from a narrative where silence would lead me out to the universe and to souls, although my night walks were the essence of that.

Being deaf made me a listener. Hearing and listening became tasks without knowing that my brain committed my eyes to the process as well. Hearing and listening as activities have changed a great deal in terms of their meanings to me since I have become a writer.

Sometimes when I teach, students will interrupt, unable to contain a response that excites them, making them feel they have discovered a central meaning in the text. Someone else will approach from a different point of view, and often now women hold their ground, especially when they are being interrupted. The person who spoke first—often a man, but this is not the point I wish to make—will interrupt again, to demonstrate or defend a point of view that he considers right. There, at this crossroads, listening becomes something I am fascinated by. It is extremely common that the bright cheeks, the deep frown, the shaking head signal that the person cannot bear to listen. I realize this moment is the chance for preaching conversion, a possibility to change a way of life: how to learn first listening and then hearing, hearing what a person is really saying. We are all deaf to a certain extent, but as often as not, anxiety leads the interrupting person to talk, to initiate, because hearing takes concentration and piecing fragments together. Like physiological deafness, listening becomes one of those situations when we must allow for uncertainty. We might miss what is out of range unless we hold ourselves open to unknowing or observations different from what we think.

If I turn the hearing aids on, snow and its noisy temporal side effects enter my ears. Click. The storm changes.

I turn them off and feel immediately what I no longer hear. I am behind a wall, more alone, as the world assumes distance that I cannot describe. I listen for hidden truths that my eyes can pick up. I watch snow blown horizontally across the hill in a blinding sheet. I wonder about the white heron and where he has taken shelter, since the lake is close to freezing over. The park is closed after dark. A vague collective worry, some time ago, overtook the town's people, a fretting about dangers lurking when there is no supervision in the park. The park is not available to us at night when snow and sky might feel more like something attached to a universe. The centuries of history when this land was alive with Native American Siwanoy is buried under the snow. With my hearing aids off or on, I still do not have the liberty to join the silence of the heron navigating darkness with his special ways. The night sky, with the park off-limits, is closed in by apartment buildings and the parkway.

Sometimes when I walk in the park, like the twilight hour I spent to escape the heat in the apartment the night I began thinking of writing this book, I realize that snow is a term used often to signal a dysfunctional blast of gray fuzziness that covers a TV screen when the signals are scrambled. That snow accompanied by an unpleasant buzz is a minor reflection of how far the word has been distorted. What snow meant to the Siwanoy, or to James Joyce as it fell on the Dublin in his mind, or to Orhan Pamuk in his imaginary village in Turkey, is interesting because of its different shadings. The snow used to describe the TV's loss of signal is like the devalued snow in Bronxville the day after it falls, when salt, sand, and car exhaust have transformed it into heaps that are already black.

The storm in Bronxville, one that came early, while the trees still were covered in colored leaves, the storm that was announced as fierce, dangerous, darkened the sky at the end of October. It was brutal, full of force, icy blasts, and the snow, buffeted by winds, fell as if dump trucks were pouring it out. Mighty and dark, a wet, gray, slashing bully of a storm, it filled up the streets like waves of shifting, slapping, skittering sheets of sea.

Listening to the howling winds, the size of the storm and its domineering presence, slicking the streets to white ice and obscuring the streetlamps with heavy, wet, massive flakes, dumping icy moisture, bringing with it no feeling of silence or peace, I did not listen to what it was announcing. It was disruptive, invasive, an intruding marauder, but I insisted on leaving the house, crossing the bridge over the river, trying to catch a glimpse of the heron. I was deaf to the storm. Deaf to my daughter, who telephoned and warned me not to go out.

The storm was real. It was difficult to see even a few feet ahead because of the blowing wind. Utterly explosive and turbulent, spinning snow into blustering blasts, the storm immediately wrapped me in a feeling of aloneness, putting my shoulder to it. It was far greater than me. Its indifference to me, how it blinded and pushed and howled, making even a few steps ahead a challenge, did not overly impress me at the time. I thought I was self-sufficient. I almost loved the feeling of getting lost because I actually thought I knew where I was.

La Verna, a monastery built into steep terrain in the Tuscan Apennines near Arezzo, a place where Saint Francis received the stigmata and a vision of Mary, was land originally given to him by Count Orlando di Casentino of Chiusi, as an isolated, savage, and wild area suitable for those who needed to do penance or who wanted a solitary life. Dangerous ravines and dark caves mark it. The mountainous boulders where Saint Francis sheltered and prayed are unyielding and cast deep shadows, narrowing the sky to a shaft confined by insurmountable stone. Standing as a visitor or pilgrim on retreat, looking up from the place Francis did, impenetrability surrounds it. The boulders and the harsh view beyond any human scale embody the reality that Blake made so simple in his poem "The Tyger" when he addressed the terrifying cat. "Did he who made the Lamb make thee?" Out in the open, in harsh winter conditions, Saint Francis prayed in silence for forty days.

The impenetrable silence in the boulders, the distant narrowed sky, the abject posture of asking and listening, are palpable if one chooses to look up from the bare, now grated space, imagining the silence of Saint Francis.

Simone Weil, an esteemed twentieth-century French philosopher and member of the Resistance, spent different periods in her life as a Renault factory worker, a field worker, a supporting member of a revolutionary unit in the Spanish Civil War. Much of her philosophical thinking constructed arguments about the nature of God and suffering. Her thoughts on finding the moral basis for action drew the conclusion that sharing the human condition was crucial. Weil, who was a Jew, explored, often in correspondence with a Catholic priest, her relationship to a personal Christ. I have learned much from her questioning of suffering, not only as personal suffering and affliction but as a reality for others with whom it must be acknowledged or shared.

In *Waiting on God*, her few pages on the Lord's Prayer gave me the possibility to understand its power. She analyzed the prayer line by line, using its Greek version. "Our Father which art in heaven" had always startled me. Naming a place where God resided, heaven, made it seem a story, a myth. Her clear and strong interpretation made sense of the words. She simply states: God is beyond our reach. That is what we accept by praying the first line and it is what we accept about our own existence. We are created, as is the entire world, and it is beyond our comprehension. Her interpretation of belief seemed to fall like a ring around the conditions in which Saint Francis prayed. It burnished the meaning of the Lord's Prayer that Jesus taught twice to his followers and disciples. He said: "Pray like this."

Absolutely without willing it, and, absent from my conscious thoughts (to the extent that I am aware of them), I understood in the two days I spent at La Verna that the silence

Saint Francis maintained and approached and reached for was silence as Simone Weil expressed it: present, to be addressed, but absolutely beyond our comprehension. Weil wrote that we do not find silence until, by waiting over the long emptiness, silence finds us and fills us. Saint Francis's long wait was answered after forty days with the sign of the stigmata, blood appearing in his palms.

The storm in Bronxville affected me in a similarly surprising and disproportionate way as the days in La Verna. When I finally entered my apartment, having walked to the other side of the building and come in the more formal front entrance, I was a person who had changed. My vivid childhood picture of snow as peaceful was changed. Without knowing it, my feelings had shifted. For decades this cold, white peace had translated in my adult mind as Joyce's images in *Dubliners*: silent snow swooning slowly, "falling faintly . . . and faintly falling." The sublime way Joyce used "light taps upon the pane" as the baton to turn Gabriel Conroy to the window and to extend the view of silence—"Yes, the newspapers were right: snow was general all over Ireland. . . . It was falling, too, upon every part of the lonely churchyard on the hill where Michael Furey lay buried" was reframed during the Bronxville storm. The somnolence, the hypnotic amnesia, the mystical view of death and snow in Joyce's story swerved that afternoon. My new sensations about the silence embodied in snow altered his fiction, a beautiful mood and metaphor created on paper leading us back into historical Irish memory and the graveyard. The idea of silence still implied burying but it had been enlarged to include physical force, sudden destruction, violence, disorientation, blind change.

I had gone out in the storm that I had been warned about. Obstinate, I ignored what was not only well-intentioned advice but offered because of dangerous and exceptional conditions. When I returned after an hour of whiteout, oblivion, slipping, sliding, blindness, and growing apprehension, the apartment building was out of reach. The steps, where an hour before I had left traces of my boots, were blockaded.

The maple, which was a green, shady pillar in front of the south wing of the building facing my windows, sprawled like an overturned semi, its contents scattered everywhere.

In the same hour I descended the three tiers of stairs, a maple that was six stories tall, covered in autumn leaves and branches that spread in the air across two apartments, was made unsustainably heavy by ice and snow on each leaf. It had no base with which to compensate for and support the accumulating weight as the snow and wind pounded. There was no course but to thunder down. Sweeping the air with hundreds of branches, its roots tore up the soil, uncorking a patch of earth the size of a table for eight. Some of the secondary roots snapped and the rest of the deeply buried arterial systems were yanked out of the underground. Still partially connected, skeins of rusty, hairy, unsevered chunks of roots were visible.

On the tree's way down, the maple whacked the black iron handrails lining the tiers of steps, as if they were hairpins, burying them under its foliage, bent and broken on the ground. It snapped in two the black steel lamp illuminating the steps and tossed it into the air. So vast and sprawling, the branches toppled the tall streetlight on the sidewalk below, breaking it and leaving the lamp swinging like a pocket watch. The tree smacked open the roofs of two cars, smashing the seats. Like a tower of a size that could not have been imagined while the maple was still standing, it tipped over everything underneath. It smothered most of the hill of the lawn; beyond the crushed cars, it spread into the street and blocked the road. The steps were gulped down; two trees on the other side of the stairs were knocked by the maple's branches and they were stripped, adding to the nets and caves of branches that at the maple's dark center on the lawn made a tangled impenetrable nest taller than the first floor of the apartment building.

My knees trembled, as if aftershocks were still shaking the ground. The maple, covered in snow, with more snow falling, so that its tangle of branches would surely soon appear to be a cruel thicket, continued emitting signals. I felt the violent beating and death—my neck snapping, my spine breaking, my head cracking.

One hour before I left, I thought I was capable of challenging the storm facing me. I perceived it as I remembered earlier storms, romantic, quiet storms as I told them to myself. In the cars whose lids seemed pulled apart like tuna fish tins, the streetlamp dangling in the wind, swinging, I saw things turned inside out and the contents like drawers emptied by thieves. The mountainous tree on its side and the hole in the ground groaned with a silence that was unapprehended before I left the house.

Helen Keller lost her sight and her hearing because of an unknown illness when she was less than two years old. Nearly five years of despair, rage, and frustration before the word "water" spelled on her palm turned into a clear understanding of the substance and the abstraction of the symbol for water. The mystery of language came alive in that moment of physical connection, organizing meaning and casting out chaos, revealing the world to her. As she wrote, the experience of understanding language "awakened my soul, gave it light, hope, joy, set it free!"

She acquired words then for things, for actions, for feelings. She had a way to order the world and order it inside her own self. More important still, she had a way to speak her mind. The silences she defined for the world, the barriers she outlined, have a different etymology, if you will, from the Yonkers storm. Her story of a particular silence, a deep isolation leaving her without language for communication, is a new story, covering territory that had not been told as human history. Certainly there were stories of barriers between Tribal sign languages and aural ones, but this was a story about a brain that could no longer access information using two principle senses and how, through human patience, imagination, science, and determination, vast and complete systems of thought could be translated by touch and brought to the brain to elaborate as comprehension.

Unsurprisingly, for many reasons, it is a personal story about women, a relationship of a child and her teacher, above all. Eventually, Keller's insights and discoveries, her superb education, her passionate nature led her to radical and well-founded political views of equality. Then, as a woman propounding those views, her socialism was dismissed, and she was described once again by a press that had adored her brilliance and courage as a person with handicaps, a woman who lacked the ability to speak of issues outside of disability. By then she was a radical who wrote: "There is no king who has not had a slave among his ancestors, and no slave who has not had a king among his."

Experiment, *patience*, sacrifice, *patience*, love, creativity, *patience*, conflict, persistence, impatience—the teacher Annie Sullivan's relationship with Helen Keller grew like the most intense and nourishing mother-daughter relationship until both needed more independence to use their gifts and tendencies. The years in which they were closer to one organism than two needed to be revised, the roles examined, but the relationship, genuine and unique, grew, changed. The devotion to one another and the understanding of what had been uncovered from the silence was never abandoned by either of them.

In elementary school we were introduced to the language of Braille and taught a few letters. We were shown a book of the embossed configurations. Our fingertips, with occasional jolts of recognition, touched the letters, mostly without understanding.

I was fascinated then by how Keller used her fingers to touch people's lips and to follow them as they spoke to her. It moved me. Thinking back, it was odd that a child would be drawn to such a practice, tracing, with her fingers, the contours and moods on faces. The patience required both of Keller and those communicating with her by allowing her to touch in order to find the dimension in things, without knowing why, always seemed beautiful to me.

My eyes followed lips closely, but I don't know if I really would have been happy if I had been allowed to politely invade people's faces, signaling to the person that he was being followed eagerly or that she couldn't escape. But as a story, I would have liked to touch the faces in our family when I was a child, to interrupt their coldness and distance, to check their words and ask, Is that what you said, is that what you meant? I had trouble understanding words, perhaps hearing them was part of the issue, but besides not hearing, I still struggled with what people meant by the things they said. Words often were arbitrary mysteries and by listening hard, I never found the reception Helen found when she acquired a platform for dialogue, spelling words out in a palm, receiving a direct answer, having someone so close listening, explaining, responding by letting her feel lips vibrating.

The snowstorm in Bronxville, which knocked out electricity for as many as three weeks for some people in Yonkers and Westchester, created a soul movement in me. I cannot say how except that it was like tracing the lips of the word "snow" over and over, and knowing I was tapping new dimensions in the word "snow," and tracing with my thumb ever more fervently the words "falling," "roots," "unknown," "cold," "danger," "fear." The storm and the blizzard, the tree upright and the tree down, the disc of roots exposed and taller than myself if I stood up against them, said to me: *Now you are paying attention.*

Inside the building, looking out from the fourth-story

window of my apartment, the tree lay like live wires over most of the lawn and the walk. At the level of my window, the maple once covering the south wing was no longer blocking light. I could see all the way to the end of the street. People watching television down where the street curves east were in plain sight. I could see the bricks framing the windows, the windows far away but lit with distant lives. As if my mind were the palm on which someone was spelling words I could barely catch, I took a deep breath. For the first time since my mother died at age ninety-six six months before, I felt a small crack of grief in my body as I breathed out seeing the effects of the tree's death. My view was clear all the way to the end of the street. I breathed cleanly, fully, seeing how much had fallen, letting light in.

The day my mother died, the only book I have published in Italian arrived by special courier. Its cover was one that the publisher had given me a chance to comment on, and then perhaps regretted his willingness to listen after I requested one change after another. The translated title of the book of essays is *The Ocean Is Within Us*, and the subtitle is *Literature, Poetry and Music Between America and Europe*. At a certain point in the process, since the designer had introduced a pair of glasses, an open book, a butterfly, a ribbon bookmarker, and a pink rose, I thought we had too many symbols. I asked to move things around, and to soften images like the rose to a misty blur. I asked that he remove the monarch, a cliché that he'd lifted from the internet. I introduced a butterfly with personality. Finally, I dared to ask that he change the slightly magnified Italian text under the pair of glasses to an English text. My book was about cross-cultural territory and the contents were essays originally published in English. I felt a message was lost if the enlarged text on the cover was in Italian.

After a few gripes in which the designer complained that he had never worked with someone who had requested so many changes, he graciously acquiesced. Then there was a truce. The designer said, *Basta*. Enough changes. Otherwise the process will never end. I hadn't seen the final result, nor had I seen the English text that would be placed under the eyeglasses until the courier arrived and rang the bell.

The words under the pair of glasses were not taken from my essays in English. I had requested that the very perky orange-red butterfly near the rose be moved and placed near that text. The designer complied. The butterfly with spiky legs and zebra-striped mazes on its wings was settled below the text. In that position, its spidery right antenna migrated into the print, almost as if to indicate a word in the otherwise blurred paragraph. The butterfly's silky pointer nearly touched a name: Winifred. That was my mother's name. It belonged to a text that the designer had chosen.

On the day she died, thousands of miles away, Winifred and the butterfly were touching. The text the designer used exposed only a few words. Along with her name, the other visible words were "black chiffon," "evening," "always used," "for up." The butterfly was there, eager and alert, as if Emily Dickinson had written about it: "Because I could not stop for Death— / He kindly stopped for me."

Another butterfly that skimmed and seared a certain January afternoon was part of a book that I wrote. The handsome volume of fifteen poems called *Bees* was printed in Parma. Its gray cover had yellow marks flying up as if golden bees were being released. My daughter had designed the cover and I thought its elegance, beauty, and motion were an amazing solution.

I picked the books up from the printer on a freezing day in late January. The slim copies were wrapped in brown shipping paper and rested on a chair while we ate lunch. I meant to open them afterward, midafternoon, while my daughter and I were spending an hour waiting to attend a Mass for a boy who had died some years earlier whose parents still celebrated his birthday with a memorial service.

She and I were discussing our understanding of the Mass and also whether we believed in saying prayers for the dead. I found myself resisting the ritual and stepping back into silence, the Quaker tradition I had participated in at many points in my life, community as silence, silent prayer as love migrating. As we talked without a clear point of view, we decided to open the brown package and look at the final form of the book.

The cover was just as we had imagined it. Clean and with a yellow spattering that could be pollen or stars and the shape like a moving crescent—moon or swarm. I took the book in my hands and opened the rather stiff cover made of heavy paper, similar in weight to cardboard. As I turned to the inside pages, a yellow butterfly flew out into the January room. It flew from the pages, sprang I would say, sprang out, released, escaped from being pressed flat inside. It fluttered around and eventually landed on my finger, where my daughter, sharing my attention, took a photograph, as if we needed to give in to the world of proof, the world that needed proof, if we were to tell the ineffable story again.

The yellow butterfly exists in a photograph that I eventually gave to the boy's mother. There is just one copy of that pair of wings. But it really doesn't exist there. It exists as a poem about reality justifying poetry. It exists as a winter appearance and a light, brief, zigzagging notion of silence and how it can touch us and make a path. In my heart, it exists as a mysteriously living transformation of the word. It exists as silence finding us.

I don't have many regrets to elaborate about my writing life. I am sorry, though, that I have not written more poetry, used its dedication to feelings and events in motion, expressing them simply, deepening their significance line after line without saying I am this, I am that. The fact that I have written so much prose proposing writing as responsibility is almost a regret for me. I believe in the inspiration of poetry, the economy, the white space, the silences in the unsaid, and the untranslatable captured. Poetry gives us a chance to be the other, or to point to the other. It is a form of grace answering silence. That surely is justification for art, especially in times when suffering and injustice are topics crying out for words, as well as new hopes and cries for joy asking for form. Life in poetry dares to open eyes and ears to adventure and mystery in language, freeing submerged lands resisting light.

Today, while I was still considering how to bring the relationship with my mother to a truthful place, as unencumbered as the altered view from my fourth-story windows, I couldn't envision more than the size of the tree when I tried to link it to what her death meant.

The disk of soil penetrated by roots was painfully impressive, as were the roots still deeply embedded in the hill. As large as a table for eight, a banquet never held, such were the tree's networks over such a long life. It took three days to loosen and remove the skeins and threads of water and cellulose aboveground in the disk and below in the soil.

A crew of eight Asian workers—who pulled in unison while their ropes tied to the roots led to a pulley that was being cranked on a truck that drove forward into large enveloping clouds of unburned exhaust—shouted and fell and reconnoitered from sunrise to sundown. The unseasonable storm was gone and the weather sunny and warm. The engine ran nonstop except when the men paused for lunch, sitting where there was a bit of cleared wall. Three days, with the men tumbling on their backs and tipping over, slashing roots with handsaws and power saws after the battered Chevy pickup had lurched forward to extricate and drag the roots from the ground.

The underground connections, contrasting with the empty space all the way to the end of the street, suggested a way of approaching what had taken place. Cleaning the roots and bundling them was an excruciating process, not easy, even for eight men. Exposed, the roots and rhizomes were as vast as the tree. Touching each branch, sawing each secondary root, the men grappled with the enormity of the life and remains of one maple.

While I searched through feelings, an email from Rome distracted me. An American doctor whose book I had blurbed wrote announcing that a section of her book had been excerpted in the *New England Journal of Medicine*. It discussed grief and how her mother's death helped her to understand the process. There it was, the overlap between inner and outer worlds put together by our mind seeing connections. In a few paragraphs, her description became a pietà, a beautiful expression of her feelings for her mother and the experience of losing her. Her mother, also a physician, died in her arms in Rome unexpectedly, and she as a daughter and doctor breathed into her mouth and pumped her heart, uselessly. From there she described what she learned about loss. She wrote about grieving, loss, nearly going mad in the months following her mother's death.

The image of the author holding her mother in her arms and trying to breathe life into her was a powerful, intimate, and moving way to cradle the last minutes of a body slipping into nonidentity. I was filled with envy, with the unrealistic and completely human wish that I might have done something like that. Also, I respected the physician's training. The email arrived as I was planning to start my page. I didn't want to circle back into recriminations, I didn't want to look at how many shadows and roles my mother had cast me into. I accepted the unknown and the strange, often-stated dissatisfaction with how she lived. I'm busy, she would say, but I know it doesn't add up to anything, not even a hill of beans. In my own way, I knew as each root was sawed that it was not up to me or to her to say that. She lived, she touched, she did her best.

As my mother began losing her power of speech, from old age or dementia or ministrokes, she was no longer able to use words with clear direction: perhaps she had always used them in ways she didn't mean. Somewhere far earlier, she had disconnected from words' borders and inside that disconnection she resisted dialogue. Many of the cruel things she did made no sense and were impossible to explain in any simple way. Her words deepened wounds with surgical skill. Daughters came in for more of her meddling and drilling and outright cruelty. The wish to take care of her, what a normal daughter would wish to feel, was always complicated by obstructions, provocations. Yet the feeling that time was running out made the search for peace more crucial still. As the older daughter and the older girl, I had carried responsibilities of nurturing feeling and relationships among all the siblings. I'd been assigned the role, but perhaps its importance was enlarged by my need.

I was very unhappy that Mother was not going to die at home but in a cliché facility of modern, certainly American, middle-class family life. Once it was called "the old folks' home," but now it was referred to as a retirement community or assisted living, with fine print about legal responsibilities, schedules, and paid services, and very little that was personal or unregulated. There was a price for nail cutting, a price for stool softener, with computers helping to compute the lists. She was not one, though, who would collaborate.

From Italy, I found my way into that residence, every day,

where she was captive, left alone in her confused state, never to leave the premises. I forded the seven hours of time difference, calling her once a day after all of us in the family had decided to move her from her apartment into an elegant residence, where her room was then reduced in size twice over the years she resided there, because other people wanted the bigger rooms with windows. She was evaluated as less and less able to actually care whether she had windows or not. That calculation was unnourishing, if not to be called what it was, a commercial decision to satisfy a potential customer who would be attracted by as many windows as possible. The invisible effects of remaining in familiar surroundings were ignored as she entered a cycle of withdrawal, each withdrawal taking her further down.

In the years my mother could not converse, or would not, I struggled with how to stay in touch. I had read that people who couldn't converse still might sing. Oliver Sacks, among others, had written a book full of the hopeful and odd configurations of people's brains and capacities to understand music. In a seminar on depression, I had heard an Irish woman speak and play the mournful and insistent dulcimer that took her into refugee camps, crammed with people fleeing war in Bosnia. Discouraged, lost human beings who were angry, who felt abandoned and penned in, were circled by the sounds of her voice and her instrument for two consecutive days. Miserable and cold as they were, standing in an open field in the rain, she asked them to sing. For long stretches there was only her voice and the dulcimer and the rain. Many shouted at her with curses of disgust. But in the rain, other voices slowly joined and turned the sounds into Serbo-Croatian, home, letting out feelings kept inside. More and more eventually followed the notes of fire, hills, love, and hate as they found satisfying jigs and began to dance, letting mud fling from their devilish stamping.

I asked my mother if she would like to sing over the phone. I had purchased a book of songs. Every day at the same hour, with seven hours of difference between us, I would call and suggest a title and then slide into the notes when she agreed. They were songs as soupy as lace valentines and as familiar.

> *Let me call you sweetheart*
> *I'm in love with you*

Sometimes we would try a peppy one.

> *Toot-toot tootsie goodbye*
> *Toot-toot tootsie don't cry*

Or one with a clear melody and a slow pace.

> *Down by the old mill stream*
> *Where I first met you*

The war, the first one of the twentieth century.

It's a long way to Tipperary
It's a long way to go

Or the songs sung to sorority girls.

The girl of my dreams is the sweetest girl
Of all the girls I know

In the groove of songs from the 1920s and '30s, played on pianos with groups of friends crowded around them, songs that wobbled from gramophones, and nothing later than the early forties, nothing where it got too damn hot, or too close for comfort, or baby it's cold outside, nothing further in time than those tempered, laundered shibboleths and fixed roles which, for all that, still led to broken hearts and soldiers leaving and being killed and women being sung to by men who defined them. The difficulty of trying to talk misted over. We lifted up out of days in an old folks' home where she was often not taken outside and ate with people who had no sense of where they were or how even to swallow. Those few minutes, which my younger brother insisted she never remembered, represented to me a few minutes when her life migrated to another place and time, where nostalgia reigned and we could ride in the silly up-and-down rhymes of a merry Oldsmobile. She could find words, and her tongue made them come out straight. The words matched mine. The melodies carried us. Sometimes we even took the risk of harmonizing.

Every day, I called and repeated the request, Would you like to sing? Every day she replied, as if for the first time, a bit of surprise, a bit of enthusiasm, Well, that sounds mighty nice.

What should we sing?

You pick.

"Down by the Old Mill Stream"?

Well, that's just lovely, dear.

There was usually some throat clearing. That pause or gulp I had known since a child, where pitch is about to be declared, not too high, not perhaps even a key that would fit my voice, but right for her and her contralto.

> *Down by the old mill stream*
> *Where I first met you*
> *With your eyes of blue*
> *Dressed in gingham too*
> *It was there I knew*
> *That you loved me true*
> *You were sixteen*
> *My village queen*
> *Down by the old mill stream*

She could pronounce every word, bringing them up from some layer that we couldn't see. She could find and meet every note.

Lovely, she would say when we finished. Do you have time to sing it again?

What was the song, dear? I know that you know. You know it. I do, too, but I just can't say it.

Inside loneliness, who isn't scared? Who is to say that she didn't understand, at least partially, her condition? In earlier times, she had tools to help her escape, and to cover up fear and vulnerability. She was flirty then, able to get out of speeding tickets, out of doing things the proper way, using her beauty, which was wasted somehow in disappointments and lack of direction, wasted because she thought it was something seen from the outside, not a serious raw gift to express.

We siblings revealed our lack of a common plan or discussion. The way we scattered her ashes at the cemetery—where my father and my son and the paternal grandmother who set off the myth of my links between life and death are buried—we showed our unfamiliarity with many silent feelings, including sharing thoughts on religion or the afterlife or bodies. Should the ash be tossed or dropped? We had not prepared together, so the reality of the white dust, the small envelope of snowy minerals, came as a shock, so sanitized and transformed it erased our mother completely from links to an elegant body, even in a gym suit, in her last years. Unlike Italian ashes that still show pieces of bone and dark clumps, either because of more elementary technology or a different relationship to the process, Italian ashes are closer to a life that cannot be manipulated away from its bodily presence. We offered no prayer, adding some uneasy laughter and useless sobriety as a solution of tolerance for all the possible differing beliefs that might have been assembled among those in the family.

We opened our palms to have some of her remains poured into them. She lost all shape as she was blown upward. I could hear her half-hearted, ironic self-assessment at the lack of ceremony and recognition. That's me, fluff, I'm nothing but fluff. How many times had she repeated that depressing attitude, never considering what it meant to those who needed to identify with her life? What do you think, she'd ask with her sharp, wounding knife, if I willed my brain to science so they could figure out what was wrong with me? Often, she followed that with the quick, defensive barb: I've taken intelligence tests, you know. I'm pretty smart.

Fluff, her white body wasn't fluff flying against the sun. Each sparkling speck caught light as it swirled in the bitter north wind. All that she might have been disintegrated and dispersed her confused interpretation of a woman as secondary, unproductive, un-transgressive, unable to dig underneath to find a direction that was hers and her. The elements that had once been a life for ninety-six years fell onto each of us, her body burned and freed from all that it was. Some was lost in the air, some on the ground (it was excruciating), but that which fell back, clinging to our collars, our coat sleeves, came with us as we got into our cars.

Understanding where you stand is crucial in life and writing. "We have to learn . . . to let loose what is hidden in our depths, to expand rather than to condense prematurely. Rather than making an intellectual point and then devising a form to express it, we need rather to release the face that is sweating under the mask and let it sweat out in the open, for a change" (Thomas Merton, *Echoing Silence*).

Merton's many works touched me and millions of others in the era of the Vietnam War, but in the noise of our internet age, when, hauntingly, he can be found on YouTube, inviting dialogue and communion, his strong, round face speaking in Bangkok hours before he will be accidentally electrocuted, his thinking and writings in our era of profound transition, by stark contrast, reveal much more to consider about patience, insight, interior and nonverbal meanings. In his notebooks on writing, he explores subjects not hoping to learn how to write but why and how to become a better writer through quiet, meditation, the courage to let the face sweating under the mask, *sweat in the open, for a change.*

His tone suggests a certain amount of egoless freedom, as if he were someone composing in sand, barely ahead of the tides that will cover the truths. He adds greater depths to simple words, letting them wash in to our questions and rhythms, to be found in different shells, alive and challenging appearances, flocks of hermit crabs racing along the shore. In identifying that space of transformation, he asks himself and often readers, and all voices at the margins, poor people of all colors, prisoners, poets, monks, people who know darkness, fear, injustices, solitude, and strength to "go beyond the dichotomy of life and death and to be, therefore, a witness to life."

One of the many paradoxes of writing about silence is that the poet and the monk seek something in muteness they must name. The closer the poet and monk draw to expressing the transcendent or divine, the more difficult language becomes. By claiming precision, they must give signs that they are unable to penetrate or to re-create in words the silence or divinity being approached. Often light and other visual images, the heart of the rose or the preciousness of gold, are called in as images as close to approximating communion as the poet can get.

The same exercise of seeking something in muteness means nearly the opposite for the marginalized, and who are they, besides the hidden or invisible parts of ourselves? The marginalized are those in collective groups who are without voices: people living in poverty, people who are abused or repressed within families, people who are unacceptable to the religious groups that claim them. There is overlap, of course, for the monk, the poet, and the marginalized. It collects in the action of taking off the mask. Muteness for those who are at the margins means finding a voice, breaking silences that are not necessarily close to transcendent. Courage is a requisite, but I have come to see showing a face requires the basic condition of trust. Someone listening to the muted person is crucial.

The exercise of seeing and hearing how many ways the same words can lead to different stories is the polyphonic meditation that lies at the heart of this book. "Who," as Bernard says in Virginia Woolf's *The Waves*, "is to foretell the flight of a word?"

When I wrote about reading Dante, I was able to spell out thoughts that would never have found space in an everyday conversation. Never Dante in a trattoria, over a rushed meal of green salad, prosciutto, and fresh bread. Never Dante when the news feed about the collapsed bridge in Genoa or the floods in Mississippi blip off the smartphone. Only sustained writing can give Dante the space needed to suggest intricacies inside a composition like *The Divine Comedy*.

The word *volgere* in Dante's *Divine Comedy* transforms from its transitive to its intransitive forms even within single cantos. It changes direction from the verb form meaning "to face" to the verb form meaning "to turn," to the form meaning "to go towards." This transformation of a word's significance occurs endlessly in the poem, in which Dante establishes the dynamism in the common and new language, Italian, bringing its potentials to poetry and to people excluded from Latin. This Sufi-like movement of words changing positions shows them reaching their limits and migrating into spheres of sound where they become music transforming slowly into a sense of eternal motion, turning toward and turning away, returning, chaos finding order in changing, the turning of the self and non-self, the turning helixes of our genetic code, the turning of the earth, the endless and varied turns going on simultaneously. Marguerite Yourcenar said that the written word taught her to listen to the human voice. Eric Griffiths and Matthew Reynolds in their book on the poet, *Dante in English*, point out perfectly managed transformations occurring from line to line in the poet's written voice, new life, recombinations, like the genes that words are.

Today, I shared the book of photos on conflicts in Africa with the Nigerian women who come to the library to spend a few hours perhaps illuminating something in their present lives or perhaps in the lives they left behind. Last week no one came. No one notified me. Often the explanation given by the host organization is that the women come from a culture that doesn't respect time. I find that not to be true. Thank heavens the effectiveness of our meetings has not been evaluated by attendance. The door remains open, without counting heads.

Today, the photograph of St. Theresa's refugee camp, opened in 2014 to provide shelter for thirty-seven hundred people fleeing Boko Haram, pulled the attention of the youngest woman in my class, who is now nineteen. It captured her so deeply that she began rubbing the photo, touching the little heaps of makeshift huts covered in rags. She said nothing and kept turning the pages, her head drawing close to many of the large, often dark photos. Her fingers traced faces, soil, waves, trees, soldiers; she traced them and they led her into deeper silence. Finally she said, This is what Libya looked like. We were in a camp like this. No food, some water, but not even clean water. We were kept in the desert, and one woman got so sick she died there. They buried her in the sand. But our Boss told us not to think about it. I only wanted work, like I had had as a hairdresser, but there was no work when I got to Kano. A woman in the store told me she would get me work. I believed her until after I boarded the bus.

For each woman, the trip taken was an individual story—a different village, a different religion, a different contract, different eyes. But each woman had seen other women violated and beaten. The same basic journey had taken one woman to prison, captured by guerrillas who were shooting at the truck she was in. Each remembered periods of feeling that she was a slave, given no food, locked up, slapped, wanting to go back but going forward, place to place in the desert and villages, no fresh clothes, no beds, skin growing dryer and dryer in the scorching heat, crying and crying and praying and finding a way to have courage.

Never, said one of them, never will I tell my children what happened to me. They treated us like animals, worse than animals. I won't ever forget what happened. Never. Some of the men deserve to die. But I won't tell it to my children. Not even about the tears. I want them to see me as I am, someone with courage.

The women in class, in the lovely abandoned quiet of the library named for a woman who had been murdered in Somalia for her investigative journalism, responded to the photo of the refugee camp in an unexpected way. A level of silence we had never touched (it had been assumed but excluded) suddenly found voice. The list of words I had provided for an exercise in imagination became magnets for feelings and facts of untold months.

DUSTY ROAD

The Sahara Desert where I slept in dust like an animal and my eyes burned endlessly because dust and sand blew into them.

DARK

It reminds me of Libya when I was in prison and needed all my courage not to give up.

THIRSTY

I was thirsty throughout my journey in Libya most especially in the desert. I was so thirsty I drank dirty water and even begged under the hot sun to drink dirty water.

BARE FEET

I walked with bare feet in Libya when my shoes got spoilt.
I continued on walking on stones, burning sand, and
sharp gravel.

BLUE SKY

Each time we saw blue sky in Libya we always said that
the weather was perfect for sailing to Europe.

RED

Most times I think that red signifies danger because in
Libya there were some men we saw sold. They tied red
pieces of cloth around their hands.

CRY

I cried and encouraged myself not to always cry in every
hard situation that I found myself in and will continue
to find myself in.

BOSS

I didn't know anybody. I was sixteen years old. We were
many in the bus. Soldiers asked for money. They said
if the woman who said she would pay for me didn't
pay there would be no water and they would leave us in
the desert. Without water, I saw one woman die and be
buried in the sand. The Boss said he wouldn't move. So
another one came. It was a very bad situation being in
Libya. I had gone to Kano for work, but there was no
work and the woman said, come with me, I am going to
Libya where there is work.

Their writing was strong. It was nonfiction in a way that makes much nonfiction fiction because of forcing contingencies into rational order. The Nigerian women's stories were vivid, with photographic details. There was disintegration, no real plot, no climax; nothing, though, needed to be added. The violence, the integrity, the human condition, the corruption needed no other voices to frame or interpret their months of being caught between uncertain borders, as women whose resources were largely faith, crying, dominating deeper and deeper fears, and finding a few human beings to trust as they made a passage through hell.

Research for writers remained to be done—research on the way the camps worked in Libya, the way payments worked, the way rival groups took possession of the refugees and trafficked them—but the life stories held up in their own voices and details, kept so carefully folded inside. The days and nights were hard to touch. Often slithery terror surfaced on their faces in the library. It was difficult to put one's mind back into the conditions, choices, and options. They talked because these memories were still part of their lives and someone asked them about what was waiting to be told. The choked silence inside was met by the silence welcoming them to the room.

He waved a fresh edition of *Lotta Comunista* in my face. Dark eyed, young, he insisted, Read it, as he held out his other hand for money.

You need new ideas, I said. We tried Communism. We don't need ideology. Italy doesn't need it. You're young.

He closed his lips and frowned like a bulldog.

You don't know what you are talking about.

I do, I said, I am old enough to resist ideology as a solution.

You're a fool, a *scema*, he said. Just buy my paper.

You aren't listening, I said.

Good day, he said, glaring at me. You say you know Communism, but you probably never read a single book.

We need new solutions, I said.

You're an old windbag, he said, holding up his newspaper and moving on.

Two nights before, Paolo and I had stood in the same square, having gathered in a piazza at the west end of the city and walked up the long avenue illuminated by the artificial light of streetlamps as store lights turned off. More than two thousand of us walked in solidarity with the Kurds who were in refugee camps and fleeing because the United States was withdrawing its critical troops from northern Syria. Many of the banners were nostalgic ones—the Communist Party, the PCI, and the unified Partito Democratico, the PD; they were waved like long tapestries, and at many points, their standard-bearers turned on portable mikes and spoke from their particular point of view. We reached Piazza Garibaldi, blazing in lights, and then the marchers bunched into a thick crowd, forming a semicircle. A woman who did not identify specific politics spoke of the tormented history of Kurds as pawns in recent years. She spoke of women and children, suffering, lack of food, lack of supplies, lack of solutions. The need for solidarity and calling attention to the human emergency was her primary invocation. Smartphones were held above the crowd, and marchers took photos without seeing their subjects. The little screens were something like candles blazing or firecrackers going off. Women, the speaker said, women are the ones creating solidarity.

H and over my mouth.

Those tight fingers clenching my cheeks, his palm pressing down on my closed mouth while he growled I was not to tell anyone, imprinted violence on my psyche, marking me from that time on.

The hand forcing silence and the indifferent thrusting became a metaphor that has migrated and transformed, returning throughout my life like spring buds holding on in the cold, as tight as closed fists. This scene of powerlessness has been repeated since the beginning of time, one of the overlays distorting the lives of girls and women.

More than the crochet hook the adolescent poked inside me, more than the lamb made of white basalt that he left, *Jesusss*, his name hissed, more than the terror in the event, its surprise appearance in a bright bed with flounces, and the confusion, the unknown sperm and white wetness, *what was it, what was it all*, but his accusation that somehow I had done something wrong and needed Jesus left me overwhelmed.

I had known nothing before, and now I was not to tell it to his parents, near strangers to me, downstairs. I had been kidnapped and dirtied, streaked with fear. I was barely six.

Toni Morrison observed, "Time, it seems, has no future."

Sometimes if I look back at what is called myself, it feels like holding up a View-Master—a childhood toy similar to a pair of binoculars that projected still images in three dimensions. Wonderfully close, magical to see before your eyes the Carpathian Mountains or Inuits, but nevertheless, the clunky, cherished View-Master always remained a static theater. Looking back is like that, oddly bearable, even when loss and errors appear. I don't do it often, but when I do, I gaze. I can do this and not think that it is narcissistic. I gaze because I am astounded, hungry and aware that energies are still at work and working on those events. Present time means my life can still absorb more.

W hat story serves the revisiting of that bedroom scene? Then, it took place like a bad spell in the early-morning hours when the seventeen-year-old boy crept into the guest room, where I had been left with near strangers. The adolescent with the flaming penis woke me up.

I see its effects differently now. Whatever happened and was not to be talked about would have been enough to condemn the young man, but the deepest wound inflicted was my mother's response.

I was afraid to tell my mother, but when I did, she used the identical words and moral compass as the seventeen-year-old molester—Don't tell anyone. She added, hoping to make it right: These things happen. He's a nice boy.

I had no hearing aids to turn on or off. I only felt that my mother's hand was the same hand as the boy's pressing on my mouth. It was indifferent to pain in others. I was invisible. No one was listening. She blamed women.

If I consider the phrases:

These things happen
Don't talk about it
He's a nice boy

I have the conditions for R. D. Laing's use of Rubin's vase.

In that event, symmetries emerge, exposing some roots in American middle-class values at the time. The adolescent boy and my mother say the same thing, favoring the boy over the girl, denying the sovereignty of one's body, and favoring appearances over confronting their friends.

Looking at that era in middle-class America, hair was a message bobby-pinned and clipped with social rules. Flattops for boys, a clean-cut look, with no feminine traces of curls or long hair. No ethnic deviations, no Afros, no skin-tight clothes. For girls, skirt lengths broadcast decency, halfway to the calf, and waists were like the base of egg cups, then breasts puffed out as rounded eggs begging to be cracked. Reviewing photos of whites and Blacks, males and females, the styles, the discrepancies, the assumptions about fixed roles and gender, makes silences obvious, sometimes absurd. The appearance of cleanness and order was so pronounced even young bodies looked like marionettes, and the smiles on faces a forced notion. One participated in a society where resistance meant isolation and loneliness.

W e don't know what traces we leave on others. In a life, no one can say for another how much something hurt or what impact it had. In the #MeToo movement, the collective injustices—the use of force, violence, blackmail, the monstrous in sex, the perverse, the abuses and abuse of power on children, women, and vulnerable men, people employed by people who abuse their status for sexual gains—released a spectacular geyser of sickness and guilt and exploitation. A ritual of public silence ended, and the news spread. Centuries of bites torn from the forbidden apple, at least for some months, were not about Eve but Adam's lust, brutality, and callousness.

Female victims around the globe, women in societies that threatened stoning or disowning them, some in dictatorships, found strength in the collective cry to overcome censored shame and fear and to come forth in larger numbers. The Western media loved it more than the people who were committed to the protests because the media particularly likes scandal and movie stars. Meanings permutated often with instrumental intent.

The stories of abuse contain similarities but each is different, needing to be lifted from ideology to its rightful significance. Otherwise the intricacies of these unequal stories are lost in ideology, which is not adequate to build a new collective language about sexual power. If we are to tell our stories, we need to collect them humbly, recognizing emergency levels of danger and different levels of violence and retribution against millions of people—children, women, men, the LGBTQ community, for whom there are few listeners.

When your child dies, the only person you want to comprehend your pain is your partner, the other half of your soul, in the excruciating disorientation that surrounds. Like Adam and Eve in Masaccio's frescoes, cast from the garden, trying to cover their nakedness, a parent who has lost a child knows that she or he will never enter the garden of innocence again. No feeling cries more loudly than you must stay together. Grief, as if it were a thousand sticks flogging, is unrelenting in its pursuit.

My first husband offered, some months after the death of our son, to be more discreet. I will only have affairs with women you don't know, and when you are not around, was the conclusion he reached in response to the death of our child. My first husband's words, spoken as if I were invisible, were said truthfully as the single change he could think of to bring us closer.

His sincere conclusion made me ashamed of the censoring hand on my mouth. It propelled me with blind courage to face all the emotions that were keeping me exiled from my feelings. In the dark, fumbling to find the covering hand, I felt many. I recognized my introverted fingers and took them off first. Then I took my mother's hand off. It was small with short plump fingers. Then the adolescent's, muscular and smelly. Then my brothers', perhaps holding their hands for the first time. Then the stiff, cold fingers of my first husband. Limp, there was my father's duty-bound hand, along with cobwebs, nets, rationalizations. Then silence spoke. Before I could utter a word, I felt hands returning to cover my mouth. It was fantasy to say patterns disappear. When my little son died, grief gave me no choice other than needing to live my life truthfully. His death cleared that path for me.

It is past midnight. I know that emptiness is circulating in the Parma cathedral. Unwitnessed, unheard, it is moving up and down the stairs to the crypt, to the altar, to Correggio's dome where Mary, with uplifted arms, waits to rise into heaven. The emptiness is moving unheard, and certainly not recorded and broken into wavelengths. Its silences are far from a composition. They are something, however, because they have been thought about and put into words. But why, what kind of words, and for what purpose?

Paolo is asleep. He is usually the one up at this hour, watching the History Channel, where the Second World War or the First or Vatican Councils or one of hundreds of horrible massacres are documented in grainy footage where people move like puppets dressed in strange costumes and clothes. His methodical mind finds the evidence a very satisfactory way of making judgments. He has nightmares and I have never been able to convince him to find less troubling material before he goes to sleep. Before his stroke, he had nightmares, states where he woke up and then reentered the same dream, as if he could not escape the stinging swarm of issues. After his stroke, in these many years, the nightmares seem more frightening, more inescapable. At breakfast, he often feels he is still inside a nightmare.

I am awake. I feel better when I get up and come to my study. I like crossing the house, turning on the light, and admitting worries in a factual way. Writing at my age or at any age is a onetime chance to take new risks. Proust wondered how anyone could die without having really known what his or her life was. That means not just observing or telling but expressing one's own being in language. When we come to abysses, having trained but suddenly admitting to ourselves that we may not have the strength, we may find we fail and fall. That is when we realize we are like others, and we join them.

The subject of *The Silent Woman*, a book written by Janet Malcolm in 1993, is difficult to intuit from the title. In the current atmosphere, it could be a book about sexual repression or abuse or discrimination or a sex reassignment. The words don't quite tell us, and until we have more information, the context basically is inferred from the present. In the year it was published, the title character might have been a spy, or the wife in a love triangle.

Instead, the book is about Sylvia Plath and the various biographies that attempt to tell her life. She remained the silent woman because human flaws and social attitudes made objectivity and research difficult. Neither Plath's extensive self-conscious documentation—journals, poetry, letters, careful fictional constructions, her psychiatrist's notes, the histories of her hospitalizations for schizophrenia—nor materials her biographers uncovered can be compressed to a point that her marriage and her suicide could be plausibly reconstructed. In the end, each version becomes a story, with caveats, assessing degrees of blame.

The biographers picked Plath's life over, shaping it as a central myth of twentieth-century womanhood. It stands as an American story, like the suicide of Marilyn Monroe: a fascinating, vulnerable female talent destroyed and exploited by the world. Success, a particular version of it or its lack, was generally interpreted through the lens of male prejudice and competition.

America gives great value to the personal interpretation of an individual's life. The pervasive right to grow, to reinvent oneself, is a cultural feature of American democracy and its experiment to define the right to happiness. Janet Malcolm's approach showed that those diving after Plath's image invariably, intentionally or unwittingly, slanted the story. Each fine-combing by a biographer left a reader with some new material and insights, some industrious detail. Each story perpetuated or argued against other interpretations, depending on how the other characters were able to develop and speak.

The biographers, pursuing their own vested goals, endured lawsuits and obstacles that initially made getting material difficult and problematic. Unlike other suicides of twentieth-century woman poets—for example, the Russian Marina Tsvetaeva or the Italian Antonia Pozzi, where sexism was not the key applied to interpreting their ultimate act—Plath's history and context were rarely tugged beyond the reflection of a specific culture and time. The fixation with her private life seemed normal, that is, ordinary, because it was an American story. The consciousness that this fixation was not one common to all cultures went unnoticed. We can't know, if we don't realize that we don't know. Each of us in our own way produces our own fictions.

I remembered a line from Plath's journal about her industrious and frugal pleasure in sewing for her daughter. When I was reading a review of the most recent book on her life, those few words leapt from a poem where this same red material flies blindingly and menacingly from the steel needle of her sewing machine. This suspended moment of paradox brought me to the intense literal sincerity of her passion to put life into words. It stayed as an image of her as a person, a *fabbro*, a maker of art, and a woman with enormous emotional conflicts, who wanted many different things from life and from art. The needle, the blood, the wish to be economical, to be a perfect housewife and mother, her rage in illness, the impossible demands on her artistic time, the cloth flying blindingly and menacingly were all genuine; the furious reds were not those of martyrdom. Do we need more in order to feel the intense, tragic throb of Sylvia Plath when she was alive?

Natalia Ginzburg, whom we read earlier describing maternity as "beautiful, happy, traumatizing . . . strange . . . It can be out of hand, too much love, too much fear—fear of losing something—losing the child, losing self," in two sentences came close to capturing conflicting or, perhaps better, coexisting feelings general to motherhood. The picture might be enough to make us think about and imagine Plath's motherhood without speculating or prying. It might make us doubt if we need to know how far into the oven she placed her head after she had taped the door leading to the children's room. It might make us question our ability to judge Ted Hughes's sincerity in wanting to protect his children.

Malcolm's book cut a strong path through the industry of Plath biographies. She argued about limits to the integrity of pursuing a single life as a biographer. In some way she argued that nonfiction becomes fiction, the same way we talk about the Vietnam War or struggles in the Middle East as if they were a single or simple thing. We say it is fact, but using set attitudes over and over, invested interests as well as incomplete understanding, we often are on the edge of fictions that can get no closer to being real. Perhaps we need to recognize our contempt for respect, even self-respect.

S tanding at the bus stop this afternoon, I watched a middle-aged man, dressed rather conventionally for Parma in a beige pullover framing a white shirt with a tie, open the disconnected refrigerator, which is an additional repository for the Little Free Library. The fridge, painted a light mauve, has all the documentation on the door: the rules for taking books.

He opened up a shopping bag and began putting hardcovers in one by one. He glanced around and happened to see my critical eyes following him. There they were, those eyes that have done so much observing for me, eyes that I forget can make people feel stared at, making him feel x-rayed. He turned his back as if to block his action as he continued dipping into the refrigerator and filling his bag. When it was bulging and heavy, he turned, his eyes meeting mine then quickly darting away.

He crossed the street and waited at the corner for the bus to appear.

My mind judged him. Twitching with curiosity, I wondered what the story was. Was he abusing the system that I had such idealistic investment in?

We got on the same bus, he at the back and I at the front. When he got off, it was in front of the used bookstore, where rightly or wrongly I assigned to him the act of stealing books in order to sell them. He did enter the store.

It is easy to say—well, not entirely easy—that I still don't know for certain what he was doing. It is easier to remind myself that I am not the policewoman for the Little Free Library. It is more difficult to decide, if he was selling the books, was that a bad thing? By selling them, was he putting them in circulation? Was it wrong to be taking them from the Little Free Library if, like so many people in Parma, although he dresses well, he actually needed the money? Or was it a bad thing because he broke the spirit of the library and could drain it of all the attractive contents? Was he a rotten apple? If he were an immigrant loading a bag up with books from the Little Free Library, would he immediately be considered a thief?

What does depend on the mauve refrigerator, grazed by hands opening and closing it, near the bus stop, as our minds and what we bring from our culture evaluate?

I had no training to speak of. I had come back from Oxford as a young married woman who had already been in the civil rights movement at the University of Michigan. Poverty programs initiated by Lyndon Johnson were under way. Quite innocently I assumed that working for the New York City Department of Child Welfare would help improve conditions for the people who were ghettoized.

The exam offered by the New York City child welfare department consisted of a few general knowledge questions, an eye test, and lifting your skirt to see if you were knock-kneed or had other problems that would impede you from walking distances. There was no hearing check. I was to wear walking shoes. I was given a paper map.

I chose child welfare as my interest, having no idea of what that meant other than children in poverty were victims. The summer my father died, I had been working in inner-city Pittsburgh, living in a church basement with other university students, painting sides of houses, repairing fences in a Quaker project of home repairs and voter registration. We often shared fresh coffee in people's neat kitchens. We attended neighborhood Sunday services, where parishioners spoke in tongues and voices shook the wooden rafters in the church. The neighborly arrangements in inner-city Pittsburgh did not suggest, and thus prepare me to imagine, that New York City poverty would be much different.

From my earliest childhood memories of Josephine, the maid who worked in the house next door to ours, sadness in her shoulders, her eyes, the way she heavily walked, I carried a physical sense of social injustice.

At the University of Michigan in Ann Arbor, once we were taking part in marches and sit-ins in front of Woolworth's un-integrated lunch counter, I was asked to work on a panel with the president of the university and his legal staff to examine the statutes of all the sororities and fraternities on campus. Each one had restrictive clauses. Each one defined its group in ethnic, religious, and gender terms. Our work was to root out offend-ing discriminatory clauses in private charters. If they were not eliminated, the use of federal funds could be withdrawn from the university, since it was a public institution. The year spent on the committee opened my eyes to unchallenged evidence of secret locked doors perpetuating and enforcing ideas of iden-tity by giving ethnic groups or religions the power to exclude. Under our fingers, we touched those hidden points meant to be secret and initiated the discussion with people who were going to have to learn that their keys to those doors were no longer valid. It was a good moment, gathering around the long table with educators and administrators wielding power and inter-preting it, letting us, as students, recognize the responsibility and long hours necessary to look underneath surfaces for in-tractable messages. The committee gave language a close look and a chance to renew itself in good faith. The level of com-mitment to change clicked open new possibilities in the world.

My beat was in the Bronx, beyond the Grand Concourse. I worked alone as a caseworker, riding the subway and then entering dark halls and banging on doors after using a map to get me back and forth between Lexington and Fifth on wide sidewalks that often had people sitting on stoops. I never worried about being there. However, the poverty inside the houses, what was not seen from the streets—the walls shiny with roaches, the rat bites on children's faces, the urine stench, the holes in the wallboard, the blackness and grime and grease on linoleum, broken windows, cracked gas rings, needles for heroin on kitchen tables, guns in broom closets—was beyond what I could fit in my limited experience of America. The silences around poverty, the conditions people were living in day and night, did not suggest solutions. They exposed structural rot that came from so many ways of perceiving human beings as different and unquestioningly believing those perceptions.

I was to follow children, with a special focus on children who were being abused. They were often captives in households where women and men who couldn't take it anymore tortured children, put salt in wounds, kicked their little ones, dropped them down stairs. A minor percentage of my caseload was abused children. These instances were noted when social workers paid humiliating visits to determine fraud, false claims for pittances including counted numbers of toilet rolls.

There were always the witnesses, most often grandmothers, who tried to support, to intervene, to protect and herd children to school and to meetings. Often the level of chaos was difficult for them to overcome. Not all those visited by social workers were abused children. Only a terribly unlucky few were the tragic physical and psychological victims of poverty that had descended into violence, drug use, and untreated mental illness.

The silence around poverty that breaks people's spirits is an obscene one. The strength of those who carry on fully functioning emanates from remarkable people who are not recognized and are spoken over in terms of societal assumptions and programs. As I remember them in my caseload experience, in spite of all obstacles, many elderly women had ringing, crystal-clear minds and religious principles that illuminated families. Some were charismatic leaders large enough to illuminate whole city blocks.

G wen was eleven years old when her sister's husband raped her. She was put on my caseload and I was to follow her through the last months of her pregnancy.

The turbulence inside this little girl, shy, frightened, unable to speak for herself, was sunk deep and muffled. She had been assigned to babysit her sister's children. She generally didn't go to school. Her sister hid her shoes so she couldn't leave the house. Like people who have been tortured or witnessed too much violence, Gwen could hardly speak. When she did, her voice was so quiet it was difficult to know if she had said something. Her eyes didn't meet mine until we had known each other many months. It was as if they could only look sideways.

I ask myself now, Did I make up the scene on the hospital stairs? Gwen gave birth on the stairs of a New York City public hospital. She was brought in at the last minute and did not reach the delivery room. The little boy was pushed out then and there, in chaos, by a child who was so terrified that she repressed every minute of the event. Her mind disposed of all her pain, the rape, the sister, the excruciating violence of contractions and being alone with people screaming at her, and that thing screaming and people telling her to put him to her breast; it all tumbled into a heavy silence inside her that was confused and raw. She shut down everything. And the little boy was cut off from his birthright and wrapped and left in his bassinet, fed by nurses.

When I saw her in the hospital, she had no memory of giving birth, no memory of having a son. The baby boy went home with her, into her sister's apartment, but in a matter of weeks he was removed and institutionalized. She could not and would not take care of the strong little child who kicked and cried and wanted to be fed. Her sister did not want the little infant, and Gwen, with the softest of voices, would say, I don't know who he is. I've never seen him before. He was erased in her existence after Gwen erased him, unsure from the beginning of what it was, much less who it was, growing in her body and then screaming with hunger.

How it has all happened is now beside the point. It has. This morning in an email, an Italian friend from California mentioned Manzoni's novel *The Betrothed*. Because it's written in her mother tongue, and because she was taught the novel for an entire year while a student in *liceo* in Milan, deep connections to the author and text are hers. She knows much by heart. Alessandro Manzoni understood the history of plagues in human civilization and chose to translate the historical plague of 1630 (which killed a million people, or one-quarter of northern Italy's population) into the biological, social, and political horrors of his characters' lives. He used history to fruitfully explore his time and place, by inference, since his novel was set in a historical past. Manzoni does not use the pandemic as a metaphor, although the plague's cataclysmic effects do open up passages for considering the nature of God as well as politics. He published the book in 1825–1827. From the beginning of his fiction he alludes to other plagues, like that of San Carlo, which occurred fifty-three years prior to the one that decimated his characters' lives. Once the book was published, Manzoni continued writing and revising it, publishing a definitive version in 1840.

In another email this morning, a translator who is officially retranslating Manzoni's classic sent me his twenty-five-page condensation of the pages about the plague. He has combined parts for various reasons, he wrote, but basically to eliminate repetitions, hoping that it would read more easily.

The American translator knows Italian history, but it is not his history. He sees how Manzoni used the plague's factual sides. The individual is swept into the collective. Barriers collapse and human beings are leveled beyond class, but many are victims because of government scheming. Probably the translator made his edits recognizing, in Manzoni's grasp of the politics, parallels to America's onetime reality with a leader who failed to comprehend the gravity of a deadly virus and sacrificed people for delusional gains. In the beautifully translated pages he sends, there is Manzoni's most excruciating condemnation and the most famous page in the novel. The scene depicts a woman who dresses her lifeless daughter, Cecilia, and hands her over to the porter collecting corpses to dump into a mass grave. She bribes the man to carry the girl of nine, undefiled, making him promise that he will lay her gently composed in the pile in the ditch. As the mother places her daughter on the cart, she bids the porter to return for her and her other child by evening, when they, too, will be dead.

Gwen was the reason I finally quit my job with the Department of Child Welfare. Deeply frustrated by my lack of training, I realized that I could not, simply as a well-meaning individual, contribute what was needed. Working for the public agency, I was too young and impatient to accept what it offered to those in need. But I am skipping steps.

Here is Gwen's narrative: one tiny person up against a society and protected by a cumbersome institution that can't get close enough to people who are exceptions. I will tilt her story, tilt it past the crack of hope that is the usual American version, her persistence, her wretched climb out, her seeing the light. Her saga, bathed by light seeping into the crack of hope, is the angle an American writer is expected to bring to life. Even better would be if the person who lived that tough climb wrote the tale and sold it herself. But what if that story, the story of success, of the individual, of the person who accepts the system and enters it, what if that story is a mantra that prevents us from hearing or listening to stories that don't have clear endings and won't sell. What if money has another function and meaning?

What if the ambiguous stories were brought out of the silences? What if we put faces on failure and suffering? We probably couldn't bear them. We probably would find distances and guidelines and refer to our own measures for willpower and sacrifice and find ourselves judging the pain of individuals who failed because, in our scheme, they didn't try hard enough. What, instead, if there was no solution but spending time listening to terrible inequalities and conditions and starting from there?

Recently teaching creative writing and the memoir in New York City, I wondered out loud to the students, Are we close to reality, close enough to justify our work as nonfiction writers, if we do not scale a life story to a broader context and structure? How do we illuminate silences that need to be understood before changes can occur if we back off because of their intrinsic pessimism and criticism of ourselves? One of my students said: We don't want to be depressing like Emily Dickinson.

The Grand Concourse was the starting border of my caseload and it extended to about 160th Street. Burned-out buildings, trash idly blowing, permanently abandoned areas, the worn-out dumped innards of rooms, broken, stained, ripped, were part of the landscape. Nevertheless, lots of blocks were more or less like many other blocks and felt completely normal.

To round out the context of local history in the mid-1960s:

1. The Great Society was a drumbeat heard in many places, including abandoned lots in the Bronx.
2. Generations listening to the Beatles resonated to the lyrics—"I don't care too much for money, money can't buy me love." Joan Baez was singing, too, her voice rising in higher and higher ranges about the resistance to war. Motown voices were showing whites that they had much to learn about romance.
3. Rachel Carson had published *Silent Spring*, her book about our poisoned environment. She broke a taboo, introduced a new language, and changed and alarmed the entire world. In a society that thought of goddesses as movie stars, she remained uncrowned,

our Tethys, the goddess and protectress of fresh and salt water.

4. Jane Jacobs had written *The Death and Life of Great American Cities*, extolling, among other things, the significance of sidewalks and how diversity composes different parts that contribute to an orderly whole.

5. Hannah Arendt had written *Eichmann in Jerusalem: A Report on the Banality of Evil*, analyzing the personality of the Holocaust organizer Adolf Eichmann at his trial as a normal man, thoughtless and disengaged, unable to think from the standpoint of someone else. His deeds were inhuman, but he was a normal person unable to explain the depth of evil he'd generated.

6. Susanne Langer had written *Mind: An Essay on Human Feeling*, arguing that language and dialogue use language not simply to communicate, but to produce symbols that humans use to create their own reality.

7. Maya Angelou was a few years from publishing *I Know Why the Caged Bird Sings*, a story that broke a silence with a most unforgettable voice. Her voice was finding its pitch and courage in the more open society surrounding her. Angelou, like Gwen, the girl I was to follow, lost her voice. For years after she was raped as a child, she could not speak.

8. Rosalind Franklin had died, leaving her crystallographic images that held the secret of life. Thus, she could not have shared the 1962 Nobel Prize with Watson, Crick, and Wilkins, even if they had been forthcoming far earlier (they were not) to credit her

work as central to defining the double helix, whose sublime structure is the key to biological inheritance.

9. Jane Goodall was on the reserve in Gombe, forming close affectionate bonds with chimpanzees and studying their social and family behavior in the wild. She named the chimps, rather than giving them numbers, raising eyebrows with researchers who objected to changing their criteria for objective science. She crossed barriers that brought chimps' intelligence into light that broke stereotypes.

10. Toni Morrison was in the wings, nearly ready to break up narrative with stories that started where they started and, without magic realism, gave breath to Black lives that were unexplained particulars of existing worlds. *The Bluest Eye* was the first to come. Then ghosts and myths in lives became visible presences.

At first, I tried to work through the system to have Gwen removed from the home into a place that might help her, some months after she had given up her son. She needed to be examined by a board of evaluators before she could be placed in foster care.

She could not answer their questions. The questions could not answer her. They fell short, like balls hitting a net.

What did you do for your birthday? Shyly, hunching her shoulders, putting her eyes on the wall. I don't know.

What color is a banana? Black, she said.

The circumstances of chaos and denial of the separate world that poverty generated could not be accommodated. The questions were for people who lived in a more orderly culture, or for whom the cues for that culture were known. The evaluators gave her a number that said she was of subnormal intelligence. She could not be removed from her sister's guardianship.

The institution failed her, but the institution that I had been raised to think about as the vehicle for equal opportunity was education. The story it leads me to is culture and testing. What about lives that fall through the cracks of testing so that the answers to questions cannot be heard? Under what circumstances can a banana be black? How can a voice be so low and mumbling that it can't be heard as shy and traumatized? In our multiple choices, there was no choice for what she had to tell. If she used her brain to tell what she knew, it could not be measured. Like poverty itself, we would have needed to imagine different questions before concluding what was the right answer. Maybe multiple-choice questions could be usefully perceived as bistables. Even as bistables, both yes and no are clearly not completely true or false. It depends on your history.

What color is a banana?
    a. yellow
    b. red
    c. black

What color is a banana?
    a. slaves
    b. a refrigerator ship
    c. Try it. Black is sweet.

Banana is to history as
    a. money is to colonialism
    b. green is to yellow is to black
    c. Standard Oil is to point of view

Maybe we should visit the LIGO website and listen to the sound GW150914 again: the gravitational waves, the black holes of matter collapsing into one another. If for twenty years teams all over the world tried to find the sound of poverty, if we could catch that first sound of the collapse and all that its traveling brought in its wake, if we would construct the tubes and use the numbers and wait for the sound to prove that poverty exists, would we hear it break through? Would the chirp of poverty be something we could finally say exists? Could the chirp be a child, a little girl, an abused boy? And if we heard a chirp, would a child ask us first for a pencil and then a pair of shoes? If a chirp were a child of poverty where schooling, fresh water, and hospitals were missing, would he ever feel so free and lighthearted to ask for an ice cream before asking for medicine for his father? Would she ever ask for violin lessons as a normal wish? Are the gravitational waves so silent that we do not realize that America is crowded with such children?

*A*ngela's Ashes, by Frank McCourt, was rewritten in various versions over twenty years. In order to publish it, much less to make it a bestseller, he had to find a voice that did not make poverty seem unbearable. He needed the hope that he eventually found in telling the story from the standpoint of an adolescent boy who is returning to America and its implied hope and way out of poverty. America is happiest reading about itself, above all, when the narrative confirms America's uniqueness and its vigorous capitalism as a place of opportunity.

Once Helen Keller expanded beyond her inspirational writing as a blind and deaf woman who learned to break through those barriers, received education, and became a writer and speaker, her passionate mind soon reached further. She gave voice to oppression that most working people endure in order that "the small remnant can live in ease." Once she extended the meaning of blindness and deafness to owners in capitalistic systems, her achievements as a radical intelligence became suspect. The same woman whose brilliance propounded universal human potential was disparaged, and the truths used to praise her were reversed. Her attitudes as a suffragette, a pacifist, a supporter of people in the working class suddenly became framed as the mistaken positions of a person who, because of her handicaps, was unable to properly assess the world she wrote about.

These observations were made earlier in this book. Perhaps reading them now there is a slightly new angle in the discussion. Maybe now we feel a little more uncomfortable because we can see Gwen and the cultural confines of testing. Or we can understand Manzoni's plague and its latest translation in 2020 as including the contemporary context of Cecilia.

Ligabue, an Italian expressionist painter who, like Van Gogh, suffered bouts of mental illness, insisted that madness was poor people's response to poverty.

L ast night in Parma I met a genial friend I hadn't seen in a long time. We met for a coffee. The bar, which had changed locations, was always one of the best bakeries in the city. Both of us used all our discipline to resist the rows and rows of beautifully colored and decorated sweets, little towers of chocolate, rectangular edifices layered like Lego parking structures filled with zabaglione asking to be chosen. We sat down, drew in the richness of the smell of espresso, and began to catch up with where our lives had been.

She started with her current pastime of reading original texts that she had studied more than forty years ago, when she took her degree in ancient Greek and Latin. Now, she said, I am visiting them for pleasure. We had passed the spring equinox, so the light outside the large windows, even at six, was still promising. Evening was approaching like the softest of mauve veils.

You know, she said, what the ancients are about?

Auden's famous line about the Old Masters never being wrong about suffering came into my mind. But she was saying something else.

Listening. Really, they all are about that.

She cocked her head. She shook it as if she were both answering and surprising herself. Yes. Listening.

The Greeks are about listening and finding silence by entering into their propositions. Reading Plato is being alone with thought that is not your thought but a dialogue with someone with the knowledge and the method for conversing.

She smiled again with surprise and satisfaction.

The Greeks teach listening.

A book is a conversation with someone who is not you, she repeated, her face growing ever more fervent. As you listen to them—the others who have committed to rigor—as you grow to understand and feel what they are saying, the comprehension and the questions become the you who engages. You become aware of not knowing. You face your own ignorance and the noble pursuit of truth. Listening admits that knowledge is real and beyond preconceptions. Knowledge differs fundamentally from self-help. In self-help books, the reader consumes what she is looking for. She never touches knowledge, which requires discovering not knowing, and a clear understanding that the text is not about herself. Knowledge belongs to others, who have learned from others. To become part of the dialogue to cultivate, conserve, and delineate what you can possess with hard work, you need to understand listening.

So then, what's a handkerchief? A small white proper piece of cotton cloth, folded in four. In literature, handkerchiefs have been symbols, mainly involving women. Othello gave one to Desdemona as a sign of his love, and eventually believed, through a series of accidents and manipulated reversals, that finding it in Cassio's room proved Desdemona's betrayal of him. The symbolism in that tiny piece of cloth in the play is muddled: it causes pain once it is lost and its original intent misconstrued. That confusion does not escape me. Objects are wordless and their meanings are added on by others. They may be true or false, or perhaps neither, or both.

The little white square handkerchief, embroidered with a few forget-me-nots, in the slim plastic box, was one from a very young woman to another, who was quite young herself, yet who in some ways stood in for a mother. It was Gwen's gift to me. Quiet as she still was, there was perception in the little square, a presumption of order, a sign of loyalty, affection, something to keep as a measure of us as equals. In the chaos of her home, the strewn clothes, the unwashed dishes, the dirty faces, the cruel, continuous undermining, the white handkerchief was a pocket of love, even self-love and manners.

The white handkerchief was a wing, belonging to a bird that, like all single-winged birds, must hide itself, rest, grow stronger, exercising its odd, difficult path to flight, hoping other birds won't pick it to death before it finds a way to move without appearing crippled. Like music composed for the left hand alone, the body and the right hand feel the melody they can't play. The body hears the whole song and plays it with the left hand alone.

By the time Gwen gave it to me, she had recovered her ability to read and write. Her mind had crawled out of its hole. She was twelve by then and for various weeks we had been meeting on Saturdays. Attention and support were the medicines needed to pull her back from depression and withdrawal. We took our time, both of us waiting for her to absorb something or think it over before her dark eyes would lift and she would nod. Without pressure or judgment, this concession of time allowed the sensitive girl to leave her muteness and the preposterous evaluation that she was subnormal.

I was walking her through elements that were missing in her psychological responses because no one testing her had the latitude to think what silences cruelty, poverty, and rape wreaked on a young life. The lack of imagination also reflected the blindness of cultural prejudice. It was unbelievable to me that middle-class lives in America at that time, even in urban places, could be so utterly cut off from broader interpretations of what every day consisted of for people without means. Until I witnessed it, I was unable to imagine it, although it was never hidden. It was just not spoken about.

Gwen and I started by giving names to money—dimes, quarters, the substantial Kennedy half dollars. She had never taken a subway, never been downtown. I started riding with her into the city, and then let her take a few stops alone and return uptown those few stops to find me waiting. We practiced on and off, over and over, naming stations and places: crossing over at Columbus Circle, getting off at Bryant Park. She learned the word "escalator" and then saw its metal gliding steps being swallowed up at the bottom. She eventually rode down it, open-eyed, as she surveyed Macy's counters and blocks of coats and dresses and colors. She was awestruck by the seas of couches, chairs, beds, blankets. She rode the escalator into a world that was dangled before her. She floated into what cost money.

I met with her on my own time, on Saturdays, which was against New York City welfare department rules. Social workers were to have no contact with their clients. I understood the regulation then; today it is even clearer why such rules must be enforced. However, I had the goal of respectfully developing some autonomy in her, and I could find no way within the system. I honored an abstract ideology about independence: not creating dependency, and not creating personal links that could undermine that. I planned to give her a sense of self-sufficiency as her source for hope. I knew I must obey the rules. Today I might have found a program where, more humanly, I could have remained her mentor.

Instead, she and I eventually set a date for her independence. I had had no success in having her reevaluated for foster care facilities. The subway runs, we did another series of skip two, get off, skip two more, and then ride back four. They were without glitches. I sat in Bryant Park and listened to her read. I could not get her a library card due to another tangle of rules and identification. And then the time arrived to send her back to the Bronx, to her sister, her sister's children, and her rapist brother-in-law. She was wearing her shoes, which she had learned to keep under her pillow when she went to bed. I reminded her that she must continue to hide her shoes but remember that she had the right to wear them, and to tell her caseworker if her sister's husband ever touched her.

We discussed how I would get off one last time at Grand Central and she would continue on alone. That's when she handed me the handkerchief. That's when she gave me the letter asking God to bless me. That small square of a dream is one I need when I imagine her. Hers was an innocence of poetic dimensions. It was taken from an everyday idea that an imperturbable square of decency exists and needs to exist.

What we wish to believe about people who are poor when our guilt takes us over is that Scrooge will make it right for Tiny Tim. Charles Dickens's tale cheers us up every holiday season when we turn to think about whom we call the less fortunate and how it is the rich who help them with a change of heart. If we define Eden as a place where economic equality starts from birth, our commitment is far more tepid if we think our status will diminish.

The institutions consistently failed Gwen. What can we do with the image of a white handkerchief in her hands, in her home, in her heart? When I think of tears, I think first of Tennyson, in his poem *The Princess*: "Tears, idle tears, I know not what they mean." That self-pitying confusion was not hers. The handkerchief was a wing. Just one, but it was not broken.

When I was pregnant with my daughter, I lived as a renter in Palo Alto, unsupported and looking for a job. Blue Cross Blue Shield defined pregnancy as a planned illness, and thus they made no provision for covering delivery and possible complications. It was 1975. Four months pregnant, I found work writing educational material for a publishing company. I worked until two days before I delivered, and was told that to keep my job I must return to work after a two-week unpaid leave. There was no one to help with childcare, even if I had wished to leave a two-week-old child for eight hours a day after her brother had died of sudden infant death syndrome. This story was not white, or Black, or brown, but female in the United States.

The months working on Sand Hill Road, which paid my rent, left me with a few stories that belong to the picture of education. My director believed that inner-city children could not fathom the lessons being read in white schools. To recognize themselves, according to her formulation, they needed material situated in their physically broken and challenging world. Setting prejudice aside, her view was another problem of ignorance, like the question about the color of bananas.

Two or three points will be sufficient.

Two of the African American project members were fired because they objected to the material being chosen. Flashing long, beautiful red fingernails, one of the women, praying down on her knees in the women's room that she not be fired, begged me to defend her. I did. She was fired anyway. The spiteful, arbitrary action caused pain and fear and disrupted a life.

In protest, I moved my desk out of the office onto a side patio; every day I pushed it beyond the sliding glass door into the outdoors. Like the talented woman who was fired, I could not afford to lose my job. But I needed to give a sign to everyone in the office that each of us was a tacit witness to prejudice. I worked in protest, knowing that I, too, would lose my job when my child was born. Unless I returned to my desk within two weeks, it would be given to someone else who would replace me.

The richest nation in the world offered me no safety net, no maternity rights or leave. After the birth, I corrected Advanced Placement essays, working at night when my daughter slept. Since *Homo sapiens* emerged on earth, caring for and nourishing infants in order to secure their survival and set their course has been considered normal. Assisting mothers or a parent, letting them bond and recover their strength, and then providing support for further care has not been part of the policy for twentieth-century American working women.

A few more thoughts on the silence in those times. It needs to be written out because it is so deep and is often minimized.

The first concerns the material used in the reading program I worked on. The project was built assuming that inner-city children, because they could not recognize themselves, would be disinterested in materials given to middle-class children. Their diet should remain stories about being poor, keeping order, saving money to develop middle-class values. The stories were flat and materialistic: about being able to buy nice shoes. They rarely suggested the exciting stuff of life, alternative values of altruism like those of the Haudenosaunee Confederacy, where equality existed among tribal men and women and had been lost because of European pioneers. Jean-Henri Fabre, a nineteenth-century French naturalist and storyteller of insect lives, was shoehorned into the program by me. I also won a battle over Charles Eastman, whose book *Indian Boyhood* told the story of his early life and his subsequent education as a white man. His autobiography embodied many complicated changes of loss and differences in cultural identity. I insisted on telling African American lives like Jackie Robinson's as one of moral struggle. On the other side was an insecure director who said we must show how the system worked—that is, anyone in America could succeed. More transparently, she admitted that the school board in Texas, which was one of their biggest clients, would never buy a program that emphasized Jackie Robinson's struggle with discrimination and his integrity. Nor would teachers teach it, she said. Jackie Robinson needed to be shaped as an avatar of the American Dream: in other words, no other country in the world would have offered him such a chance for recognition.

I was glad that I spent my last six weeks of work at a desk outside the office. It wasn't much, but I remember the silent disapproval at my back. The air was better outside.

Lucio Fontana, born in Argentina, is claimed as an Italian artist for reasons of his Italian parentage. Fontana's signature works are cuts on canvas, often a small series of them, or a long single slash, clean as a fencer's lunge. Behind the interrupted or pierced surface, black backing underneath or the wall on which the piece hangs release the questions of levels. Fontana's process (representing, like much modern artwork, accompanying concepts to support or justify the content) suggests that art must bridge the gap between its space and the space around it. New materials, new technology have destroyed conventional relationships to space. The illusion of art must find halfway positions between the object and the space around it in order to capture reality. Without a rupturing of the surface, no form can be special. Fontana wrote that the artist, too, must free himself from the center of his work and let motion in.

Both emails mentioning Alessandro Manzoni's plague feel like roots pushing the present into the book I am trying to write. Pushing from a book and from the present, they are turning things around.

In these days, nurses on the Italian evening news talk about patients who are terrorized by their fears of dying. The nurses often cry when they answer an interviewer. We can't really help. We don't know what to say.

On television, Paolo and I see caskets building up in long lines, waiting for a time when funerals can be held once again, since now groups must not gather for fear of infecting one another. We see tents being set up. This is not another place, or about another place, a fire, a flood, an earthquake, a volcanic eruption, in someone else's country. This fear is ours. Somewhere in the long line of closed caskets, we have a friend. This collapse is something greater, different than the last time we used the phrase "domino theory" for the false explanation of why the United States was fighting in Vietnam. Villages and regions are being infected.

There is real silence on the streets. People cannot go out. A month ago, as the mild winter rushed birds and the violets and the wheat into their cycles, no one knew silence would suddenly have an enormous presence as would the unknown.

Think of Correggio's ceilings, where the next reiterations of cosmology and knowledge, the dynamics of motion disturbing the physics of inertia, belief systems, and faith were his mission. He could not refuse his vision. It took ten years of his life to paint the two domes; the thrusting and falling forces that he saw coming were largely rejected. They were too threatening, too unfamiliar.

He introduced motion, motion caught and soon to be enacted as commonplace in art and resisted in religion and science. Soon to be brought into being, challenging the Catholic Church, a new model for the universe in which the earth moved around the sun. Correggio's torques and twists appear, in part, because the mastery of three-dimensional perspective could go no further. Verisimilitude was static unless motion could be shown. New worlds would come into being. Not just style but content drove him. He saw ahead.

His Christ, in the cathedral, his genitals seen and Mary reaching up for him, what insights were driving him to show the people below that far-distant vision of men and women living their sexuality? He coming down for her, buffeted and blown and clearly seen by the priests below, and she reaching up among all the sinners born since the original sin, ready to be taken by him? He was centuries away from a version of that uncensored and ambiguous humanist image of sexuality as an expression of human salvation.

Today at lunch, sitting at the table we set with unusual care, Paolo and I remark on how quickly the two weeks we have been inside have passed. We go as far as the terrace that is covered in twigs and sticks because a pair of doves is building a nest above our awnings. We try not to be intrusive as they sweep back and forth from the driveway gate to the column to the branch where the nest is balanced.

Paolo says, They carry those long straws in their beaks. They don't have hands to carry or to build those amazing structures. They've assembled them from what's around. While the men on the scaffolding have stopped and the tree cutters and leaf blowers have been furloughed by federal decree, the doves swoop and dive and carry the grasses back and up all day long. They are building structures so sturdy and aerodynamic that architects and model builders puzzle over their secrets.

The shape of the week has disappeared as if it were a tent that had been folded. No more poles like Monday or Tuesday to turn it into a definite structure. Sunday used to be a day slightly different in its respite and then Mondays filled up quickly with cars and errands and meetings, and the world we called our life rushed in. Now all is still. As still as snowstorms used to be in Wisconsin decades ago. The spine of the week holding us straight up as doers, as doing the bidding, in part, of others, has broken for the time being. We are not compelled to meet the rhythms that have dictated our lives for years and years. In fact, we are forbidden to acknowledge most of those rhythms. It is a strange freedom, a reversal, like Correggio's ceiling in San Giovanni. Christ is descending, not ascending. The virus and its required quarantine are just at the beginning of being seen for what they are. They are showing us frailties we never imagined and powers that we had forgotten.

Paolo went out as far as the backyard. Swiss chard grew through the winter and he cut a large patch. He chopped it by hand, and green, a strong scent of fresh green, fills the room. He explains: Each tiny piece of chard, having four sides, allows it to fully release its scent. The chopping sound is clattering, knife to wooden board at great speed. Silence has gotten here; how and what it is this time, it is too soon to say. It seems to be seen as an invading army with fires at night. But it is showing us our lives, full of clutter and frenzy, and for all our motions, strangely not self-sufficient.

When I attended the university, the questions around how art and life reflected one another and reflected society were not yet being examined using the light of glaring omissions. The foundations of a specific literature were taught using linear surveys divided into categories of style and social history—Classical, Romantic, Victorian, and so on. "So on" meant: of course, cause and effect, and this is all true. Literature was taught in historical contexts, and history was most often taught as economic transitions stimulating or causing changes that then were reflected in what authors were writing. It was a useful structure at the time, teaching how to make links and how to understand place.

Once the basic works had been identified in chronological order, studies of genre or author became more specialized. When omissions became an imperative topic, an extensive reformation of the curriculum began, starting from the social movements in the 1960s. Voices unheard and viewpoints unseen began to crowd into commonplace considerations. Tom Stoppard's play *Rosencrantz and Guildenstern Are Dead* deconstructed a play that had been examined and interpreted in every century without looking at what remained silent beyond Hamlet and his dilemma.

Toni Morrison, James Baldwin, Adrienne Rich are examples of the revelatory voices that suddenly ruptured complacencies in required reading. Otherness from this social perspective became commonplace and one's own story a default narrative that obviously had not been known before the author decided to tell it. Women began writing personal stories without doubting their literary value. Movements and upheaval soon suggested new genres and physical forms to writers like Anne Carson, who published a book as a series of separate booklets that could be read in any direction. Fracture and flow took over from the logical linear line. Chronology began to be mixed, time erupting on itself.

The literary curriculum I studied was almost entirely male authors, as was the faculty. Content was not yet an articulated issue of political importance, but form, how things could be told, was an exciting discussion nevertheless.

Shifting borders, like Fontana's slash, began to be a part of content. Works existed in other eras and appear, the way Renzo Piano and Richard Rogers put the mechanical parts of the Pompidou Centre in full view on the outside of the structure. Instead of hiding the mechanical guts of the structure behind panels and corridors, the practical realities of the building became narrative that overtook old views of institutional beauty. Laurence Sterne took that path two centuries earlier. Herman Hesse introduced a physical break of a Magic Theatre inside the novel *Steppenwolf.*

Czeslaw Milosz in *Unattainable Earth,* a book of poetry written after he had absorbed the utterly different realities of Poland, where he grew up, and California, where he resided, introduced a dialogue about influence onto the page. He placed poems that influenced the poems he wrote, a world we generally do not see, into direct relationships on facing pages. The book opened windows, lifted curtains, without explaining how art comes to be made. The theme of borrowing, of quoting, of tradition released a different idea of truth, reality, and invention, which spoke without words for itself.

By introducing photos into books that seem to be novels on the one hand and nonfiction on the other, W. G. Sebald relied on photos to provide a sense of documentary evidence for the stories he told. He wanted seamlessness: veracity and memory and fact blurred together until they metamorphosed into a fourth genre.

The new directions in form were embraced by ever-growing numbers of women, who were full participants in creative worlds by the late 1960s. Their eruptions contrasted sharply with women's work in earlier periods, not just distant centuries. Jorie Graham deconstructs poetic lines into unfinished parallel propositions.

In earlier centuries, women's writing was often a single voice or collective direction breaking into silences and censorship. Hildegard von Bingen is an example of a writer who used her visions, music, and philosophy to show the joyous complexities of her faith. Her work had roundness and echoed unselfconsciously the feminine place in creation. Simone Weil, eight centuries later, was still arguing that human beings were living in a state of emergency in which we must respond with our whole lives.

The sense of women's writing for many centuries was not that materials were new, but that existence, at the most basic level, had not been fully defined or explored for society in general. Women often wrote using an inclusive reach—romantic and platonic love, perhaps for noble, educated women, or social conditions and religious faith. The realities of life for women meant that consciousness of their state and injustices because of their sex still needed to be articulated by conventional means. They were drawn to reflecting upon how they lived and how they wished to live in the world.

On the following page you will find an example of Fontana's suggestion to let surrounding reality into the object and to free the artist from the center of his work.

You, the observer, will be invited, once you get there, to participate in the reality seeping through the page, behind it, inside it. To let in something, possibly silence changing dimensions.

Evidently, reader, you have not turned off your phone. I hear a *pling*. Resist the next *pling* or Fontana's work will fold into all the rest.

You just want one peek. Instead three messages wait.

Oh, a plane has crashed.

Oh, a certificate of deposit is coming due.

A friend has just delivered her baby boy.

The idea of a slit piercing reality is minimized as your eye moves back to your own little screen, again, where your fingers feel in charge even though you actually know next to nothing of what is going on under your fingers. You know little of the language, little about the algorithms, little about the consequences of cookies and how we are being used and our information sold, but the speed with which we are being fed a sense that we exist, that someone is listening, that we are learning, are addictive illusions. The *pling* has pierced like a slit—leaving a slit in your brain.

Have you ever been on a 737 MAX?

What will you decide to invest in with the money from the CD?

Because you've known that little Justin was a boy for months, now that cute little soccer ball you bought on sale for him can be sent.

All this means that you stopped listening to the constructed narrative of this book.

L ucio Fontana's insight:

The world is what the artist makes it." Mark Rothko wrote that.

This page is intended to suggest the gauze backing for many of Fontana's slits. The backing in his installations appears all black; the closeness of the weave gives it the illusion of being a solid. Fontana's slits open to produce an elsewhere, an underneath, an unknown, another dimension, something—once a rupture or opening breaks a surface and the underneath throws back a bottomless response.

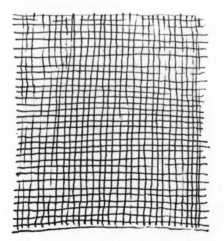

I can't look directly or for long at the photo of the whale, butchered and autopsied once it was found dead on the beach in the Philippines. More than 175 pounds of plastic were found in its organs. The photo was accompanied by a request for money.

Plastic does not break down. It does not disappear, having no obvious way to decompose. Many levels of the sea are suffocated or suffocating. It reminds me so much of what takes place on the computer, where even if we erase something, which is often extremely difficult, it remains owned as data belonging to companies and governments. Large powers keep things in the cloud, where they, in theory, can be retrieved, recalled, or recycled. In the cloud, however, they will not die. The meaning of the word "cloud" has been changed, its function as storage changed. The real clouds have changed. The weather has changed.

As frightening as death may be, as inevitable and indomitable as it is, what cannot be broken down, what does not die but accumulates as inestimable amounts of material waste or unintended verbal record, babble, trivia, is more frightening. The meanings of permanence or forever have been flattened to something meaning impossible to be rid of. Plastic won't die.

The communications we send on electronic devices won't die. Both thoughts condition me, without knowing what might usefully follow those two sentences.

The whales cannot sift out plastic as they ingest what they need to live. Whales faced extinction when they were hunted for their oil. Now that exploitation has been nearly stopped. Now another peril threatens their existence.

D oris Salcedo was a name unknown to me before my sister and I, on another of our visits to museums in New York, climbed Frank Lloyd Wright's ramps at the Guggenheim once again. Discovering Salcedo's work was part of unknowing that is not ignorance in its most shaming definition, but rather the natural human unawareness of existences—in spite of internet, air travel, documentaries—carrying on in other places. Museums were constructed precisely to offer other versions of the world to citizens. We were asked to become voyagers, *flâneurs*, ever since the mid-nineteenth-century French poet Baudelaire named the occupation. Narration by way of exhibits, themes, points of view, are integral parts of the experience.

Yet allowing the gap, the fresh air, as it were, to come in as a nod to the borders beyond the museums, to all that is out there in other countries, other villages and cities, other times differing qualitatively from that of discovery seems essential. Seeing an exhibit like Salcedo's makes the need for context obvious. It's a big leap to the context necessary to understand her work, just as it was to actually understand the result of the LIGO project. Years went into the hypothesis of the Salcedo exhibit, years into the funding and it was finally found.

Listen to the whoop.

We know artists are individuals working everywhere in the world, but the hum of our lives and the way things are often presented to us pre-interpreted, prejudged, means we seldom stop to ask what we do not know. We lack the silence, the free time sitting with no thought, to expect that we have not yet heard of something. We forget, it's only natural, that what we hear most often are the stray thoughts and passions of our own minds.

S alcedo's work was not exhibited in the spiral part of the museum. It was settled in the back so-called tower rooms. My sister and I were aware of Colombia's years of strife and armed conflict but could not have put precise dates to violence that basically took more than a quarter million lives over fifty years. The words "torture" and "rape" were words we associated with prison systems, with U.S.-involved Central American wars, with drug lords, but were we really aware of the history of those years in Colombia and the powerful feelings of Colombians who experienced fear and of those who found the courage to resist? Memory as a process, individual and collective, and as a process at a third-hand distance are different. Salcedo offered art as the bridge between lived experience and third-hand distance.

Entering the rooms with her installations of everyday objects mixed with her individual interpretations, tables sawed in half and reassembled, metal cabinets, desks with files, disfigured by soldiers entering, worked into scars by her hand carvings, we pushed into the pain and loss and violence and pushed out as if we had touched the victim's terror in ordinary lives disrupted by conflict, abduction, murder. We exited scenes of abrupt interruption and emptiness and entered again the individual and the collective reaching out to us from these familiar places that once belonged to everyday lives.

Salcedo re-created memories of the civil war, of prisons, of racism, colonialism as ongoing effects leaving trauma and pain in a society destroyed by social forces of corruption and violence. Each room spiraled us into an installation created from real objects found or left behind and then altered—a child's garment, stacks of ironed shirts, human hair in strands that ultimately the artist wove into garments, adding to the silence of people who have disappeared. One creation inspired by the deaths of three children killed by guns in the United States were three gossamer shirts, shaped and suspended in air like angels or spirits of the most fragile kind. The fabric was exquisite, the delicacy of the weaving an image that moves directly without translation into the reality of a child's fragile and beautiful life. The fabric was a mixture of silk, steel stick pins, uncountable numbers of single fibers, light and beautifully complex, working as nearly royal loomed cloth. But full of pain for anyone who would dare to put on a shirt made of thousands of pins that draw blood. The garments that seemed alive, invisibly animated, were made with the painstaking participation of the weaver, agreeing to give form to the impossibly precious but difficult combination of material. The artist accepted the burden of commitment to complete such a task, never losing sight of art as beauty—the sacred beauty of life itself.

Salcedo's handmade additions to the installations are presences that are personal interactions with objects that have lost their context and voice. She brought offerings from the world of nature, the world of the living to such objects. To recall the more than two thousand women who died in Colombian prisons from beatings and rapes, she decided to express their existence with the material of rose petals. She worked months in order to find a solution to preserve them without losing their red color. She did not want to embalm or dry out the petals. She wanted nothing funereal for these women. She wanted the petals to appear and be associated with the women when they were living and beautiful: red roses opening in the air, bowing on long stems and held up by deep roots. Once Salcedo found the solution, she made a river of the petals. They poured from a source and rushed out, the petals like waves, wavelets of red. She reached from life and history and the dark reality of torture across the river of death to leave a living river in memory. It undulated with breathtaking sensuality and beauty, and it required the viewer's resistance to the perception that it was a river symbolizing murderous blood spreading from the back of the installation until it reached us, stopping just short of our feet.

S tamping a tiny foot" was the way Theodore Roethke, an American poet, described Louise Bogan's poetry. He was not alone in his confident evaluation of the limits of women's poetry when he wrote his review in 1960. His narration, like any that generalizes about a group, was even more terrible because he never questioned his assumptions. A doubt cannot be a doubt unless one holds it as a possibility.

Roethke criticized Louise Bogan's poetry for "its esthetic and moral shortcomings," which, in part, he described as "the spinning-out; the embroidering of trivial themes; a concern with the mere surfaces of life—that special province of the feminine talent in prose—hiding from the real agonies of the spirit; refusing to face up to what existence is."

Boasting on the one hand and ridiculing on the other were meant to define value systems, using "mere" and "tiny" to scale women's realms and to set their perceptions apart. These observations and judgments are now the exposed ghostly files of a male regime written to keep women's work from an open chance. The preconceptions meant to establish the bars around culture, identifying those inside and outside of it, have been swept away by women who have made the word "tiny" into an indomitable fabric of knots in a gleaming net. Roethke's

condescending reading was a perfect foil placed against Salcedo's work.

Salcedo shows us the power of that outdated, maligned
lexicon for women. She insists that the spinning out, the embroidering, the mere surfaces of life *are* life. They hold meaning and community; they cover and fill our days; they hold
our memory. Salcedo shows us what happens when they are
touched, disturbed, destroyed. By touching them, she allows us
to identify and empathize with the experience that emanates
around and from them. Using tools that are about making,
joining, stitching together, ripping apart, she faces up to what
existence is, at least in part, when the same object undergoes
metamorphoses in a different reality.

Her vocabulary could not be clearer. The objects, the mere
surfaces of life—tables for eating meals, beds for sleeping, shoes
for walking—have been used with a woman's utter familiarity
with the power and importance of objects and shown for their
silences. Thin pale blades of living grass grow between the slats
of the abandoned and violated kitchen tables. Blades of grass,
unrepressible associations of life that evoke graves, as well as
hope.

My sister and I leaned on one another at a certain point.

Neither of us needed to say anything. We were left breath-
less by the beauty of Salcedo's works. She was a lifter, one who
rose above systems, power systems, industrial systems, and put
the objects into places where they could be seen in their metamorphosed states.

Her language might be one of tears, tears for the momen-
tous and violent ways oppression needs memorials designed
to release the lives of people who suffered but who also lived
normally, joyously. She joins tears from the victims and mixes

them with those observers entering her scenes. She creates what has not existed in those objects and synthesizes what might be made from them, reminding us of a powerful beauty.

An installation on immigrants, on otherness, presented by photographs in the exhibit, showed a sharp crack of more than fifty yards inserted in the floor. It diverged into a forked set of tributaries, of cracks. The initial crack magnified, breaking into other smaller ones. Separations widened and became obstacles. The image, the organic reality of an earth split apart, the geological process, carried a female perception of splitting, the effects of birth after the explosion. Then the repercussions were ripples, spreads, micro-actions continuing after the event. The original split was a profound, widening separation finding ground. The silence around the act of becoming an immigrant being separated from what came before filled the room. The enormity of the act was present, teetering—as the crack became an abyss and reconfigured geographies. The land was becoming a new configuration and would need a new map.

The silences in "tiny" could be as welcoming and tender as the fingers of infants, the transparent fingernails peeling from their scaling newborn hands. Why give "tiny" a diminished meaning? The terrible size of the silences in "tiny"—that include fright, surprise, terror, and challenge—women know in their bones, not just disremembered like being alive and not able to participate, but as seeds that are allowed to grow.

We could all learn to recognize "tiny" as a world without end—from the microcircuits we take for granted to the steel pins Salcedo showed as fastening things together, forming angel wings that, if felt, tear at the skin. Insignificant, trivial, but who says so? The small space of taking in and expelling breath marks how much there is always, until there is not.

Now "tiny" and "virus" are linked. Growth, virulence, speed are turning "tiny" into an enormity bringing one world to a halt while locusts in the Horn of Africa are adding still another scourge to lives that are not being spoken about as we focus on the pandemic rupturing reality in the place we are in.

"Tiny" is also tilting silence into new translations including stillness as a fact—now present, having taken over our streets and closed the doors of shops. This morning, as it has for weeks, the Italian TV channel Rai 1 broadcast Pope Francis offering the morning Mass from an empty chapel in the house of Santa Marta, a social dormitory where he lives. When communion was offered, the cameras moved slowly from the pope to the altar where the Eucharist had been blessed. The church was empty. There were a symbolic flock of four priests and nuns. The acolytes were missing. The scriptures were kept to a minimum before he announced that the communion would be a spiritual one, given the circumstances. The camera moved slowly in silence, and for fifteen minutes, an eternity if advertising revenue is considered, the fixed space was broadcast: an altar empty of doing facing an empty chapel, with the round host, held in a gold sunlike lunette, framed by two candle flames brushed by the currents in the air.

Yesterday is a near silence, yet it is difficult to catch, even a few details of it, unless disremembered objects appear. Yesterday Paolo cleaned up some boxes of books stored in the basement. Forgotten and discovered inside were Italian road maps from the 1930s. There was a book written by Carlo Darwin, the one we know as Charles. There were two published scientific papers on lung capacity, one carried out on human subjects, the other on sheep. These paper treasures, age coloring them a sandy soil color, belonged to his father, a tuberculosis doctor when there was no cure for TB. His father died of TB, malnourished, exhausted after the war, before Paolo ever knew him.

The silence of his father, the physical silence, meaning the absence that never can quite be forgiven because his father, by dying, abandoned his family who were desperate and badly needed him, followed the devastation of the war. Those few items—maps commissioned in Mussolini's Italy; Carlo Darwin's thought, a blasphemous possession, although as Paolo noted, one-fourth of the pages had not been slit open by the nominal Catholic; the two published experiments on human and animal respiratory physiology done under terrible wartime conditions in a remote village—together were a silent story of his father, the doctor-scientist who broke through the low level of medical instruction and was searching for truths more rigorous and empirical. Paolo held in his hands his father as he knew him from myths. His letters, his photos, personal things had been burned, fearing they might be infectious. Paolo's father was his own version of them, invented, clung to, needed. Paolo imitated his father, often citing the two experiments and his father's wish after the war to go to America to do research in a university lab. And here he was, having followed in his footsteps, even teaching Carlo Darwin to his university students in Parma.

All three kinds of documents could be turned into stories—true or false in part, set in historical time—and the personal story, the pathos, the gap, the touching emotions and inspiration found in those few yellowing pages would then be turned away from and made meaningful to countless others. The meaning of those documents, in my mind, is revealed most closely in the personal story—we see three lines of a portrait, incomplete but authentic details of a father's life. Taking them from the box, as long as they remain in the son's hands, we cannot help but perceive beauty in that silence held in the box, in his hands, and brought to life by finding them.

Raised as an Italian Catholic, Paolo had been conditioned to perceive personal narrative as minor, the stuff of egotism and women's tales. Instead, he sees how the present has brought us to a place where those silences have value, and we know that the voices of slaves, prisoners, woodworkers, coal miners, mothers, factory workers, chefs, soldiers, gay people, lovers, children, artists change and fill in stories about life itself. "Tiny" is the beginning of mighty and knowing. "Tiny," though, often needs enrichment by a personal voice—the recovered torn cardboard box needs a son's emotion to make it come alive for us. It needs context, too, in order to grow until understanding time and place and a voice bring it alive in a way most people recognize the details as speaking to them.

I n Bronxville, for several days I was awakened in our modern Shaker bed by the sensation of a wet pillow. My nose spurted blood, which I caught in my palms as I rushed to the bathroom, leaving bright red blotches all along the way. I worried for those three days when each morning I caught handfuls of blood. Then on day four, my pillow dry, I woke up holding a dream in an utterly different dimension: clear, in order, and vividly present.

The dream was not one to be mined for its symbols. It was charged with psychic content. It has centered me with little analysis, at least until now, with a scale for human existence. The dream organized and left me knowing that I cannot grasp the whole of reality but I can act nevertheless and I can know something of my own size in the story.

The dream, more or less, because it does change slightly with each telling, is as follows; in some ways it hardly matters to retell it:

I was on a long, slow train that was traveling on a high ridge above a city. The city below was wholly visible. The life of people was going on in the streets, lined by redbrick buildings, early Victorian. They were not located necessarily in England, or even in Yonkers, which has lots of redbrick copies of Victorian structures. The city was somewhere. The view from the train was nearly 360 degrees. I was traveling in a circle and could see the entire valley below, spreading out and circumscribed.

I got off the train and descended into the city. I wandered in the slow-motion streets and, on a road that led me out of the city, came to an altar, white marble or stone, so high above me that I could not reach it except by pulling myself up. Out of time, it was an archaeological feature from another civilization. The altar loomed several feet above my head. Let me skip ahead, as the dream did, leaving those odd jumps in the narration.

It took all my strength to pull myself up and climb. The shiny marble surface, worn and worked, was flat on the top. I stood in the open on the massive four-sided surface and looked out at a dry, dusty, barren landscape. Not only was I in a different, more ancient culture, I was in a different dimension of time. Standing on the altar, I was exposed to the sky and visible to anyone who might be approaching. The strangely delivered sensation of reality made me aware that the structure was part of the act of worship in the civilization that had built the altar. Part of the act of worship was looking up at the sky. The surface also suggested that it might have been used for sacrifices, human and animal. Before I could even process a next step, a shaft of light pressed down on me. It was beyond blinding. It was an abyss. It blocked out all the landscape with its presence. Its brightness terrified and comforted me. I could not look at this light directly. I felt a gaze that was so powerful its light was far brighter still than that enveloping me. It perceived me. There, too, the scene broke.

In the next one, I had returned to the city. In the street, I immediately met someone I knew in real life, a woman of great professional accomplishment and rational integrity. I tried unsuccessfully to explain what I had just experienced. She nodded but had no interest. She pointed to a redbrick Victorian church with a tall steeple and insisted that this was what was real and was the scale at which we could live.

The dream ended there. The woman I met in the street who pointed to the church was, in dream logic, probably the real starting point. She was an esteemed person whom I recognized from my life in America. Yet as is often common practice in interpreting dreams, at some level the woman I met was a part of myself. She was immersed in actions and institutions. She dismissed my explanation of what I had felt, especially about the gaze, and asked how I could assume to understand such an experience except in the reality of everyday. The question and dialogue opens along the border of its narrative: What is the woman who points to everyday life to make of the dream?

Almost all of us live long periods of doubt or with a frustrated sense of going through the motions of life. Certainly, the stroke many years before—which had changed Paolo's life and our life—the crack that left chaos and a sense of simply coping, was not made easier by cultural differences. As was true for me at many points in my life, just as I thought I might set out in new directions, I was called back in to serve with courage, instinct, and bravery. I believed in the acceptance of all responsibilities that seemed to fall to me, but they pulled me back into believing, for a while, that my life as a woman was defined by this.

The dream in Bronxville settled in the space that was empty. It seemed to say to the woman in the Victorian city, What are you doing here? You have stood on the altar; you have felt being seen. You are all twisted up if you think you are central to how life proceeds. Go ahead. You are not in charge of life. Be all that you are, and that is not an earthly measure.

The experience of the dream remained without confusion or drift. Perhaps we are always missing some essential element. Our mind continues to search for invisible links. In the dream, the stepping down, the looking up, the scale of the two worlds, the archaic altar, the sacred, and the return to a life where the sacred was institutionalized rather than violently experienced waited for me like a puzzle that had all its pieces. The images were like those found in chapels in Italy, century after century, a story of progressions. From the train to the altar and then back to the city, I was between two worlds. Light in the dream broke through to my real life.

I was realigned that morning in Bronxville, pulled back to reality's magnetic pole. The stirring gaze inside the incinerating power of the light, light that by its quality was cosmic, was not scalding or brutal in any way. It was far beyond my capacity to search for words for the light. But I did not doubt its presence. It was love.

Until now, it has remained unquestioned. I have nothing to do about that. It does not depend on will, and perhaps one day it will no longer be such a simple thing. Just as I accept sunrise and sunset as fixed features of the earth without reviewing them, I accept that the dream filled a space in me, filled it with silence that invites me to listen, to remain still, to accept my capacity to know only a small part of what I live every day. I often forget it. I often forget about it. But when I remember, I understand that what is consuming me, what I am carrying and worrying about, I can't know more than I know. I must move in the dark.

In the darkness last night, sleep was distant. I was cocooned under the feather quilt, warm and wide awake in the brisk unheated air. Darkness was embracing, ample, holding everything in the room. The darkness had qualities, and they were not the same as many nights when the darkness in my mind (because that is where or how I perceive the room) is unsettled, damp, filled with impish terrors and long lists of concerns, physical complaints, family worries, political thoughts, imaginative plans and schemes, escape routes, willful decisions.

Many nights my mind riots, choked with half thoughts clogging the processes of a loyal brain that deserves to plunge below the surface in order to sort and clean what is extraneous. Instead it can't shut off and becomes a noisy thing, annoying and intrusive like a leaf blower, stirring thoughts and spewing them into darkness, lit by the thin, illuminated hands on the alarm clock. My mind, desperate to pace itself, searches the time for directions—how many more hours till dawn?

In the dark last night, I rested in its enormous stillness. It was quiet, close, beautiful. Without dimension, I was in it. The dark of rest, the dark of not knowing, the dark of acceptance. I rested in silence.

I was nearly thirteen when my sister was born. The minute Mother announced that she was pregnant, the word was "bets." Let's bet on when the baby will be born. Let's bet on the date, on the sex, on the name. My brothers and I were in the living room, lined up on the evergreen-colored couch in front of the fireplace, and we bet then and there. Betting was our default solution for obtaining justice or resolution or authority.

I didn't do that.

I saw you do it.

Want to bet?

I didn't do it.

How much do you want to bet?

A nickel.

That isn't enough. How are you going to prove it?

Bets were serious business, duly inscribed, witnessed, and signed. My brothers both opted for dates in September, the month that Mother said the baby was due. I'm not sure about the rest. My mouth opened and a date in mid-August flew out. Of course, she would be a girl. Of course, her name would be the one I wanted. We wrote all the facts down.

I collected twenty-five cents on that set of predictions. All three were right on. Born three weeks early, in mid-August after nine o'clock at night, the successful bet was another mosaic tile in the myth of my father's story of my connection to passages between life and death. It was nothing but a gloating victory at the time. I never questioned it as strange.

But looking back, I see many similar times. It's easy to say, well, you forget the times when your bets didn't come through, you block out the times when predictions were flops. That's undoubtedly true. It is easy for me to admit that.

But this does not negate the many times that along a border I do not see, I encounter information that utterly takes me over and I accept it as a basis for action.

All over the globe, women giving birth and carrying life face death along the way. Globally in the last two centuries, one quarter of all children died before reaching their first year, half died before reaching adolescence. Most birth stories belong to mothers who carried the child. But not all. A few years ago, I listened to a man in his seventies recount how his mother felt contractions when she was in the forest gathering wood. She lay down on the forest floor and gave birth to him. She walked home with him in her arms. Most of humanity has been born in fields, on forest floors, in huts. Rostropovich insisted that his mother did not want him, did not want to carry him. She tried to rid herself of that pregnancy. But, he smiled as he told us that day, I was too strong and came into the world anyway.

I remember the morning in London on Oxford Street when tears began to sting my eyes. Struck by sadness, I entered a flower shop, the first I passed. I said, I would like to buy a bouquet of violets for my grandfather. They were indigo purple, with yellow stamens. Their soft stems were tied together with a ribbon. A telegram arrived later that day after I reached my apartment. My grandfather had died in Pennsylvania, after a stroke. For three days scripture had been read to him until he stopped breathing.

In switchboard-phone days—days when phones were so costly one didn't make calls across borders—from Paris I had plans to visit a friend in Florence. I was in the Gare de Lyon to buy my ticket and depart. I had a rucksack with T-shirts for a weekend and a couple of what were called shifts, light, flowery cotton dresses like short sacks. As I spoke to the clerk, the words coming out of my mouth startled me. I said: A one-way ticket to Oxford. Within that second, the intent of my journey changed without any plausible explanation.

I was unable to even think about how to contact my friend. In pre-cell-phone days, people worried, but expectations adapted to the reality. Youth was given some slack for being thoughtless or caught up in other worlds. In general, the attitude was, well, if something bad happens, sooner or later you will hear. My absence on the train headed to Santa Maria Novella in Florence was a silence that didn't really seem catastrophic to me then. My friend would meet the train, I wouldn't be on it, and she would assume something had happened to make me change my plans. Her response would not have been to alert the police but to wait for me to call. Often the line of reasoning was, she has probably met a boy. Parents, too, in those years, let children travel sometimes for months without hearing from them. The mail was understood to be slow.

Skip ahead to the middle of the night when I finally knocked at the house where my brother was boarding. An alarmed woman opened the door, but didn't have the heart to chastise me when she heard my name.

She took me in. You're his sister. Thank God. We had decided we couldn't take the responsibility any longer. Your poor mother is in America, and she has enough worries, having lost your father, but I would have been forced to call her. Your brother is in the Radcliffe Infirmary, his life in great danger. But now you're here.

If I chose to underline the parts of my life where I have changed paths because of life and death, I could tell many stories. I often was drawn in like a moth to light where there was to be a crossing, a slit opening onto another plane.

Three weeks before Paolo had his stroke, I was teaching in Geneva, and he was there keeping me company. He visited museums, walked around the lake to get to know the city. We were staying at a friend's house while they were away. Coming down the back stairs after we had locked the door, I turned and was shaken by a sensation of a heavy cloud passing over us. The sky was blue and empty of clouds.

Nearly buckling over, I shouted, Paolo, something is coming toward us. It's dark. It's traveling toward us and we are in danger. I screamed.

What is it? he asked, as if there should be an answer to such an alarming cry.

I don't know, I said. But it's coming. It's like death.

And another crystal-clear sensation was the moment I realized I was pregnant with my first child. A feeling took over and settled in. The baby was connected to my father. It was a certainty, not a hope but a conviction. It was an opaque thought, obsessive, closed, always with me.

He is buried next to my father, his little grave the only one that breaks the pattern of the traditional family markers and the central stone covering all the people buried there under my paternal grandfather's surname. I had a stonecutter hammer out my design.

My encounters with the heron and the butterfly were experiences of transformation, metamorphosis, spiritual shocks with varying degrees of impact and confirmation. They dance around the doors of life and death. Hibernating a toad when I was nine years old was an opening offered to me by my aunt, who helped me catch it behind a woodpile in northern Wisconsin in summer, and by my fourth-grade teacher, who suggested that we bury him for the winter, and, of course, by Toady, who came to recognize me and stay in my hand. Its power, which is about the power of nature, has remained a pillar of truth.

Toady was humble and quiet, no match for the heron that would come to catch my attention with its spectacular wing-span of five feet. The heron was earth water sky. The humble toad that wet my hand with his defensive poison when I first tightly held him as his heart beat in fear pulled me close to the beating heart of life—possession and relationships.

In human lives, metamorphoses are realities that some people perceive, and their consequences vary. We each have understandings that, perhaps, we can unify as an image of self, but even within a family, we discover that we have lived entirely different experiences in the same space. Each of us makes something of the chaos and we privately get used to owning our own stories as the ones that are real as we change and move on.

The relationship with my toad was one of a full silence, half to the border between understanding and being understood. Witnessing Toady's life gave me a sense that a life has order, much of which was hidden until he caught my eye, betraying his memetic cover by moving in the woodpile. Because mine was a child's experience, it was pure, uncluttered. The idea of waiting in darkness for long periods of not knowing became central to my understanding of life.

Miss Hornburger, my teacher, rallied for and engineered Toady's descent into the underworld. On the proper day in late October, we ceremoniously filled half an empty one-gallon paste jar with dry leaves, put Toady in the center, then made a layer sandwich out of other oak leaves until he was cushioned by them below and covered on top. She punched holes in the paste jar lid. The janitor dug in the schoolyard for a couple of hours. The hole was nearly four feet deep.

The jar was to rest below the frost line. This was best for him, Miss Hornburger said. This is what he would have done—hibernated all by himself using instincts—if we had not snatched him from his world.

With a rope fastened around the neck of the jar, the janitor lowered him and covered the jar with soil. A funny little dime-store flag, the size children waved in patriotic parades following the war, marked the spot.

It was April before Miss Hornburger finally nodded. It's time to bring him back to our part of the earth.

Miss Hornburger believed adults should be examples. She challenged us to contests sometimes so that we could understand how little we were and how powerful she was. Her face grew bright red and her steamed, rimless glasses were taken off as she forced herself to eat the twenty-nine PTA pancakes that would prove she was as great as the Norse gods who habitually ate and drank too much, grabbing the school victory and earning our respect forever. Like too many talented Wisconsin women, forced in those years to retire when they married, may her name not be forgotten.

The anxieties of a child living through six months to discover if her toad was alive were an excruciating test of faith. Time stirred memories and feelings, but never changed its pace. Gray squirrels left light feathery paw prints like seeds across the snow. Dogs left their amber marks. Avalanches slid down roofs.

This was best for him, I reminded myself. This was love, Miss Hornburger said, this letting him live his own way. The underworld, Miss Hornburger said, had lots of stories we needed to learn.

I often found ways to stand alone in the schoolyard where the little flag fluttered. I jiggled its stick, back and forth, calling, uncertain if Toady could hear me. Sometimes I bawled.

His sides were caved in. No puffy air sacks.

His spine a thin twig. A dry piece of brown wood, blending with the leaves.

She said, Touch him, very lightly.

He blinked, the way matches do when struck.

One eye popped open, and then the other.

He filled his lungs, blowing up to more than double in size.

Each little hair on my arms tingled and rose.

The class clapped as I refused the box to carry him home.

Once settled, Toady stayed only a few weeks. In one of my evening visits to the backyard, I discovered him utterly engaged, his back legs pushing something over his head and his front legs tugging and steering and stuffing the long transparent fabric of dead cells into his mouth. He'd changed skin.

He was older. I found him on the lawn. One evening soon after, the large zinc tub for leaves was empty. I cried hard, knowing it had ended. Visiting him had always seemed like a magic theater.

Miss Hornburger told me it was better that way. He was free to live in his own world again. Toady was not the fiction of *The Wind in the Willows*, she said. He was where stories took place. It was different, being buried, eating your own skin, calling to a mate and finding her.

His soft velvety body, with eyes that let some form of light pass across them, led me into a new place. He was authentic. When he disappeared, consolation was beyond my understanding. But I had grown, could feel the bruise, the loss, and the amazing discovery of his self-sufficient and fascinating life. Knowing that in spite of being tamed, he was not tamed and was free to go gave me some sense of nobility for my own position of accepting the greatness of life.

Mary Ann Evans, known as George Eliot, extolled "unhistoric" acts, acts that contribute to balance lives by people "who lived faithfully a hidden life, and rest in unvisited tombs." Rebel that she was, she still acknowledged the tiny, unnoticed threads as crucial to the fabric of life. In *Middlemarch*, she extends this thought to give it its due: "If we had a keen vision and feeling of all ordinary human life, it would be like hearing the grass grow and the squirrel's heart beat, and we should die of that roar which lies on the other side of silence."

Toady's life gleams as a silent thread of time and renewal in a Florentine garden in the novel I wrote at Yaddo.

For more than two years after his stroke, Paolo could talk, but his words were detached from feelings, as if his brain contained partitions cutting feeling centers off from rational ones. His stroke took place in the brain stem. A physician in Parma pointed out that if the stroke had been a mere hair different in its location, he would have been on artificial respirators for the rest of his life, his vital autonomic systems incapacitated. Instead it hit the center where basic survival emotions—anger, fear, sadness—register before they are sent on to higher circuits in the brain to be processed and scaled. *Is the fear I feel seeing that tiger real or caused by a film?* The higher brain functions resolve the question. However, if the tiger seems present in some indefinable way, the rage, terror, and fear released in the mind confuse it to the core.

I still tremble looking back on that period.

The nightmare of deciphering words where connotations have been detached from feeling and meaning required more strength than I ever realized I had. Add the fact that we had two languages to traverse and that, because of deafness, I had extra sensibilities. My way of understanding words meant that I leaned on them, trusted them, squeezed them, learned to ponder and question them. I cared for them one by one, tasting, testing.

Paolo spoke clearly even a minute after the stroke. However, words that were correct in terms of syntax and vocabulary were without riders. He didn't evaluate their impact. His temper, a part of his warm personality, became ungovernable. He didn't perceive himself as split as he kept moving. Who was the screaming, trembling person who huddled in the corner? Who was the person who needed help? Certainly, it was not he. What are you doing here? Leave me alone.

More than two years after his stroke, he returned from Milan after psychotherapy (he was going four days a week) and breathlessly reached me in the kitchen. Did you realize that I had a stroke? I was the person who did, he said incredulously. I had a stroke more than two years ago and I never knew it until this morning. Knowing meant that today was the first time the event coincided with his awareness of self. It meant that after two years he thought for a few moments in a way that reached him and wondered what I might know or feel.

TINY.

Was the blood vessel that burst tiny?

Was the space tiny between where we started and his perception when he finally unwound the confusion that nearly killed him? Was the word "stroke" and his understanding a single meaning, and was that meaning "tiny"? Was the life spent to reach that perception, the long years of studies for the neurologist, the psychotherapist, my support and stubborn passion, Paolo's strength to endure while stumbling toward integration again—was all that time, knowledge, commitment, suffering, and love in societal and personal terms tiny? Was the hope tiny, was the rage?

The stories of how repair and change never cease, on their own and with others, are silences that fit in mosaics of great importance. They reside in part in families, in the ordering of the commitments of society. They are not simply material for complaint, for confession. They are intrinsically flexible material and can be used in many and new ways. And women carry the basics for enlarging and centering these focuses crucial for society as a whole.

The fragments in Paolo's and my life that had broken forever, and those that instead left gaping holes in walls with rubble, needed sorting out. The work of admitting despair but not accepting it as a reason for giving up shaped our relationship.

Stroke. Stroke—a touch or a blow. Or a forward movement, a hand dipping an oar in water and pulling against it. A shutdown and death of a cell. Which is it? Or is it all of them invisibly tangled and being considered by living their shifting aspects, collecting them in silence, and seeing small changes, tiny changes turning toward day.

The Nigerian women's stories of the sea followed me as I traced the crescent of the empty shore near Tarquinia, a city famous for frescoed Etruscan tombs that provided inspiration for many writers. How could I stop them from sounding in my mind and raising questions?

In Tarquinia, I was stepping into a small extension of sea that is still sea. As I write it is smooth; I am immersed in a minute of silence up and down the edge between the water and the black volcanic sand. There are no other people here. Yesterday, waves were high and I hesitated, moving inch by inch into the water. Children and dogs were daring to dash in a few feet and then run out. In my mind, the Nigerian women continue to ask me, as they did on the last day of class, might I, could I teach them to swim. They crossed the sea knowing that the boats had a limited number of life preservers. The human mind opens and shuts so often to get past risks. The Nigerian women's dreams were not those arriving in sleep. Theirs were wishes they were willing to act upon.

Every morning for these two weeks I will look to the sea's tidal rhythms and messages. The water is uncluttered by boats, except yesterday, one white fishing boat so far away it seemed like a handkerchief suddenly sped up and made a rapid, furtive landing to dump trash.

The nuclear plant rises to the north, part of a skyline that never came to be. People voted against it, and it remains a converted electric plant. Those who voted for it still fume, certain that any explosion from nuclearized France will certainly drift as far as Tarquinia. It is impossible anywhere to escape thinking about enormous events. Looking north, a few hours from this wild, unkempt beach is La Spezia, the place from which Frieda Lawrence had her piano shipped.

D. H. Lawrence spent nine months in Liguria in 1913 and 1914. Frieda, who had been forced to leave her three children with her husband while waiting for her divorce, traveled with Lawrence to Italy. The couple lived in a white house on land rented from peasants in Fiascherino, near Tellaro. In a small book published in Italian in 2012 by Cinque Terre, I discovered Lawrence in letters that made him as familiar as if he were sitting in the room. The letters were to English-speaking literary people who visited him in Italy like Katherine Mansfield and John Middleton Murry, and also letters written to and kept by the peasant family of Ezechiele Vallero, who hosted him. They were mirrors with angles that assumed intimacy and dialogue. Letters were a pleasure like sketches or watercolors where a unique intelligence captures something in time and makes it visible to someone else. Then the walk or the journey to post the letter in Tellaro added another element to making the piece of writing a significant effort. The journey from Tellaro to England was still another leap in time and effort and culture. The letters were "made things" from those times, and the interval from putting pen to paper to being opened by another pair of hands was one of weeks if not more.

Lawrence's letters growl, explode with laughter, and spew forceful opinions reflecting natural life, the work of peasants, the seasons, his love for Frieda, spelled out with attentive precision to how days passed. They have the force of identity, someone writing to someone else, wanting a reaction, wanting to share or jostle another mind. Some events are simply surprising, for example the complicated importance of finding and renting a piano in La Spezia, loading it onto a boat, followed by arranging the logistics of unloading it in the bay, where peasants lifted it and carried it up the hill on their backs to move it into the Lawrences' four-room house because Frieda wanted it. Besides the scene of privilege and social class reflected in the task itself, the picture of Frieda, mourning the loss of contact with her children, is tempered by the strength of her personality, willing to engineer the transport of such a cumbersome instrument in order to express herself through music on hot summer evenings. She knows how to get her way, how to keep up with Lawrence. Imagine the sound of sonatas floating out into the fields and to the sea.

In the details of their days, we understand the intensity of their equality. Along with many comments on her paintings and her letters, we see his getting closer to her and observe some of the powerful dynamics of their relationship as well as his discoveries and opinions on the rhythms and mutually respectful growing communication and appreciation of peasant family life. Lawrence happily serves as the witness for the bride at the wedding for the peasant's son, Silvio. The deep and spontaneous link represents the freedom that Lawrence so treasured. His account of the marriage glistens with details of the celebration, his disapproval of its lack of passion and its pragmatic basis, and the abundant feast, down to the stupor and admiration about the wildlife hunted for the occasion.

If we were to read about a similar process or event now, life among peasants or a year in a foreign place, it would most likely be pointed toward finding your way around or understanding customs or teaching something. It probably would be an analysis of behavior to obtain a practical goal. The reading-self who chose such a book would, in part, consider herself a consumer, a listener in key with the writer. Money would possibly be part of the vicarious focus, of what you the reader could get or buy by following in the author's footsteps. Instead, Lawrence's letters written in Fiascherino are like fresh blossoms or crashing waves because he believed his observations had weight and carried silence that murmured: I want to make you feel this, the color of the soil, the hard practical goodness of the people, my own eyes opening to my feelings because they will continuously change or fade or disappear. Some will be nearly eternal or universal. Some will end when I leave or, even earlier, when I lift my pen from the page. The tissue of feelings is a living thing.

As the son of a coal miner, he was comfortable with people who lived values that were not bourgeois. On the pages, as in many of his poems, he reveals himself in simple ways. His intensity loses its doctrinaire sides and often shows his luminous vitality.

He could not write this way if he were imagining eleven thousand Facebook friends. He could not write this way, in this voice, even in his novels, one of which, *The Rainbow*, he nearly completed during his stay.

D. H. Lawrence, in his book *Etruscan Places*, often wrote about the sea I am writing about in Tarquinia. He saw it then as still carrying traces of history that brought people to the shore. "Even before the fall of Troy, before even Athens was dreamed of, there were natives here. And they had huts on the hills, thatched huts in clumsy groups most probably; with patches of grain, and flocks of goats and probably cattle."

In a city less than thirty kilometers from Tarquinia, Tuscania, less famous because, in part, local politics determine which locations create high profiles in order to attract tourists, I saw a set of tombs, twenty-seven burials in all, fifteen women and children, from the Curunas family. The burial chambers, starting in the fourth century BCE, had been constructed in three separate stages. By some stroke of luck, all three remained undefiled by pillaging and dispersal. The tombs were fresh and complete.

Upon opening the first tomb in 1970, as light reached the musty walls inside, archaeologists found sarcophagi in place as they had been arranged. The reclining figures faced one another; the effect upon entering was that of joining a banquet where people were enjoying a feast. It's easy to imagine the emotions of breaking in on a party that was still going on. The banquet expressed by life-sized reclining Etruscan men and women, each with specific features, each with a place at the table, expressed a vision celebrating life in eternity. There were life-sized photos in the museum of the sarcophagi in place.

The faces on the sarcophagi—bulbous noses, tapering fingers, quizzical eyes—were neither haunting nor gloomy. They overflowed with secrets that were lost to us even at the time the tombs were found. Yet narrations of the death of children, the wounding of animals, vases that drew male and female bodies in positions like those in the Kama Sutra, and vases celebrating homosexual love evoked the life lived by people in the tombs.

The archeological photos of the Etruscan finds generate the haunting feeling of standing among these sarcophagi and hearing Lawrence's demand to present-day people in response to the Etruscan culture: "Oh build your ship of death. Oh build it! / for you will need it. / For the voyage to oblivion awaits you." The walls, depicting athletic feats and singing dancers, leaping leopards and gravid vines, celebrate life and provide a world for the dead and their souls to rest in.

L ast November, young people organized a flash mob parallel to a rally being held by a right-wing leader in a city in northern Italy. They called themselves the Sardines. They wanted no particular continuity or adhesion. They counted on electronic SMS messages and insisted on not having their narrative taken over by anyone. They attracted more than fifteen thousand people at the first gathering, ten thousand at the next. When the wife of a prominent politician announced that she was among them, lost in the crowd, they said they didn't want names, didn't want people hoping to communicate. They wanted community, simplification, restoring and expanding politics so that people know what is right and necessary for humans to live well. They caught politicians off guard with their spontaneous reactions to fascism. They broke into a surface of government as professional politicians and presented a gathering that was not a protest but a general call for citizens' physical participation in democracy, voting being a first response. The Sardines were little fish swimming together. They used crowdfunding only for basic expenses. A few handheld mikes, some modest ads. They were not interested in the idea of winning, they announced, nor in building a movement based on the need to collect money. They wanted to disconnect money from the power to win an election. They wanted to take elections away from paid teams of image makers.

A whispering conductor reprimanded me because I was speaking in a normal voice to my granddaughter. And was my cell phone turned off? I was unaware that there was a silent car on Metro-North until I inadvertently landed in it. Since then it's become a habit.

Like James Q. Wilson's broken windows theory of slums (things deteriorate further until conditions are improved and maintained), with respectful, quiet borders restored, the right to privacy comes along. We don't know one another and don't need to know. We acknowledge we share a space with limits.

The silence in the space works as communities do. We enter and exit it. We are outside it or inside it. Implicit is the sharing and at the same time the recognition of boundaries for behavior.

Public space as silence on Metro-North is not defined by economic privilege. It isn't acquired by collecting points, creating a deliberate sense of being above others in a tiny ping of stealthily constructed tinseled privilege: boarding first, free drinks. Without knowing anything about one another, it is natural to assume we have things in common since we have chosen silence. Silence is a physical condition with attributes.

We drop abrasiveness, drop pushing. Our opting for it enforces standards and rules. It is not a commodity. We only need to choose the right carriage.

Since the neat, brown-haired girl sitting next to me was answering her phone, turning it off, on, as we sped toward Florence, her activity moved onto my lap like an uninvited dog. She was checking something. Then checking again. What would he be wearing? The color of her plaid skirt?

A nun faced the girl and me, but her mind was with a clerk checking on a pair of shoes. On her cell phone, she was pursuing her proper shoes, black, closed with laces. She wanted to know when she could pick them up with their new soles.

If I had possessed a headset, I might have escaped without a second thought. Instead, my silent presence in their actions had a toll if not a meaning.

I was zoning in on a low-key devaluation of the word "witness." How could I pretend I was not sitting next to the schoolgirl? Or the nun? Or overhearing both of them? This was 2017, when so much had changed so fast.

Each of us knew that the invisible phone booth didn't exist. Everyone could hear everything. I could not admit that my silence was indifference. The girl was silent about us knowing. She was also silent about the value of her life. The nun and I did not exist in her communal space, either as authorities or grown-ups.

Silence on my part translated as nonintervention while vicariously being part of such wretchedness. As I read about Lila, woefully transformed after her escape to a life in a sausage factory in Elena Ferrante's *The Story of a New Name*, without meaning to, my mind stitched together intervals in the girl's comments. She was meeting someone and she was to be paid for the meeting. How much? How much? Perhaps she was thirteen. She had a backpack, had gone to school that day, and this meeting was a secret. The internet had entered in. She wanted money.

Exposed to the situation for two hours, I had time for it to work on my brain and chip away at assumptions, including my place in the scene. Face-to-face, we each acted indifferent to those around us. Something was tarnishing life's luminous halo that Virginia Woolf identified as a "semi-transparent envelope surrounding us from the beginning of consciousness to the end."

The moment the pink-cheeked head of the Partito Democratico appeared, running from a car, looking energetic, looking in that moment impossible to be accused of being arrogant, the men and women in the Parma crowd, who were restless, began to kick and push. Aggressive hateful shouts rose far above the capacity of the young head of the party's voice to carry. Anger erupted at the disruptors and lines were drawn between positions as the disorder began to feel dangerous. A tall, heavy man in a baseball jacket pounded into my back and fell forward, pushing me into a metal barrier. My foot, recently broken, slipped off the curb. There was no place to run. A small group from a rising party, the Cinque Stelle, the Five Stars, had infiltrated the crowd and planned the disruptions, hoping to create minor chaos and even violence.

They were fake participants in the rally. They wanted to stir up uncertainty, conflict. Play with fears. The warm autumn day lost its easy feeling of simplicity. The glittering ginkgo tree flashed the sun in its gold, lobed leaves. People were still facing off and screaming as the prime minister was rushed onto the train.

I limped away, feeling touched by something that is growing and has no particular words. It has no focus. No one is trying to put it into words except by looking into the past—Fascism, Nazis. Something I had never experienced even in dark years in Parma, the "Years of Lead" when terrorists blew up tunnels and buildings, had been added to the rally in this small city, which for ten years had rejected left-wing governments. The agitators had come in from the outside and their purpose was to create confusion and unrest. Television didn't cover the disruption or voice an analysis of its deliberate and yet fake presence. In many ways it was similar to events taking place in the United States, and how they were not being analyzed for their obvious manipulations. Instead they were taken at face value or identified as movements similar to the past or a new populism that reflected the needs of people looking for a strong leader.

On the instructions of the organizer of the Russian trip, I had packed a money belt and a series of small locks, along with a mental chain of assumptions about the Soviet Union, the Cold War enemy of our education as children. I had little locks not only for my suitcases but for things I would keep in my room, always under lock and key. The flurry of alarms and warnings fluttered in my head and settled as a stiff neck extending to my shoulders. It cost me a lot to approach the event in such a defensive way. It was a perception of our having wealth and *their* wanting what we had to the point of being willing to steal or be violent. It was ignorance largely amplifying a possible reaction. All along the roads toward the outskirts, people huddled next to small piles of arranged household goods—samovars, linens, cutlery—the contents of their lives being bartered for tourist dollars. The danger emanated from the police who would confiscate their goods if someone alerted them that they were accepting dollars. It was November 1991.

Nadezhda Mandelstam wrote two books about her experience as the companion of Osip Mandelstam, a Russian poet who was imprisoned and ultimately executed for images and words that defied superstitious Stalin. *Hope Against Hope*, her first, and the second, *Hope Abandoned*, trace the painful direction of events. In these relentless masterpieces, she describes the cancerous aspects of survival when society adapts to the pressures of a regime. Besides enduring inhuman periods of persecution and terror, she lived the progressive degradation of society created by petty lies, crafty betrayals, rationalizations of silence in the face of injustice. She suffered and described the personal heartbreak, conflicts, and fears of being forced to reckon with people trying to survive, including herself and artists like her husband. She was altered by the pain of watching people lured into complicity to gain and get ahead in a totalitarian system. Fear and material deprivation reduced people to practical compromises—a better regular allowance for meat, a few more square feet in an apartment in exchange for a little information. Complicity and ambition finally demanded many make immoral choices as the bargaining between power and survival grew. Many acquaintances became spies and some murderers.

A slow poisoning of a population may take place when those in power deliberately foster an atmosphere of confusion and suspicion, turning the meaning of right and wrong vertiginously inside out. The lie, personal compromise in service of a system, exists, at first, as a small aggression, but it exists for some gain of power and control. Until it becomes ingrained practice, and thus one is immune to its erosion of conscience, it stings as a tiny humiliation, where one must quickly forget its significance in order not to become paranoid knowing anything might happen inside the system being watched by others.

S ome lessons of the twentieth century are clear. Some lapses clear. But our period is not the same as the earlier periods. Valéry, the French imagist poet, wrote, "The time is past in which time doesn't matter." He observed this more than one hundred years before our time was tattered by speed and instantaneous connections. Remembered life is important but it can't make sense of real life in the present.

We are always learning and relearning. The girl sitting next to me in the train with her cell phone is not the same as the tall skinny one who was amazed by the written offers in phone booths. The young Nigerian women who know life on the streets in their cities told me that they had never heard of the Nazis. The marches led by Martin Luther King Jr. are not the same ones as those for Black Lives Matter. That is perhaps why rallies now no longer have the effect that they did when Martin Luther King Jr. organized.

Zeynep Tufekci in a recent book suggests that tactics, not emotion, carry the success of movements. Rosa Parks becoming the symbol of the Montgomery NAACP's bus boycott was made by a committee as a strategic choice. The first woman to defy the rule of sitting in the back of the bus had done so eight months earlier. The organization did not allow the young eighteen-year-old young woman to become their symbol. They needed someone more robust, who could handle hatred, obstruction, and infamy when it would be heaped upon her. They needed roots in place that could sustain action that was going to require sacrifice and time. They worked silently for nine months before Rosa Parks sat down and caught the interest of news reporters.

I n November 1991, I landed in Saint Petersburg with other writers from several countries, most from America. We were on a two-week mission to meet with writers, editors, visual artists in Saint Petersburg, Moscow, and Odessa. Narration was of primary interest to the Russians in our discussions. How do you define truth and approach it when it has been tightly controlled? How can you pretend that words are not political?

The consequences and effects of the tabula rasa facing writers, journalists, and artists when Yeltsin climbed on the tank in front of the White House were not precisely those that we had romantically envisioned. We held as nearly sacred the oppositional myths and sacrifices of Osip Mandelstam, Anna Akhmatova, the truth-telling prophets hungry for human rights. Instead the writers, largely members of government-sponsored writers unions, were angry, frustrated people who had made their adjustments, most with reservations. We heard poets sobbing because their work, often the only poetry to be found in official bookshops, would no longer be printed in runs of two or three million. Many agitated middle-aged men raised fists and shouted at us to stop mocking them as specimens in cages.

Some in our group criticized these fraught displays, whereas for others it was possible to imagine, in some unthinkable parallel situation, similar tensions if our livelihoods and safety nets had been destroyed in a matter of months and at the same time we were scrambling to make existential sense of our lives by applying new rules. Would we be any less desperate? But, of course, we were there because our system was the one left standing in 1991. The great counterweight to capitalism, Communism, had collapsed.

The magazine editors and journalists had attitudes different from the writers. They were more excited about the official defeat of limits on thought. They were eager to explore restructuring their fields. How do you write about AIDS when the population has been kept in the dark about it? How do you describe gay lives and the horrors of the disease without a cure without setting off more persecution? How do you rewrite your national history when much has been destroyed? Do you ask others from the outside to tell it for you? Once political lines are questioned and extricated, how far back do you go in Ukraine, for example, to say this is where we start? And which criteria do you use? The journalists conveyed near terror about the importance of the responsibilities of a free press. They feared its dangerous repercussions as well as new forms of manipulation from private ownership. Skepticism kept brakes on proposing possibilities clearly thrilling to most of them.

In 1991, we brought some perspective to how accurate information was critical to any democratic system. The war in Vietnam and the battle over the Pentagon Papers were within memory as an example of when and how lying was used by the U.S. government to build a convincing but knowingly false image. Facts selectively presented to the public by government meant that the risks of fake numbers and false definitions of containment and winning were difficult to grasp. Manipulation of facts when contradicted by journalists made it possible for government to suggest that no factual statement could be made without also introducing doubt. Once that bulwark was established, blurring truth and falsehood became commonplace. Official government press releases were used to institutionalize a form of lying meant to restore goodwill and a readiness to believe a patriotic story. We had a lot to say to our Russian friends about opposition and a free press.

Most political opinions can be sold or bought with the right pitch in a democracy. This, we told them was nothing new. But when the levels of trust are deliberately polarized, with the institution in control sponsoring the official and false version, to break through false narrative, exposing it, requires knowledge, conviction, and making peace with personal fear. Some in our group objected to us voicing criticisms of our own system. They resisted what they called "negativity."

We witnessed many acts of personal courage and sacrifice among people we met in Russia. I often think of where they might be now and what they have concluded about the enormous unwritten promise and the way opportunities were deformed. Many of the experiences, different in scale, feel parallel to the challenges for Western institutions to function effectively in present times.

Many personal encounters and the spiritual responses of specific people still urge me to be more committed. The deep revulsion toward corruption stands out in their responses to uncertainty.

The temperature was so low, our breath danced in front of our eyes in the abandoned squat where, after midnight, we joined art students in Saint Petersburg, hoping that darkness would prevent our being followed. The artists were operating as a coop, sharing supplies bought with earnings from a few who had captured the attention of Western galleries. Timur Novikov, whose tiny human figures engulfed by huge red backgrounds, often the Soviet flag, was one who had made a name.

What remains of that midnight meeting, all of us huddled in long winter coats, heavy scarves, woolen hats, large stray dogs sprawled like rugs on the floor, is a sense that artists, explorers of other kinds of truth, are lucky to be artists if they use their gifts. In the freezing cold, we Westerners, too, touched some of the basic reasons for being artists, not as professionals wanting security, not as complainers about insurance and retirement, but as participants in the existential process of creation.

When someone spoke, breath condensed. The intruding scent of unwashed dogs was part of the reality of breakdown, homelessness, and elaborating our common, uncertain hopes for the importance of art.

We stayed until after three. Before the collapse, the art students felt they were free, certainly given the knowledge they had of the U.S.S.R.'s dark periods. Self-censoring never entered their minds. Only after the Soviet Union collapsed did they discover that they were conditioned to discard many ideas a priori as not belonging to their system. They expressed stupor at their blindness. Now they saw choosing either A or B as impossible. They were choosing both. Their discovery of not realizing how they'd adapted to the system until it broke down stunned me then. It seemed utterly true, a principle all artists should review. There has never been a year since in which I did not return to its obvious revelation. We are easily distracted and lose our awareness of what originality is, either because we conform, or are fearful, or forget its demands.

B efore the workmen have settled the spruce-colored couch bed against the living room wall in Yonkers, the phone rings. How would I grade the workers? The two heavyset men are handing me a paper to sign. As the door closes, I am asked to choose a number for the robust pair by the person on the phone.

I can't quite believe the intrusion. Not a minute has passed, and I am being rushed and pressed into unwilling service.

I don't want to grade the workmen. I don't know enough to have an opinion. I don't like arbitrary power. I don't like grading people without saying something directly to their face. I abhor, in the whole of our electronic world, my sensation of not knowing what I am in when I participate. I don't like blindly feeding systems.

Do I want to say that they scuffed my floor? Perhaps, but only if I know the meaning and costs of my remarks.

My impulse is to stir rebellion in the script-reading voice, the one who is possibly being monitored for any deviations from his text. I want to prod him, yet I know he, too, could lose his job. I want to ask, Are you acting as a spy for the company that is paying you with scarce loyalty for your needs? Do you know if the two men—who, incidentally, had mud on their feet and left it on my carpet—need their jobs or have hernias caused by this heavy lifting and your company's small carts? Do you know if they have children and are without health insurance? Will you tell me their stories so I can understand what low numbers mean and if bad marks will remain fixed to their records like chains if you record them? I would never choose to ruin someone's life for a bit of mud.

A large bronze bust of Giuseppe Mazzini—full head of hair; wide, serious forehead; shoulders broad enough to carry responsibility and to lead—rests in a special commemorative circle outside an ice-cream shop in Tarquinia's town center. When Mussolini introduced a policy to melt every scrap of metal his citizens could contribute for making bullets and arms for his war, the stately bronze bust was an obvious provocation. Besides its historical significance, its material was too tempting to pass unnoticed. Since minute gold wedding bands were being extracted from wives and melted for the war, Mazzini's head and shoulders were surely good enough for a cannon.

Each day the bronze bust goaded Fascists to topple it and melt it for the greater good of *Patria*. The grandfather of the owner of the local farm we stayed at, repulsed by the symbolism of desecrating a great statesman, decided to oppose the encroaching sacrilege. When the moon was a sliver and thus night was as dark as it would ever be, he and a friend risked their lives, unscrewing the patriot from his pedestal. Mazzini, the bust, disappeared in a few tense minutes to wait for better times, when the war would be over and his positions about liberty welcomed. The two men artfully and quickly covered the bearded head, tilting it and lowering it into the family well, where the bust remained, silent in darkness. In the morning, the vacant half pillar defiantly faced windows all around the square, any one of which might have had someone spying behind curtains. The audacious act signaled that resistance existed.

The family that runs the farm in Tarquinia nurture roots that have been in place for more than one hundred years. They tell the story about the well as defining not only their history but a sense of being on the right side of history. The owner's father's grandfather was a Republican, supporting Giuseppe Mazzini's ideals for creating a popular democracy in a republican state. A revolutionary and exile, writer and thinker, Mazzini in life fought with various alliances, believing that the final goal of a democracy must not be individualism but rather collective equality for all.

Virginia Woolf kept diaries from which she then took small parts and developed them into essays and fiction. The sea in Tarquinia and the setting of the farm made me want to write about many of the changes I saw in the two weeks we were there.

THE LANDSCAPE AND ITS SILENCES
PUT IN A NONFICTION SKETCH

A swim in the sea is my destination in Tarquinia each morning after a one-mile walk through wheat fields and melon fields, my eyes absorbing the green of watermelons, the yellow of sunflowers, the greens of potato fields, the sheep sheared until pink skin shows, past Angus cattle with black shiny pelts, Cotentin donkeys with a single white stripe on their hairy shoulders, the china red of tomatoes, forest-green marine pines with clouds of lighter green growth. Except for the donkey braying for a female, the early-morning walk is lavished by a silent view of 360 degrees, unobstructed by buildings.

Today, as on previous days, many of the fields with melons smell of rot. Wheat fields, heads broken and stalks bent, are brown, wet, lost. A month ago, two hours of steady hail broke the crops. Ice balls pummeled the fields, burying them under a deadly frost. The brutality of an unexpected storm did not spare this farm, even though the owners believe in climate change. Thousands of melons, lying in ditches like cracked skulls, are quietly decomposing. Many hundreds have been tossed to the sheep and cows that dance when they hear the truck coming. How can words be used to penetrate government and journalistic silence around the changing climate? Observing is not enough. Maybe only poetry can reach us with the sorrow and awe needed to make us want to redefine taking risks and changing our lives. We must identify a feeling in ourselves that nearly everything we touch needs attention.

On the morning walk, sometimes there is the noise of a tractor, or voices working through the rows of whatever can be salvaged of the potatoes. Some sound is necessary in order to create silence. Giving space to sound in music means giving space to not sound. The pause. In polyphony, voices come in and then stop to let others in. The pause. The establishment of tempo is determined by how much time will be given to silence, the space that is not sound. So the fields are silent because of small amounts of noise. Is the opposite true of silence around climate change?

How sharp and bright the smells and colors are: blue butterflies, red poppies, purple thistles, and spicy oregano and alfalfa. All the way to the sea, I can follow a line of the water's blue. Here I have never seen this water as azure, indigo, navy, sapphire, or aquamarine. These sea colors belong to advertisements showing exclusive resorts.

My walk shows me sky-blue sea at a distance, most often, and gray blue, powder blue, teal blue, until I cross through the wild brush and face it directly. Then usually the sea throws down teal in the morning and royal blue with whitecaps in the afternoon, with various strips and shadings changing toward the horizon.

P aolo woke up with a searing headache. He rose from bed so as not to awaken me. The house was dark and quiet at four o'clock. His heart was heavy because his sister had had another psychotic episode. Facing the family were unknown approaches to bringing her back using new drugs that made her tremble and robot-like at the same time.

He turned on his computer and flipped from site to site looking for distraction. He read a piece on music therapy and found himself deeply disagreeing with the argument, the logic, although he had hoped to find it useful.

It was the first day of March. Our front yard in Parma was dazzling with tiny white daisies and soft dark violets, a carpet of white and purple knots. He went out into the darkness and heard birds just waking up and getting their messages across while there was still some silence. He heard the blackbird, the finches, the sparrows. Each sound was a bit different and some birds did tentative repetitions until they flooded the dawn with arias. He listened and realized with each minute how much more there was to hear, how much more he was hearing. He leapt into the hour of song before dawn. He gave up the rational mind that was so irritated by the website and the argument he could refute. He listened to songs he could only vaguely understand. Their ardor moved him.

When I got up at six, he was fixing coffee. I told him I was reading a chapter in a book on death the night before called "Who Am I?"

He smiled.

The blind dog next door barks a lot in the night. He barks a lot in the day. It bothers me more in the day, when I am trying to write. Without my hearing aids, I really can't hear him at night.

But all three dogs—the setter, the dalmatian, and the spaniel—bark some days all day long in spite of the fact that their owners have lavished on them their own underground heated apartment and given them the full run of the yard and all the organic pet food and drinks a dog could wish for. Still, they have escaped at least four times into our yard, digging holes under the fence and then dashing wildly up and down in my flower boxes, breaking the geraniums, smashing the cyclamen.

The story for a moralist would be that the grass is always greener on the other side, in spite of being blindingly, obscenely green on their side. They are not happy. Something is missing. It is human attention.

Following from the idea of fences, I link them to the people renting the apartment facing our bathroom. They have acquired two birds with crests that suggest to the inquisitive eye that the yellow-and-white pair might be cockatoos. The cage is small, the birds large, and they scream at each other for hours on end. The perch seems to be the issue. Who is on the little swing and stands higher than the other? Today, for some reason, the white bird is on the perch and the yellow one is barely visible below. They are quite close to quiet.

What might it be? Could it be cooperation? Could it be defeat? Is the cramped cage an issue? Is it the bars that get on their nerves? Are they mating or competitors of the same sex or lovers of the same sex? What brought about the truce?

In front of the building hosting the caged birds is the man who cannot walk and clings against the fence every morning. He's done this for more than a year.

Are the stories the same? Who is more confined?

The wine store owner in Bronxville and I had had a conversation about dreams several years ago. We were alone in his store. I can't say why the topic arose. It was soon after I had the dream about standing on the primitive altar. He wanted to talk. To better explain his dream, he recounted an underlying experience. He described a month he had spent while still in service as a policeman.

Following 9/11, he and many of his colleagues were assigned to cataloging any bits collected from the masses of materials that might pertain to a human life. They sifted through stinking, burned, mixed matter created by the explosions, collapse, and fires of the violent fallout of that treacherous day.

Just as archaeologists identify events that occurred thousands of years ago after finding a deposit where bones and trees and boulders and fires fell on top of one another and burned and sank, the police, with little physical or psychological preparation for the shocks and tolls of poring through human loss and destruction, were to reconstruct evidence of bodies and personal possessions. Each scrap testified to an existence.

I am reconstructing here. I remember his stories, yet I may have lost or inadvertently changed some of the facts. The police worked more than eight-hour shifts. It was hot, the room overcrowded, noisy, and airless. Their superiors screamed at them. I remember that he said they could not take breaks. Obsessively sifting through charred, decaying, uprooted fragments of human life, he said that the destruction, the atmosphere of tension and anger, drove him nearly to the breaking point. His sense of futility deepened until he could not cope.

Every day as he opened the door to the sorting operation, he felt nauseous. He had walked into hell. Touching death in tiny fragments, a tooth, a scrap of cloth, a bit of skin, bagging each tiny sign with a label, hoping to connect it to another piece that had a name or a number. After more than a month of this activity, paralyzing despair saturated his being. Suicide became a suggestion in his mind. Then a dream changed his life. The dream was light-filled, with magnificent flower-brimming meadows. He stood up from his beaten position and walked through them.

At the time, he evaluated the dream as a curiosity. He wondered if it could be believed as an omen. Perhaps it was a sign, he ventured. Like someone said. Maybe Ionesco. Words are not the Words.

The day Paolo met me at the Metro-North station in order to buy wine at the ex-policeman's shop, the open-faced man was glad to see us and began to chat. A few sentences here and there as we fingered bottles of Chardonnay and Nero and theorized about the worth of the bottles of Sassicaia, then it was as if we stepped into another place. Suddenly the ex-policeman was asking what it all meant.

A few customers made purchases and left. We waited in silence and then the conversation resumed. When we finished our conversation, twelve bottles were lined up like bowling pins, waiting for their 10 percent discount.

We're ready to pay, we said, handing over our credit card.

Nothing, he said as he ripped the bill from the adding machine. I want to make a gift. His smile was shy, almost apologetic. He surprised us both.

No, we said. You can't give us these bottles. We even have champagne, a few vintages way above our range. We don't want that. Doing business doesn't prevent us from being friends.

Look, he said, I do fine in my business. What I don't do is really care about most of it. This conversation gave me something. Really, it's nothing. I want to give you the wine. It makes me happy. You get what I mean. You can see the difference between the way we are talking now and the way we were talking just five minutes ago.

It was only or it was really or it was just incredibly twelve bottles of wine given to us as a gift. The commonplace, the ordinary direction in things reversed. The instrument of money was free of expectations, free of the self-importance of charitable giving. Like being inside a traffic circle, there were judgments to be made, not red and green lights telling us what to do. The screaming ambulance sirens stopped, the dark magpies flew off, the cash register had stopped ringing.

When Paolo and I visited the Louise Bourgeois exhibit at the Museum of Modern Art, it was the third visit for me. The intensity of her freedom made my sense of wonder grow. The work primarily referred to her last two decades, when she was in her eighties and nineties.

The last rooms displayed a series, "À l'Infini" (2008), that she created using watercolor, colored pencil, wiping, soft ground etching in attenuated tones of blue and red. In the center of the room was a large neoclassical gold statue of a naked female, bent backward and open, like a bow pulled to full strength. The sequences of male and female love-making in expressionistic progression on the walls were long, large journeys of desire, acceptance, process, and climaxes interpreted in wandering and often watery images with vein-like biological tangles and connections. The lyrical series, without strains, flowed into many silences, filling the unexpressed with her visions. Like her works on the family, the body, cells, and seeds, she naturally defied covering over physical reality with symbols. The "À l'Infini" series suggested two bodies, the lines and movements interior feelings transferred as relationship. Think of Picasso's scenes with Dora Maar, or De Kooning's portraits of his wife; you see relationship from a single point of view. Bourgeois, in this series, expressed a point of view that transcribed both male and female positions from the interior feelings of a woman, as well as from the biological processes and responses of bodies.

Paolo, who is always precise, insisted before we had even looked at any of Bourgeois's large prints of sheaves of grain on the walls that the so-called twelve-foot spider in the first room was not a spider. It's a daddy longlegs. It doesn't have a spider's six legs. I am surprised, but don't interject. It's a daddy longlegs. An arachnid; anyone knows they have eight.

That is the beauty of a scientific mind. It's always observing, always ready to make a case. A good scientist rarely uses time to simply stare into space. Paolo analyzes, he links, he extrapolates, he questions. What he has just said about Louise Bourgeois is revolutionary to me. I struggle with my own knowledge. Don't spiders have eight? He insists that they do not. I go silent and continue thinking, as he adds to his identification. The daddy longlegs has two types of males: alpha males and betas, who mimic females. They don't bite humans. Some sorts even graze. If he is right about his general classification, a whole line of observations about Bourgeois's symbolism alters: clichés characterizing female spiders and women as venomous and as overpowering their male counterparts. It's impossible, I think to myself, that not a single critic has remarked on that.

The twelve-foot sculpture contains its prey, its prize, which is an installation of a lighted, solitary domestic room. It's a cage, some walls created of torn tapestry of fables and women's lives, a lonely chair. The word in my mind for the little scene is "trapped," its dark domestic frustrations inevitably under the power and control of the huge arachnid. But the type of arachnid has assumed more relevance, in my eyes, with Paolo's observations. It is now an open silence. If the eight-legged arachnid were a spider, the interpretation of the installation would gravitate to women. The relationship of the inner-lit room clasped by the spider would imply mother and daughter, predator and prey, given that Bourgeois put forth quite a few thoughts and objects to explore that specific relationship. The legs of a spider, we mythologize, are ones that strangle her victims. What changes if the arachnid belongs to the order Opiliones, as Paolo says, and is a daddy longlegs? Those long metal legs appear then as vulnerable, easily torn. The awkward creature weaves no steely webs. Then the cage, the house, the ideas surrounding women and domestic life would support other interpretations.

I don't have the energy to bicker about the number of legs a spider possesses. Not now, in the museum, but sooner or later the arbiter will be the smartphone. Yet Paolo's observations, in spite of his lapsus on spider legs, contain lots of new information. His knowledge makes me think.

Beyond this remains a deeper sense that I don't like the push-shove form of bickering: I'm right and you're wrong. I like the silence in listening, in thinking, in fitting pieces together. Seeing the eight legs as belonging to a daddy longlegs adds something interesting and important to the figure Bourgeois created. It's a very modern interpretation. And we need time to evaluate the sculpture's power in our imaginations with its relationship to living arachnids as well as social constructs.

M y two brothers, my sister, and I went to public school. The school was uniformly white, mostly students from modest economic backgrounds. To my knowledge, it had no national ranking. We walked more than a mile to school, dashed home and back to class in the hour for lunch, and then walked home at night after band or theater practice or volleyball. There was no Advanced Placement; we all had language requirements. In the first year of middle school, girls made aprons and white sauces and boys sanded wooden bookshelves and wired simple electric lamps. Both sexes were offered conventional ways to work with their hands. More than 80 percent of the graduates pursued some kind of further education. We were taught to be proud of attending public school. Good education meant building community and discovering that varied manual and technical skills, musical and athletic skills, were as necessary as history, language, math, and Plato's *Republic*.

A student a half year ahead of me, a bookish kid with glasses who was friendly in the halls as we changed classes and visited our lockers, became a world-famous maker of sculpture, painting, and installations: Bruce Nauman.

One of my older brother's friends, who sang in the choir

and played saxophone in the band, often visited our house. His father supported the family of five children on a single salary. My mother put in a word at her alma mater and he went to a small Midwestern school on scholarship, torn between music and science. Decades later, as a professor at Yale, he won a Nobel Prize in biochemistry.

The last time I met Tom Steitz, possibly forty years ago, our conversation, not surprisingly, turned to language and its specialization. He appreciated the irony that he and his wife, in fields that were closely associated, did not communicate easily using a common vocabulary.

The degree of specialization that he described made clear why I didn't possess a single one. Technical languages were not about the Tower of Babel. New processes that needed names generated new terminology within an existing language. Fine-tuned man-made words have built new worlds, which, like other languages and other nations, cannot necessarily be translated without knowledge of differences and the main roots. I imagine that of those who can write in these languages, there are a gifted few who use syntax in a sublime way.

G iven our hectic pace day to day, it's unlikely that we ever pause to be amazed that human beings, at a certain point, began to speak. To imagine such a time would require silence, time to step back, and then a sense of reverence as well as horror remembering events and regimes when words worked as coercers and instruments of terror. Language can easily be diverted to justify an oppressive order or to create one.

Given what we know about the disproportionate power of public speech in a media age, it is all the more stunning that an educated population in a liberal democracy allowed a president to use public office to traffic in false, divisive speech that incites while circumventing accepted systems requiring logic, syntax, and knowledge referring to reality.

Language is not a neutral instrument. Donald Trump, in or out of office, gives little indication that he dominates language enough to express thoughts in a rational or empathetic way. He speaks in fragments that don't hold together. Speaking from the highest office in the land, Trump successfully sanctified slang and slander to mock reason and sneer at the possibility of truth. He normalized the language of the mob, miniaturizing it to the tough kid on the corner. He still pretends he is a daredevil who is secretly feared and strangely admired as a lawbreaker. We seem to have given up on using language to unmask him. We slip into name-calling and ridicule as distractions from the powerful naming needed to reintroduce a sense that truth is necessary as well as possible. History suggests that populations like lies as much as they like hard truths. We have tolerated ignorance as if there is no such thing as knowledge.

Democratic society always faces the task of describing and fixing up the room, which is society itself. The room is the one always standing slightly out of focus, in the present but perhaps part of the future. Once we see the room clearly, a sense of reality can be established. Naming things with real names. This is the hope of democratic elections.

We are free people, empowered to satisfy our desires. Nevertheless, sources of power become further and further detached from our activities. Advertising is not an issue per se; it is received weather. We accept that and tell ourselves we're still alive, even though we are being influenced.

The fourteen billion dollars apparently spent in the last U.S. elections failed to educate us as a people about connections between our individual preferences and the collective meanings of our choices—not just A but B but C but M—for society. Unlike most Western democracies, the U.S. presidential campaign extends for more than a year. The extraordinarily costly show is lucrative for many, but it is difficult to argue that the prolonged process is necessary for democracy to work. It may even make it more difficult to be democratic, given that money and its influences are the fuel keeping it going day after day.

Meanwhile, most of us weren't educated by what was said in slogans. If we turned on the television, we just couldn't learn the statistics and analysis of why semiautomatic weapon sales were out of place in the twenty-first century. We didn't seem to be able to speak openly about how the sea levels are rising and how waves follow one another without innuendo breaking to blur facts and create false equivalencies. COVID-19 became a narrative in which truth appeared to be a matter of personal preference.

Many felt it, some said it, but believing that we were in danger was nearly inadmissible because it was against our national image of ourselves.

W hen *Sesame Street* was sold to the public, the radical idea was to use brief intervals, the length of advertisements, to teach children basic concepts. Israel was among the first to refuse to license the series as a model for instructing children. Creating a need in children to be entertained and conditioning them to expect this from learning was judged to be anti-educational by Israeli psychologists in the 1960s. The teaching model, in their analysis of the show, furthered advertising by reinforcing the resistance to learning concentration while reinforcing the craving to be entertained. Teachers were being given techniques to condition students rather than to train their brains to accept the uncertainties and rigors of uninterrupted reasoning and thinking out loud.

Years ago, when I was in California working as an editor, a woman psychologist surprised me by saying that she would not allow her boys to sell cookies for the Boy Scouts. Her bright eyes flashed. An Australian, she was bothered by the American value of teaching children the skills to sell. Where does that lead? she asked, hoping for a reply.

Pitching ideas, selling sweets. Not my boys. Building a critical mind is hard, painful work. It's a well-rounded mind that sees beyond immediate concerns or even a specific field of knowledge. I'm not willing to condition my boys to think fast. That's for robots. Wasn't that the point of Chaplin's *Modern Times*?

E very Sunday in Parma we walk from our house, choosing the same route, past the lit shrine with fresh flowers, the Madonnina receiving prayers and other gifts from passersby; past the fruit-and-vegetable store owned by the Albanians, who have flourished as legal immigrants; down the curving street repaved with granite from Via Mazzini, where the stones cracked under the weight of buses; past the university building, erected in the sixteenth century; past the federal courthouse, where the national press huddled for the verdict about the murder of Tommy, a toddler who was kidnapped (for reasons that to this day have remained obscure); turning left past the park with chestnut trees planted immediately after the war that now throw shadows as deep as a forest. Then we cross the street and walk the Lungoparma.

From week to week the river swells and shrinks according to the rains. The snowmelt from the Apennines is not particularly influential this year, and the rains push the river's shape here and there. Sometimes young trees are buried under it. Sometimes the gravel bottom is exposed and swirled by the currents into various islands where water birds pick up tidbits. For nearly two months now, Sundays have been days blessed by sun, and we have walked through the arc of the pheasant season. In high grasses that grew greener and taller each week, the small crests on the males could be seen (having shed their obvious colored markings) and we heard their cries of alarm as we passed. The fledglings had been born and an amazing series of behaviors and costume changes had taken place. We were on the road with rivers of genes making their own way.

With the sun rising always a bit earlier, we walked earlier. The quiet was such that without cars, the river sounds could be heard. The church bells. Clear. The pheasants were placed at regular distances from one another, clear territories. Two months ago, we saw ten, and then as the grasses grew, three, four, always the piercing cries of alarm. We saw a hare. Lovely seabirds circling and soaring. Down to one pheasant, and then this morning the banks had been mowed and the ten males appeared again against clipped grass. They were spaced as they had been in all the other weeks. Two or three had two or three very mimetic females on either side. The Alps were visible. Where were the fledglings? Why were the males still separated, marking territorial strips?

Today we see patches of trees farther on and Paolo says they, too, appeared after the war, as sprouts, since most trees had been chopped down in the preceding years for fuel for cooking, heating water, keeping the extremities from turning blue. Now many are sick. Old age, perhaps. Fungi. But maybe climate change.

The river, the mountains, the sunlight running between the mounds of gravel in the riverbed, and the light filtering through the spaces between tree trunks are a wordless vision of silence. Each step I take is one away from the cars, and the worries about a dying friend who knows he is dying, and the vote that has just taken place in Parliament to allow more people early retirement. Looking around, simple greatness has entered my breathing. My heartbeat is calm, feeling its part in the rhythm of the walk, steps touching ground.

A tree fell in the Ferrari park in Parma last week, striking a woman who was sitting with her family eating ice cream and drinking coffee. An hour later she died in the hospital. Most of the marvelous pied plane trees, with dappled trunks, have reached the end of their lives. Several have fallen in the new storms and winds, and several have crushed and killed people in the city. Trees that have been such silent benefactors for the city are now being looked at with more caution and wariness. The culture of managing trees is not very deep.

If the winds are strong in Parma (because before the city seldom had winds to relieve it from oppressive humidity), public parks like the Cittadella and the Parco Ducale are closed for fear of falling trees. The old poplar and chestnut trees have taken on a new life as assassins. Huge branches leap like robbers out of hiding. They have unleashed a new set of wars between the conservationists and those for public safety. Strong, gusting winds have changed parks from places of rest and enjoyment. Throughout the city, strewn heavy branches and jagged breaks in trunks look like the work of vandals. The municipal government is short of money to collect them. Danger. Murder. Trees have added to the general mistrust of change: one thing becoming suddenly something else or its opposite.

The calm silence of the trees is majestic until their leaves are whipped into furies. Even when branches are bowing and breaking, an immediate larger silence frames the storm. The mightiness—oh what is it and whence did it come?—is larger. Its unpredictability will reveal itself whenever and wherever it will.

P aolo studies many aspects of Darwin's journey. Again, at breakfast, he brings up the topic because he has returned to an interest in breeding. Early on, human beings recognized familiar traits among kin. But they couldn't explain them. How did green eyes skip a generation and come from a grandfather or, more disturbingly, from no known relative? Gregor Mendel, an Augustinian priest in the 1860s, found patterns. Peas were used for many reasons: rapid maturation and the ease of tracking their red or white flowers, green or yellow seeds from generation to generation. Colors were easy to count. Mendel's fundamental ratios, doctored slightly by his assistant hoping to please him, were not accepted until the first decade of the twentieth century as the basis of a new science, genetics.

By the time I am carrying our coffee cups to the sink, my head is spinning. From the decade of accepting Mendel's laws to the sequencing of the human genome, more had been understood about inheritance than in the previous two hundred thousand years humans had been reproducing. In less than one hundred years, humanity had unlocked some of the main secrets of life.

I saw an exhibit in Rome on inheritance. One section focused on Dolly, the first cloned sheep. A death mask had been made of her long muzzle and low brow. She had been commemorated like a Donatello or Michelangelo. The fleece of her daughter was stuffed, a mummified version of herself. Information on breeding Dolly's offspring for sweaters and meat also included a panel about cloning her for organs to be used in organ transplants, since humans were not donating theirs fast enough. The way Dolly was lit, the way her arthritis was described and her daughter also displayed, if we were a civilization that considered tomb paintings part of the ritual of passage into darkness, perhaps she would take a place among the gods on the altar built for an afterlife. But we are on a path with different doubts and noise. Our beliefs are in progress and its opportunities rather than far-off heavens.

Dolly, displayed with factual reverence, stressed possibilities rather than the darker implications of her contribution. She was an icon, a technological wonder, as well as an expression of the resilience of genes and the marvels of breeding and selection. Dolly didn't have price tags hanging from her legs. With her placid, beatific face captured in her death mask, with her small eyes so far apart, the sheep suggested how we might have millions of Dollys, putti with long ears, buzzing around her, celebrating a certain kind of eternity by cloning.

The ambivalent message of framing her as a media star and an intrepid pioneer in humanity's search for progress made the eugenic ripples and the Faustian admonitions seem like ungracious anxieties. She was cushioned in a lit mausoleum, where, as with so many things in our present world, as nonscientists we had scarce knowledge about what we were observing or that what we understood had altered in the word "sheep" or the meaning of the word "clone." Or "life." Or "death." Or "money to be made."

We haven't caught up to Dolly. Most of us still return to the little rhyme that coils in our brain: *Baa, baa, black sheep, have you any wool? Yes, sir, yes, sir, three bags full.* The bucolic song stops in a cul-de-sac of nostalgia.

Sheep: *Oxford English Dictionary*

Myriad biblical citations exist for flocks and humans as sheep, and Jesus as the shepherd.

Jer. 50, 6 (King James, 1611) "My people have been lost sheepe."

Sheep do not have a shining reputation in literature and common usage.

George Bernard Shaw (1914): "Bullied and ordered about, the Englishman obeys like a sheep."

Common compounds: sheep-faced, sheep-headed, sheep-hearted, sheep-willed.

Sheep gut was used for musical instruments. A few of us still possess tennis rackets strung from their innards.

In Tarquinia, at the farm, their wool no longer has a value. A shearer from Australia passes by once a summer as he makes his way up and down the littoral Mediterranean coast, shaving sheep. He did more than fifty in a day at the place we were staying. Once they are liberated from their suffocating wooly jackets, the mountain of tangled dirty hair that is too short to be easily woven cannot even be given away. The quality is not high enough to justify the rest of the equation. It is not used. Perhaps that does not mean that it cannot be used. Maybe some felt could be obtained by soaking it and proposing its ecological insulating properties.

But the wool is emblematic of a way of life that has disappeared in large part. How do we adapt to the words "sheep" and "wool"? Where do we put Queen Dolly? What has she brought to the thousands of years of literary uses of sheep as weak, and followers, and in need of salvation?

How do we translate "Dolly"? Part of the female creation myth? How do we approach what a sheep is in our twenty-first-century world of broken mirrors and radio telescopes?

We moderns have many other priorities that preclude worrying about the rough pelt and smell of Tarquinian sheep and the laboratory Dollys that don't show dirt and are no longer about grazing on hillsides. It has all happened so fast we have gotten used to not bothering to work out nonexistent connections. But her sisters now often carry valves that are being tested for human hearts.

We have assumed for far too long in the West that as a species we are privileged over other forms of life. There is much evidence that the primate brain from which ours evolved has coils in its deepest recesses that allow distinguishing nascent forms of empathy, sorrow, suffering, and right and wrong. Our uniqueness and solitude are not enough to allow us to proclaim that we know what we are in. Since no one else in the animal kingdom speaks as extensively as we do, it is too easy to believe in our interpretations of the silences we confidently fill in all around us.

Paolo tells me that he had to turn off the documentary on birds last night because he could not watch the wren trying to satisfy cuckoo fledglings who occupied her nest, having hatched after the cuckoo had eaten all the wren's eggs and substituted her own. Back and forth, the wren became more and more frenetic, trying to feed the cuckoos' voracious appetites, stuffing their open mouths asking and asking for more. The wren couldn't keep up. I couldn't take it, he said. I turned it off. Then, he added, since it was too early to come to bed, I switched it back on to an *il commissario Montalbano* rerun. (The detective mystery series, written by a Sicilian who continued writing even after he went blind in his nineties, is still the most popular in Italy.) I knew the plot frame by frame. An immigrant kid jumps from the ship and Montalbano jumps in to save him from drowning. But Montalbano is too late. He walks ashore carrying the kid's body. He and his girlfriend had wanted to adopt a kid like that but had never found the time or quite enough courage. It was a terrible night for TV, Paolo says, his eyes filling with tears. No one could get things on a happy track.

E arly in the morning when I am walking in Parma, in order to go within myself, I often sit in an empty church where the former priest, who died a few years ago, offered shelter to refugees and implicit support to people with AIDS. The doors swing on hinges that wheeze closed behind me as I choose a folding chair. Beggars often follow me in or they are already inside the church, bright-eyed as birds in the shadows. They wait to tap my shoulder as soon as I shut my eyes. I know that the beggars will understand and give up when I don't open my eyes as they continue to tap. In one way, I am shutting them out. I am shutting out noise and thought and letting calm take over. Blackness comes, it inevitably comes, and then a soft green fills my vision, then a mauve appears as a circle, and finally a pulsing, throbbing yellow inside of it. In this set of colors and this progression, the yellow pulsing slowly forms a benign eye looking at me lovingly. I take it as an unknown gift.

I often feel surprised thinking about this familiar experience as I continue my walk. I never know what to make of it. What took place? Does it mean anything except some brain reaction like the zigzag motions of phosphenes that often disturb me? Why is it always the same beautiful sequence, with that deeply loving eye, which eventually fades? Dante finds refuge in muteness as he approaches the Divine. Words reach a border and are replaced by light. The untranslatable presents him with a threshold that invites crossing and yet is gloriously impossible to be crossed. I accept in silence the sequence of colors I see. I have no means nor even curiosity to translate them. I accept their light.

On the street, activity rushes in: the people, the ambulance screaming, the buses, the paving torn up to put down cables and, at the end of Via Mazzini, a glass-and-steel monument containing part of a marble cornice from the tomb of a Roman military official in the first century. Death is never that far from sight. I like that reminder, not as a screaming headline, but as a discrete meditation.

Several times in my life, death appeared unexpectedly, like a hood thrown over my eyes. When taking it off, the unwished-for insistent bright light and the rough and dissatisfying answers that are substitutes for loss always pushed me. It took me several times of being knocked to the ground and realizing that I had been hooded before I recognized that when I took the hood off, blindness was my condition. I could touch things but no longer knew what I was seeing.

Heaviness, an ache, a word like "grief" engulfed me. But I didn't know much about myself or others. The concept of "self" seemed pitiful. But "soul" sounded deep enough to be independent of "self."

She called early in the morning, before she thought I would be at my desk. There has been serious illness in her family for more than two years. Her life has returned to nursing and caretaking, to giving up most of her day to routines of feeding and washing, following medicines. It's fine for me this way, she says. Better than the alternative.

But she has righted herself in the last months, perhaps as the coronavirus has added still more limits and unpredictability to life, while not lessening her routines. It was time to return to her easel. She called to say she'd cleared a white space on a painting that had been started long ago. It took several sessions to cover the colors with white. The space was empty. Nothing bled through. She'd studied it for several days and knew it needed just two brief blue strokes. They would break up the static space, but she could only make them once, just once, and they had to be just right.

She called to say, I did it. Just two small blue strokes on pure white.

Are you happy now?

With them? Yes, I'm happy.

With them, yes. But it's me.

I'm happy.

In Rome last year, I saw Artemisia Gentileschi's paintings, in a context of feminist commentary. The facts of the trial she underwent in the early seventeenth century accusing her teacher and supposedly promised husband, the painter Agostino Tassi, of rape were opaque and contradictory, as was the sentence issued. The silence, like the smell of damp mold rising from many ancient underground ruins in Rome, was definitely penetrated by the fierce and painful struggle she underwent in physical and moral examinations to assert that she had been raped by her father's assistant. Raising her voice and conveying her need to restore her identity meant exposing the effects of his violence to her body and mind to a public judgment.

For those who don't know her story, there is no single story. However, Artemisia became a painter, in part, because her father was a painter and her instructor. It soon became apparent to him that she was his equal. A daughter, in theory, was not a rival like a son, but we know from different sources there was friction. Using the subject matter of their paintings, we can make direct comparisons between the two artists, since many subjects—Mary Magdalene, Judith and Holofernes—were general material for painters.

Artemisia Gentileschi approached the treatment of Judith

killing Holofernes differently than her father. She interpreted the act of beheading that we see in paintings by Caravaggio differently. Her work is personal and expressive in a different and objective way.

In Artemisia Gentileschi's version of the subject that belongs to the Uffizi museum (she completed six paintings about Judith), Holofernes is positioned less dramatically than in male versions. His agony is a secondary focus. His face is near the front of the frame; the gore is minimized. We are not overly involved in his death. Instead, we perceive Judith's emotions and conflicts. One of the general's arms is pushing back at the maidservant, who is holding his head down and in place as Judith presses on his skull from the right. The awkward and nearly implausible position of Judith's arms seems technically strange, if not an error. Their length and prominence make it obvious that the position from which Judith yields the sword is signaling larger issues. Her arms, bathed in Mannerist light, are unlikely to provide the leverage needed to saw through the Assyrian general's flesh and bones. It is as if her long arms are needed to express the barrier between herself, her violent act, and her victim. Judith's closed eyes interpret her murderous strength as psychologically abstract. The message of her strength has been complicated by inserting its deliberate detachment.

Judith is a figure who has been interpreted through the ages as saving her people. She was the Jewish widow who, with faith and courage, falsely promised seduction and then killed the enemy in order to help her own people. The way Judith's hand-maid is pressing on Holofernes's head, we understand the gap in physical strength between the general and the two women. Instead of the triumph of Judith's plan, we witness the women's psychological determination and sense of duty. Judith's long arms announce the negotiation going on in her soul as she presses on the blade cutting his neck. Her stiff arms reveal repugnance and ambivalence. Their parallel prominence can be seen nearly as a wooden structure, the expectations of existing norms. Artemisia painted a scene that forces us to admit and puzzle over the reality of Judith's arms. They almost suggest a cage or gallows.

In one of her early paintings, *Susanna and the Elders* (1610), Artemisia Gentileschi interpreted the impact on a woman's psyche when men play on her vulnerability, assuming that she has no autonomous feelings. Well aware of how women artists were viewed by men, Gentileschi was naturally drawn to creating images of how women saw themselves or how women interpreted men seeing them. Her numerous portraits of Mary Magdalene depict her sensuously, often loosely garbed, in poses that include penitence, melancholy, and ecstasy. In her still controversial version of *Allegory of Fame*, found in the Musée de Tessé Le Mans and ascribed to the painter in the 1980s, Gentileschi renders a beautiful sleeping woman lying partially covered by an elaborate embroidered cloth, her buttocks away from the viewer. A carnival mask in her hand, her paints scattered in shadows, she curls around a space otherwise filled by the cloth draping her sexual parts. Shown from both its outer patterned side and its plain underside, the cloth's elaborate twists end in the foreground as a narrow shape like a snake's head. Gentileschi highlights the sleeping figure's knee so that it transforms into a bright white hole breaking through the cloth. There is another oblong of intense light near her bent left elbow. Unexplained as symbols, difficult to overlook, as technically strange as Judith's arms, they ask for interpretations. Where is the source of light creating them? Almost blinding, the opening in the dark cloth covering her sex seems to be presented for inspection. Was it ever meant to suggest a birth canal opening? The other light on the limb supporting her sleeping face is equally strong. Its symbolism could be many things, including her mind's potential.

As I am crossing the Via Torelli on the white zebra lines, a large black Mercedes does not stop. He and I are playing a game of chicken. I blink and pull myself to an abrupt halt in order not to be hit. The driver is talking on his cell phone. If I were reasoning like many anti-government Italians, I would tell myself that he is not to blame, since he had no free hand to downshift and let me pass. *Pazienza*. But I am not so empathetic. He knew there was no traffic and expected me to stop. Not stopping and talking on the cell phone are not really tiny infractions. They are indifference to the community's need to practice safety and respect for others. Because of the model of his car, I cast on him, rightly or wrongly, a label of corruption and wealth.

His mind and body were in the new present. He was entitled to a petty form of lawlessness and counting on a growing petty form of others tolerating it—after all, there is little to be done, no enforcement, and it doesn't matter. What counts is who is more powerful. This narrative of privilege and lawbreaking is dangerous in this knee-jerk form, but that doesn't stop it from growing.

New present. What did that mean one page ago? Since I turned to this page, the phrase has shifted in an immense way. Tatiana calls in tears because Sonia, the fifty-year-old woman she works for, has died, in the hospital, alone, without her husband or her mother, who was operated on for a tumor in her back. Sonia's mother has been moved to a hospital where the virus has not yet filled all the beds. She has not been told that her only child has died. The woman Tatiana worked for cannot even be cremated in Parma because the backup is too great. Her body will be shipped to Turin to be incinerated but her husband will not be able to accompany her on that last journey because all of us are confined to the city here. Sonia's ashes will then be shipped back to him.

Tatiana cannot stop weeping. There can be no funeral. It all happened in two days and now that sweet woman, with a kind word for everyone, who was fighting cancer, is gone and died alone. Tatiana is worried for her own daughter in Poland, who shares her workers' apartment with a Russian and his daughter. They drink, they won't clean. They won't wear masks. Her own daughter and her boyfriend have been laid off but cannot return to Ukraine and will only be paid for another week in

Poland. Through her tears, she says, It will end. It will. But the bad moment may be only the beginning of worse.

For weeks, since all travel has been banned, I feel the Atlantic Ocean as a barrier that will become more and more difficult to cross as if it were a normal event. I am sincerely struck by the question of the distance of home. The pain of having my daughter and her precious family only reachable if we make the crossing becomes acute. And the need to support one another should physical help be needed seems more difficult than just months ago. I remember looking for the American poet (and some said saint) Robert Lax when Paolo and I were in Patmos one summer with friends. A woman leaned from a window above his window to answer us when we shouted out, Is Robert Lax out for a walk? He's gone, she said. For a few months, he's been gone. Relatives took him back home. He was at home here in Patmos. But he was ill and alone. He needed help and his relatives understood that. He was not a man of many words, a monk among us. He refused to fly. They took him back by ship. Now he's in Olean, New York, his home, where he was born.

I finished rereading *To the Lighthouse* by Virginia Woolf. How radically original she was exploring her sense of identity and the reality of others from many points of view. In *Flush*, she inhabits the mind of Elizabeth Barrett Browning's dog; in *Orlando*, she mirthfully moves through five centuries of his changes from a man to a woman, as her passions shift. In *Mrs. Dalloway* and *The Waves* and other works, men and women of different ages and classes illuminate what Woolf knew about human nature and herself in upper-middle-class British society; there were multiple selves in one body.

In the novel *To the Lighthouse*, Mrs. Ramsay is a fulcrum, defining things—she narrates her life and those of others in a certain bourgeois class who are assigned roles, both as men and as women. But she dies—a stark exit, not elaborated upon. Others are left to narrate their versions of her life as well as their own. The sea leading to the lighthouse—waves and currents with motion and its subsequent erosion and nourishment—is the context for unseen worlds around the characters. The sea is the all-absorbing, moon-pulled body, holding life and death, danger and wisdom. It contains depths, secrets, danger swelling and receding beyond all the loves and hates beating in their hearts. The unsettled characters like James and Lily, outliving

Mrs. Ramsay, decide to take the long-postponed journey to the lighthouse and its keeper.

Between the Acts is Woolf's last novel. She completed her final draft days before she penned a letter to Leonard Woolf, her husband, explaining that she could not endure the onslaught of her madness again. When she'd finished the manuscript, she was still dissatisfied with it. She told her publisher she found it shallow, wished to revise or not to publish it at all. But her determination to end her life cut her free of concerns such as her standards for writing. The stoic Woolf filled her pocket with an unyielding stone and walked farther and deeper into the river Ouse. How many times had she placed her characters in front of the sea and found it larger than their lives?

When Woolf killed herself in 1941, society was falling apart; London was on fire; rules meant nothing in terms of societal niceties. She identified the darkness in *Between the Acts* as "the night that dwellers in caves had watched from some high place among rocks." She knew the part of life that had been civilized with manners and laws, and discriminating social classes, in the end, showed itself to be no more than a room, "empty, empty, empty; silent, silent, silent. The room was a shell, singing of what was before time was; a vase stood in the heart of the house, alabaster, smooth, cold, holding the still, distilled essence of emptiness, silence." Death was in the vase. War was pulling civilization apart, showing horrors and society's veneer.

In one sentence, Woolf captures her perception of life and death in a family and civilization by bringing the reader to the central place of an alabaster vase in the house. The vase alludes to the vases that held ashes in civilizations in Egypt, in Etruscan tombs, in Greek villages, all efforts to distill the meaning of emptiness before their civilizations came into being: the dwellers in caves, who before civilizations viewed life from the rocks. With the civilizations came economic systems, classes, and roles, and with roles, substitutes for feeling and defining appearances, like the bourgeois furnishings including a classical vase.

With German doodlebug bombs streaking the night skies for months, the Second World War broke up life around Woolf. She felt the depths of humanity's primitive and contradictory nature, its vestiges of civilized behavior swept away, revealing class society as an absurd piece of amusing, hypocritical theater. In her last work, she pushed hard on silences. "Oh to write a play without an audience—*the* play." "We haven't the words—we haven't the words. . . . Behind the eyes; not on the lips; that's all." "Thoughts without words. . . . Can that be?" Woolf touched ruthless, banal annihilations in history, violence, death; life's flirtations, seductions, mismatches; and the futile strange power of words to bring all lightly together in crystal-clear art as illusion. She was able to make reality and hallucination whole. She had nowhere to go.

In Parma the sidewalks outside the center are poured tar. In the spring the city picks an area and renews the walks that have been destroyed by weather and cars spinning their wheels. But the cracks and crevices, the open twists and turns, the mounds are the expression of the trees whose roots struggle to find space and a hold to the underground.

The long black tongues called sidewalks are filled with sores or volcano-like cones, as well as low undulations that crack open like a baked bread's crust. The life underneath is the cause of all this motion, sculpting, and moving. From aboveground, my viewpoint as a woman using the sidewalks, the unevenness is a hazard, inspiring daily complaints and cautious running. Never had I viewed sidewalks as a source of pity that I should feel for the trees until I read *The Hidden Life of Trees* by Peter Wohlleben.

The language of roots had never before crossed my mind. Yet roots store the experience of trees and distribute resources, as well as control the need to expand if the tree is to grow and be supported. Trees are one of our most unrecognized guardians for sustaining life on earth by looking out for one another.

The trees planted in sidewalks, contained in rough little tar semicircles, heat in summer to very high temperatures. Their poor roots are suffocated and sometimes even scalded. They keep growing until they would ideally form underground webs of up to seven hundred square yards. Bound in root cages and executed if they fall over or their roots clog up underground urban pipes, trees are hobbled and kept in a state of confinement. The root tips can change direction, but they can't get past walls. If one tree's roots are able to reach those of another, they can share nutrients as well as exchange signals about the environment. Imprisoned under sidewalks, the roots searching for space and communication among themselves are silent except for their active movements that push back against the way we want to walk over them. There is something of us in those confined spaces, where the natural instinct to reach out and communicate has been stifled, manipulated by forces that do not consider the nature of roots and their connections.

Which are the maps and the laws to be made from where we stand now? Modern Western countries seemed as if they had uncovered some remaining humanistic bedrock on which to rebuild society following the Second World War, but recently it seems as if we don't know where we are again, or who we are or were. We see, perhaps ever more broadly and sometimes for the first time, infinitely different stories when we look at histories of race, gender, religion, culture, genocide, and unending forms of oppression, as well as rapidly moving biological, economic, and technical frontiers.

How do we generate new language? Recent new sounds and cries are breaking through silences, asking for reparations for slavery and education for girls. This is not Woolf's "empty, empty, empty; silent, silent, silent." These sounds are not the sounds of an ending, but something new.

The cockatoos in the cage on the balcony across from our kitchen window in Parma stopped fighting about a week ago. For long periods of time they are quiet, and when they do make sounds now they are far softer and varied and there are no squawks of alarm or fury. One bird is yellow, with a long tail and plumes. One is white, with a strong tail and a set of long crest feathers like a droopy crown. There are two little trapezes, and they take turns. They have accepted the cage, it seems. The cage was not the problem.

They are moving. Now that they have stopped bickering, I am drawn to them when I hang out laundry. I sing a few notes that I imagine might seem like nice sounds to them. They notice.

The changes in them stimulate me. The story also unfolds around my limitations. I have had a lovely set of revelations, tiny revelations, revolutionary as well, if I admit my unknowing. Now I am interested. This interest is not simply in acquiring information about the cockatoo habits. This is about witnessing change of those confined in a cage.

The white heron had been hidden for all the weeks we had been in Bronxville. The week before we were to return to our home in the Po Plain, as Metro-North was rounding a curve and beginning to slow down to enter the Bronxville station, a white column rising from the canvas-colored Bronx River caught my eye. My brain applauded.

Two days later, Paolo and I saw *Amazing Grace* at the local cinema. We fit it into an afternoon space, because if we picked the film up in Parma, much of it would be dubbed. The songs would have subtitles in Italian, but the rest, the voices in English, would most probably be lip-synced and replaced.

The documentary recorded a performance that Aretha Franklin gave in Watts in 1972. Rumored to be a masterpiece, it had been tied up in legal battles since the two-day concert was filmed and its results deemed technically flawed. Following Franklin's death, a stipulation blocking its release expired. With improvements in technology to enhance it, its hidden treasure found a path to distribution.

Any documentary, as it goes forward in time, transforms into a narrative about reality that no longer exists. Its reflection of time begins to look more sculpted and the people more like actors in a theater.

The ordinary gradually ceases to exist in documentaries.

In the Franklin concert, differences between a commercial performance and a religious one were framed. Songs that originated in religious praise and spiritual need were brought back to the pews and pulpit where they had always found voices that brought bodies to their feet.

The film moved between the creation of an atmosphere, the atmosphere itself, and the start and stop of performance and retakes. The person Franklin, the artist, the singer, as well as practical presences of the manager, issues of contracts, timing, production, became different angles on a performance with various purposes, while bodies and voices in the congregation and chorus carried steady currents of worship: ins and outs, highs and lows, elation, sorrow expressed with close-ups of blown-out hairdos and weirdly fluted clothes that reflected the tail fins and flares of the times. A young Mick Jagger sat in the back row taking the voices in.

Sweat trickling on Franklin's forehead created a sense of agony. (Perhaps the church had no air conditioning.) Profusions of concentration crossed her face as she got deeper and further into her music. During a few of the breaks between songs she wiped her head with a towel as if she were a boxer in the ring.

Then *Amazing Grace* was over, the troubled soundtrack of the original concert overcome. The distinction between entertainment and a form of worship was established. Imperfect, hot, and impeded by technical difficulties, the struggle for fame in the recording world and the identity of Black soul music migrating into secular beats returned the music to its source, clearing out some of the scaffolding of media. Bodies rose from their seats moved by invocations of forgiveness and resurrection.

Paolo and I left the theater, heading toward our apartment,

glad that we had made the effort. As we crossed the stone bridge, in full view was the white heron, wading near the right bank of the river. Intent on his business of fishing, and particularly elegant, he was free in his own realm. There are meanings to borders, to real, to private, to religious, to official, to innocence, to coincidence, to crossing over—and they need interpretation, contexts. We nodded to each other, took the heron's presence in, and added it to the grace we felt having seen and heard Aretha Franklin.

The few days remaining after sighting the heron were busy. Several small things were noticed, and their effects were noticed in the way that a mosquito can bite in silence and then for a few days the bite becomes more and more real. An ash-blue heron appeared on the rocks. I had never seen one in the many years of walking part of the river. I mentioned it to Paolo.

Oh, I see him all the time. He seems to live under the bridge. I was sure you saw him too.

A student of mine from Baghdad, a professor of engineering who was kidnapped by Iraqi terrorists and eventually became a refugee in Switzerland, for years has been putting contrasts together in a nonfiction memoir about his life in the East and the West. He sorts through positive and negative versions of the same story, searching for how they might be reconciled.

His latest chapter reached me by email in our last week in Yonkers. He had set up his amateur telescopes and equipment in order to locate the M87 galaxy, inside of which the interior of the first black hole was photographed. He made elaborate preparations to sight the M87 cluster, certain that in his driveway he was far enough from adjacent Swiss villages to be assured of darkness. Instead, he had forgotten about the moon. Being directly overhead, its brilliance made it impossible to peer into the distances. Furious at himself, he began to dismantle the precision setup. Something stopped him. The astronomically banal moon was the only celestial body that could rescue his evening.

Once the moon's pocked surface glowed in his lens (it was easy to locate), childhood memories slipped from their confined space. The hot spring nights in Baghdad, when he and his six siblings slept on the roof, especially through the simmering heat of Ramadan. As a child, his telescope was his greatest treasure and studying the moon a source of pride.

The moon in Arabic poetry and culture was a central theme, not in the science that meant so much to him, but in art and philosophy. The moon's rough surface, which he was seeing from his driveway, pulled him closer. His powerful telescope allowed him to range over the craters and mounds in stunning detail.

The moon is wonderful, he wrote. Simply wonderful.

Science was his chosen path for life, but the moon that had delighted the young boy brought back his identity as his mother had transmitted it to him. The spell of the moon swelled with her insistent lessons and poems sweet as plums, the one overhead seen from the roof again.

That same day the Geneva email reached me, I was to meet a close friend in the C. G. Jung Institute in New York City before she gave a lecture. While I waited for her in the highly specialized library, I pulled a book at random off the shelf. Its title: *Alone with the Alone*. It was a study of Ibn Arabi's mystical thought in the early 1200s. Speeding over two pages only, I read that this God—the God who is unknowable, the unpredictable God, the God who is not—needed to know what the creatures He had created knew of Him. The God who is unknowable, the unpredictable God, the God who is not, can only be seen through God's eyes. Human beings can see God only through God's eyes by using God's eyes, which are inside of human beings. There, a human being is alone with the Alone. Arabi was not explaining a tautology but the idea that we mirror what we see.

My head felt exhilarated in some superficial way, trying to follow the turns in the couple of pages of Arabi's thought. This was Sufi thinking as far as I knew. The turning was also Dante's turning. Mystical turns where each person knows God only in the way she can see God, as the spiral deepens inside her own knowing. In this line of thinking, we will only ever know as much as is revealed in us. All that is outside or beyond our knowing cannot be known by us but it may be known by someone else, in the past, the present, or turns in the future.

As my friend entered the library, a book of photographs displayed across the room caught my eye. The book was called *The Moon*. The image on the cover was a close-up of a dusty, dry surface with craters. It was a picture of a stone.

Although we were leaving for Italy, we could not leave without one last abundant dinner with our daughter and her family, where Paolo and I pretend that our hearts are not heavy with the reality of separation. One red, one white, and the other bottles we'd been given by the ex-policeman would age in our Chinese cupboard until we returned. The roughly hewn cupboard, elegant and battered, still smells faintly of smoke and fish. If you want a piece that looks better or smells better, the Chinese seller on the street in SoHo had said to me, I'll find you something new. This must be left as it is. It is history, suffering, and survival. The wood it's made of—all of those trees disappeared in the south, after the famine of the 1840s. That's how it can be dated. The cupboard is full of hunger. I think he told me the name of the tree meant "Chinese weeping cypress."

Yesterday, I read a few more entries in Beethoven's diary. As he struggled with deafness, his despair grew worse. And then he found his balance in the forest, the peace he needed: "Oh, mighty God, in the forest. I am blessed and happy in the forest, every tree speaks to me of you."

My second pregnancy, before I resorted to a test, gave me the sensation that I already knew. In crazy circumstances, I had the certainty I was carrying life. The moon was full, and although my body was still half grieving, I let out a strange cry of laughter upon seeing the moon. I was in the unidentified, rattling space between two railroad cars, crossing from one carriage to another. There was a window, and the bright ball of the moon was bouncing along outside of it. My joy was so deep it rushed up from my stomach through my chest, out of my throat, escaping like a wild belch. A universe had been turned on, and seeing the full moon, I knew that I contained it. A living soul had entered.

Less than two years later, my little daughter, standing on my lap as we ate outside in Parma with friends, broke in with an exclamation that brought the dinner to a halt. She nearly catapulted from my arms. Moon, she cried. We shared her delight with our laughter. A word she knew from books caught her full attention in the sky. The moon, she said, feeling it inside herself and up in the starry heavens where her finger was pointing. The moon fused in her brain, the light from the sky, the image in her eyes, the word on her tongue propelling her body into complete awe of the connection.

I saw the book on *The Moon*, its stone face up close, in the Jungian library. My Iraqi student rediscovered its double sense for him while seeing it through the lens he set up in his driveway. He perceived it as an object viewed and understood scientifically but also as a jewel in the crown of his culture and his mother's heart. My daughter that night, as a baby learning a word inside and outside history, made its beauty her own. Each of us invests in the particulars of what lives in a word and its counterpoint in reality. In life and then in memory and reflection, we find as long as we are conscious, time still allows us to perceive our life in a way that is more true. In part how we organize or interpret it is by claiming the luxury of time, where actions and events can be contemplated and reexamined. We step out of noise.

I had difficulty talking with my mouth full of cucumbers and ham. He told me that he was a physician who was an abortionist. Anxiety, like a cat stretching, filled me up. His voice pushed. He was in danger, he said, and the women seeking abortions were in danger; any of them could be shot by fanatics who insisted human life was sacred. His practice was legal but he felt that he was a leper. Liberals supposedly favored his choice to do this work, and then he shook his head.

We were attending the same course in New York City, because he, like me, was interested in communication. He needed help in his daily life in order to continue performing an intimate, complicated, and much-needed legal procedure.

His loneliness was overwhelming. He identified hypocrisy on the part of others as he faced threats of violence. He did not need approval, but he resented being surrounded by judgments. While we stood up to get coffee, silence descended. He was another soldier in combat, like a veteran who was ostracized when he asked to describe the debilitating effects of war. It was not all pretty, not all clear in the details. He turned his back on me, his neck and shoulders, a hump. He turned away, leaving with me his need for appreciation as well as to be listened to and better understood. We were not in the same classes. I was sorry not to have heard the discussions that must have ensued. But it was important to have heard how he felt silenced by people who believe in the right of choice but have never empathized with how dangerous and lonely it is for an abortion doctor.

Who could think that a single beech in less than five years shall produce thirty thousand beechnuts? In the life-span of one mother tree of at least two hundred years, only one nut will become another tree that grows two hundred years.

The meaning of those thirty thousand nuts is hidden. The meaning of the surplus of nuts over one mother tree's life-span is hidden. But their presence is not hidden to birds, to deer or wolves or ants. Most of the potential trees are lost and never put down a single root or open a single leaf. Their excess is only hidden to us.

Oedipus shows us the possibility of truth lying just out of reach. Our mind in everyday life sometimes hides it from us, lest we be too sickened or frightened by what we see. Tragedy, the state of a life being tragic, belongs to a character possessing nobility. Noble beings (since we all err) are the ones whose falls from greatness move us to pity. Catharsis occurs for the character

and the audience as the result of accepting truth in its unbearable contradiction. Oedipus blinds himself once he real-
izes what he has done. The city of Thebes heals because truth
needed to be admitted, brought into the open.

At Yaddo, an artists' colony in upstate New York, I met a composer who was recording silences in churches and cathedrals. In the night hours, he set up mikes and recorders in the empty and darkened spaces within domes, buttresses, and carved marble columns in order to capture the sound of air moving across and against ancient stone walls or bricks. Sounds built up like silt in corners, they attenuated in open space. Each structure held many different silences. The stones were different, the angles different, the heights. They were churches in which nothing was happening at that hour. By that standard, they were the same. With those words and those criteria, they were the same, if this had been a standardized test with something to measure. However, once the recordings of the sound waves were broken into their separate registers and patterns, there was little overlap issuing from their frequencies. Within each structure, the vibrations that he converted into frequencies within and among churches were different. From these frequencies he made compositions. The music within the residual waves of night silences against stones was a new source for arranging order and patterns.

The vibrations of air moving were converted into sound and graphed visually by a computer. The silences contained waves carrying the intensities determined by what they encountered as walls and, altering, continuing on as different waves moving forward, becoming separated, as frequencies. I heard a few of the early recordings before the composer had manipulated and further enhanced them. There were swells, lifts, vibrating minor dissonances not considered before in churches where choirs had sung Bach, Haydn, and Messiaen.

The Baltic Sea in November on the edge of Saint Petersburg was a color, again, where the brain met the universe. It was terribly cold, terribly windy, and the sea was an open space, giving way to openness without limit. The objective on that dark November morning before the sun had struggled over the horizon was to step into the waves, their brittle foam, feel the cold, the shock, the life and death in the same act.

The feet walked into the sea. The legs braced themselves for the mild tow of the water. The ice-blue baptism, part gull-colored, part dust-blue water, washed over my feet. The color rubbed into my head.

When I first saw a heron in Saratoga, New York, when I was attending Yaddo, it was colored with this Baltic blue.

The herons in Saratoga broke through a silence in a way I hadn't expected. There in the woods I followed many birds, the most amusing being the pileated woodpecker, with its vertical motion and its intense drill. There was a flash of red. But the herons engaged, eye to eye, stopping and lifting their legs and feet fastidiously, as if they were being troubled. They engaged or I did. Before I sat down to work on my novel, a story set during the summer solstice in Florence Cathedral, I would rush down to the water to see if I could catch sight of them. I was touching something blue that I knew from the Baltic. It was spirit. The wind from that cold day. It was unspeaking sound, whirling, battering.

I drew mandalas. Poems poured from the encounters. Seams of gold from the winter sun in the Baltic, the summer gold from Florence Cathedral, the blue from the icy water going over my feet in the sea in Saint Petersburg, the crook in the necks of the herons at Yaddo, their long bodies, their way of camouflaging—all poured into my writing.

I began putting on my blue plastic raincoat for my morning walk. I identified with the way the birds hid in the reeds. I half believed, without telling anyone, that I was one of them. I couldn't sleep because I couldn't wait to return to that kingdom. I could feel in their wings, which spread and snapped open, that I longed for that kind of flight.

The corruption in Florence. An excavation of an Etruscan woman. The oil in Nigeria. This was the novel in my head, but the herons obsessed me. If I didn't see them in the morning, I was bereft.

Putting on the blue raincoat and seeing their wings—if the herons would turn their backs and express their discomfort at being observed and rise and row away across the sky, wings that suddenly were a visible expression that was in opposition to the camouflage, the stillness of waiting for a fish, the cunning blend of colors hiding in the weeds—this became a reality that raised my spirits and kept me on the alert. Nothing of all this reached the pages in any way that was visible. The words were going rather well, characters whose invented lives were catching on. Suspension of disbelief was a conscious crafting craftiness. But that was imagination, and instead the birds and my connections to them overwhelmed me. The herons and the zone of my searching for them mirrored some other reality in my mind. The awareness the herons had of being observed and my discovering them—sometimes so well hidden and so still, my eyes could scan the reeds for minutes before translating them—was like a piece of music only they and I could hear.

In that silence that was so alive, my own sense of scale—not only who I was, but who I was in relation to all else that was—defined place in a new way. Everything was interconnected but nothing was the same as anything else. Empathy, that possibility to transform and exchange places, understanding by looking out from another's place and point of view, was like my wearing the raincoat mimicking the color and shape of the herons. It acknowledged the ability to believe in a close connection. It allowed for an experiencing of that connection. But only for a brief time. The wings, those bony wide contraptions, those rebellions, those glorious flights of beauty, broke up empathy and the illusion of knowing. The seam of separateness, unstitched by moments of empathy, was tightly sewn up, repaired, not allowed to leak once herons decided to lift. The herons rowed off, out of sight, into their own realm. Out of hiding: the weeks in Yaddo were full of intense exchanges in which people admitted doubts and conflicts about their lives and actions as well as their art. There was endless listening and a few revelations.

Out of hiding, out of schemes, timidity; it's far to move from grazing in the mud, catching something to eat, to being active and letting oneself be noticed. The herons at Yaddo led me to the edge of a lake that I had touched in the Baltic Sea. It was liberty, liberty for human beings, liberty for those artists who must share what they know from their own realm. It was the flight of knowingly pulling into sky with a destination.

It's frightening to think that nearly fifteen years ago a man who lived as a painter at night and a computer whiz by day, the right arm of a CEO, had a conversation in Geneva with me that has become more and more prescient and painful. He said: We people on the ground think we are in a democracy, but it's happening in private planes, in the sky, where deals are made and no one can hear anything. That's where the power is, that's the disconnect that is unaccounted for on the ground. In a couple of hours between London and Paris, a few men decide how they will iterate a plan that officially uses some concept tagged to a tax break or a rider in a bill. Then they will use their inordinate amounts of money—words and code and product—to secretly influence and change public opinion. Besides becoming inordinately rich, they convince themselves they are doing good by ridding democracy of what they consider blights to individual freedom. They are racists. They know that technology is still an unregulated weapon for infiltration. They can lie, and do, using technological tools while working in extraterritorial skies with business people from foreign countries.

The unseen purposes of Stonehenge captivated archaeologists and historians for centuries, but slowly the hypothesis that the monument was linked to the summer solstice was accepted.

Now archaeologists believe that a few miles from the site there is evidence that more than four thousand people settled at a place that marked or observed the winter solstice. The Durrington Walls are opposite the solar alignments at Stonehenge. There are no written records, but the two locations may allude to the land of the living and the land of the dead. Huge tree monoliths forming a circle of pillars were in place and then dismantled and eventually covered over by a henge at Durrington Walls. One hypothesis is that they were part of a restructuring of worship from nature, in general, to the worship of solar movements. The change, the rejection or abandonment of a system that was so costly in human terms and so powerful, leaves us with the silence: Why are such monumental structures hidden or replaced? What causes a culture to reverse itself in a short period of time?

W hen Rachel Carson wrote *Silent Spring*, she justified her commitment: "There would be no peace for me if I kept silent." "The obligation to endure gives us the right to know," she claimed, referring to our obligation to save the earth for future generations. Her understanding of biocides and how they were poisoning the earth compelled her to write a book that would make it clear to ordinary people how chemical pesticides were destroying nature. It was an extraordinary act, singular and brave.

Once Carson began to divulge her observations and conclusions, gathered from a lifetime of experience and research, chemical interest groups spent more than a quarter of a million dollars fifty years ago trying to discredit her. "Bird and bunny lover" and "spinster" were terms of ridicule meant to undermine her knowledge and commitment. The campaign of disparagement, of placing articles that insinuated she lacked qualifications, was only the first tactic used to disturb and disrupt the dialogue she was proposing. They targeted her gender as a way to mock her authority.

Carson defined truth in the silences she would pursue. Her book was written in another age, different from the one we are now in. Carson was not asking for personal attention, not asking to be understood, not asking for glory. Her contribution was not Warhol's fifteen minutes of fame. She defined silence clearly as what was being purposely suppressed. With facts and reason, she wanted to stir waters, but not by saying one thing and meaning the opposite. She wanted to define a specific systemic silence and its effects. Her definition covered the renewal of nature as silent, meaning invisible, dying unnoticed, without protest. She implicated hiding from and repressing evidence by commercial interests who are poisoning the earth but are so powerful that they can divert attention from their role in nature's slow death.

Rachel Carson saw the danger in keeping silent—making no noise, no trouble, no waves. She, who would die of cancer soon after finishing the book, saw death as a many-headed monster. There was spiritual death. There was physical death as a sentence on the earth. There was her death. Silence was waiting for its definition, waiting to exit from its nothing state of not being audible. It was also waiting to be defined as a state beyond this life—a state where language borders on light. She wrote a book. It took time to read. It took time for science to coalesce around her observations and concerns.

Marguerite Yourcenar wrote that "the written word has taught me to listen to the human voice, much as the great unchanging statues have taught me to appreciate bodily motions. On the other hand, but more slowly, life has thrown light for me on the meaning of books."

Every angle of silence contains more than silence. We will hear the positive and negative valences in silences, the wild way words falsify and hurt and confuse. We will hear the faint new compositions already vibrating in the silence. We may hear ourselves thinking. We will see how new language always destroys some of the old. We will hear new stories of injustice, new angles on equality. That is right, but so difficult to extend and translate.

The man formerly in the United States' highest office has broken down norms that were assumed to be nearly common ones in U.S. history and laws. By using language decoupled from accountability, he has fomented a toxic climate of diminishing respect for language's importance, while creating alternative meanings for symbols of order. This has been done at a time when communication is instantaneous and everyone chimes in with their own view, which often lacks knowledge. The man formerly in the highest U.S. office has defaced the reliability of words, as the least scrupulous advertisers might, to sell products that should not be sold, and to break up carefully established understanding. He has partially succeeded in creating a blunt illusion that by having power one can define meaning at will. Our phones and computers, as well as the strange world of COVID, advertently and inadvertently have added to the new reality of a sudden sense of change, collapse, and disorientation. The connections are largely hidden. We don't know precisely which ones we need to understand. Identifying them will take pausing for breath as we test if what is under our feet can support our weight.

Yesterday in Parma, the ceremony for remembering the victims and survivors of Hiroshima, the Japanese city on which the United States dropped the world's first atomic bomb in 1945, attracted hundreds of participants. The Japanese custom of the living reaching out to ancestors by lighting candles and writing messages of peace, placing them in little origami boats to float out on the water, occurred in Parma on a hot night in which children ran barefoot and dogs flopped in the grass panting.

In Japan, many days in the month of August are dedicated to remembering the dead. The sixth of August, the day the first U.S. bomb was dropped, became an anniversary for the victims, but it is only one day among other August days to remember death, over centuries and kingdoms. The Japanese Obon festival in mid-August goes back as a ritual for five hundred years. It originated when a monk perceived that his mother in the other world was suffering.

The little origami boats, like pert paper hats, went out into the water of a three-hundred-foot trough once used in Parma by farmers to pile their stinking sugar beets for processing. Now it's a lily pond; the sugar beet factory has become a concert auditorium designed by Renzo Piano. The lights, wobbling and pooling together, a few odd boats wandering on their own but most tending to jam up, were intended for the dead, who were called upon to see them. The singular procession of flames were signs for the dead (wherever they were in the darkness) to lead them a little further.

As the boats were placed in the gently moving stream, it was easy to listen, not so easy that the water dripping from the filters at the edge could be heard, but a collective urge toward silent listening was felt.

What had become of life in Hiroshima by evening of that normal August day in 1945 was remembered. The newly invented, unimaginable suffering changed the meaning of normal forever. Traditional ceremonial drummers in the park pounded out centuries of sacred beats of excruciating intensity. The boats slid off into a ceremony that was not political. Children went first, letting their serious thoughts and precarious flames leave their hands by placing their boats in the water.

Since I had been searching through Marguerite Yourcenar in those very days, her observation came easily to me as my hands dipped: "Water drunk more reverently still, from the hands or from the spring itself, diffuses within us the most secret salt of the earth and the rain of heaven."

The dead? Where are they? The border between the two states may be different than each of us imagines it. But surely the dead travel on the waves of memory, oral history, music, written texts, tomb paintings, and love. And remembrance is not only of revenge and wrongs but the tentative beginnings of repair and healing, the messages sent out to the dead, who are wandering in our hearts, still in need of light and love.

Two more mass shootings in the United States coincided with the Hiroshima commemoration. The U.S. obsession starts all over again, the reasons, the history, the twists and turns skipping over the obvious: that the story of guns is not a need but a seed, planted deliberately in minds and fed by consciously targeted messages. It is a story of advertising, a manipulative campaign, which, among many other false narratives, has numbed people to critically resisting it with action. It's a story among many other stories about nature and civilization that are making the most powerful democracy on earth sick. As the coronavirus takes hold in the United States, citizens have purchased another two million guns as if they might protect them from the invisible enemy.

Someone sent me an email about Camus's *The Plague* and

how this current moment mirrors it. For me his novel was always about good and evil and how people must decide and join the collective, choosing to stand with the victims instead of with the cause of the plague. Saramago's novel *Blindness* touches me as a closer analogy to the present moment. It is not about morality as much as it is about an inability to see root causes. It is about ignorance on the level of a population. Saramago's narrative passes from one person, one victim, to another, to the narrator without making distinctions. They are all implicated, all unable to disentangle using rationality that favors one over another. New rules are present and the characters, who have all shared in the suffering and disorientation, will have to find their way with partial answers.

D ante used categories for each of his circles in the inferno to name sins that were orthodox ones in Christianity at the time—usury, sodomy, gluttony—and he interpreted them by placing practitioners, most often contemporary Florentines, as examples. He introduced each definition by using dialogue with one or two people confined by that sin, punishment, or state. They would then explain or interpret one or two personal experiences of that lapse. We meet various individuals and different nuances in behavior, judgment, repentance, and hardened indifference.

Dante learned on his journey, and in writing about it, he was interested in how readers might learn from these characters (historical figures or current ones) and their attitudes. He allowed the characters voices while revealing how he, on his journey, understood or rejected or was skeptical of the category or the punishment or the repulsive situation of a character who showed no remorse. He continued to go backward and forward in his story as he ascended, because he wished to recount how he felt and how he changed in time. His was not a conversion memoir like Saint Augustine's. His was an unwritten story about a journey that, when he wrote it, still was not over.

Dante, the man on a journey, the man being written about

by Dante the writer in his epic poem *The Divine Comedy*, is a strand in a series of perceptions and dialogues and events and orthodoxies. Dante the writer does not insist on defending his point of view. In organizing his poem into three sections, like many Medieval paintings, and by making love its center, he spoke to the reader about it from many positions. It's a continuous exploration of explanations. Virgil, in Purgatory, canto 17, referring to the three circles in love, mirrors this unwinding theme: "I'll keep quiet about how the three-part arrangement works so that you will probe it for yourself."

This freedom and direct address released the originality at the heart of his poem. Eight hundred years ago Dante invited readers to find their own way and to use his journey for their own purposes.

His poem, by starting from a place, dark woods, that had no physical attributions of a political place, led us through circles where historical figures, and specifically a majority of contemporary Florentine figures, were commented upon. But when he reaches heaven, Beatrice sends him back to a place where he, as a writer, will reconstruct what he has seen. By the time he actually writes it, he will be in exile.

The fluidity of a life and how to narrate it is laid out by Dante centuries before it becomes an issue for modernists. The walls of Florence, expanded by the city three times in order to protect its wealth, change for him during the period he was narrating. Once he became an exile, those protecting walls turned into walls that kept him apart from his beloved city. He turned from an insider to an enemy. The thick stone walls become "cruelty which shuts me out from the beautiful fold where I slept as a lamb." The orthodoxy, the ideology of fixed points and singular logical arguments, are shown to be limited and temporal since his journey keeps moving life forward into greater consciousness.

Beatrice sent him back to write about his journey. He will interpret it and insert himself into it, as an actor writing about himself, and thus show changes in understanding, positions in time, who he was when he was in the inferno journeying with Virgil, and who he was as a man who had felt God's light and was trying to describe a journey when the man still had not reached that awareness. He will show contradictions and human longing to get beyond orthodoxy. He will look for loopholes in dogma, for example, for an exception for Virgil, who by orthodox thinking cannot ever reach heaven. The tenses will keep changing because, as Boccaccio wrote, his narration was "a new and never finished journey of this life."

Italians then and now call nonfiction "a novel," an invented narration. Amos Oz, in defending the truth of the novel, said that as a novelist he was neither a "prophet" nor a "guide." "The novelist," he wrote, "has no political aim but is concerned with truth, not facts." He took issue with the language often called nonfiction, finding its defense of being factual rather harmful. His example of a "boiling cauldron," taken from a news report to describe the Middle East, he judged approximate and its analysis, meant to be objective, close to the worst in fiction. Tolstoy's *War and Peace* for Oz represented a precision and a fullness that made it far truer to history than most historical accounts.

That is why it is more than a joke when we admit the consequences for a nation when its president, using the powerful platform of public office, deprecates language and how it binds to searches for truth. It is why sound bites are not sufficient for helping us understand. It takes time to understand how precious understanding is.

So here I am in Yonkers. Headlights are just turning on in the cars pouring down the Bronx River Parkway. Am I deaf enough to listen to silence and touch glyphs of beauty and love? Not magic, but facts and feelings and, beyond those coins, the challenges that life, in darkness and light, offers us. The white heron and the smoky-blue heron made recent appearances. Both, when they open their wings, accept living their revolts and their places in the environment.

The smoky heron's return was startling. I noticed him sick and miserably hunched up on the other side of the waterfall. He had come back. And then tonight, on the little dune, on the other side, he was so integrated with the falling light that he was barely a shadow. Paolo didn't see him and I had to insist, tugging his sleeve and pointing him toward the river. Then the white heron swooped in, and the smoky-blue heron and the white heron appeared together, each on a separate island of sand. They stood on different little sandbanks and then flew off, one immediately following the other into the darkness. Both flew, one far more visible but then both invisible, somewhere farther down the river. The night was wide open. For some reason, I thought of that freedom and then corruption: how corruption is wide open, in plain view, and how words are corrupted, and how we have very little time left to go beyond. Our work is not to be known but to be real, not earth-shaking necessarily, but winged. There are austere challenges all around, and, like the herons, we cannot live apart from them.

It's night, nearly night, my readers. The light is changing, growing dark, and in this changing over, the herons have flown off where they can hide and rest, put down their guard. I followed them as far as I could. Now I am alone, with my own sense of direction. I, too, want to lift. And to hide and to rest, put down my guard. It will take morning light to see them again, find them perhaps grazing in the mud, camouflaged. But when the birds open their wings and lift against the sky, I can say, having gone through my own night, wings are the rhythm, wings beating, open, uncovering for anyone to see their heart.

NOTES AT THE END

The direction in silence, the temporal forward-and-backward movement rippling through this text, ends with wings. I originally came to the last page and finished with tree roots, outside of us, holding that essential place on earth. I add the silence of roots here. We need both wings and roots.

I didn't use photos as I have in my previous books. Visual material is so powerful that it has gradually altered our relationship to thought. A book on silence needed words, with their undefiled power, to establish and define a rich domain.

The spaces in the text are invitations to rest. I came to see them as similar to benches in museums, where one takes in a whole room, thinks, selects, and gathers energy before visiting the next room. It's an honor to publish a book with a publisher for whom a generous layout is seen as part of the subject.

While knowing that ornithologists might raise flags, I never questioned the name I gave to the long-necked creature in Yonkers. It was and shall remain a white heron. Books of typology explain that the white herons seen in the northern United States are most often great white egrets. Yet white herons do exist. Those at Yaddo were called blue herons, by me and other residents. The smoky fellow under the bridge is sometimes called the green heron, or an ash heron. Parma seems to attract white herons, because other birds in the same space are clearly great white egrets.

Last year when Paolo and I were in Turin, we spent hours at the superb Egyptian museum. The crowds were dense, something that now, with social distancing, seems like a hallucination. In the early rooms, which are more didactic, general explanations of Egyptian culture are offered. In the long papyrus room, thronged with people trying to get close to the scrolls under glass, a single opening appeared. I moved forward into the parting. Before my eyes, two drawings of hieroglyphs: the heron and the phoenix. The heron: hunter, snake killer, fighter of evil. The phoenix: Egyptian symbol of life and rebirth; some think it to be the purple heron. My system of names rests with that sense of nature and myth. As does my interchangeable use of Yonkers and Bronxville. The railroad tracks put us in Yonkers as taxpayers, but the post-office zip code assigns us to Bronxville.

Thank-yous also require distinctions. The crucial ones necessarily remain formal because they are public; much help remains acknowledged in a place that is private. My deep appreciation extends to Jonathan Galassi, an editor who offered me support and freedom—a near-fabled combination that called me to attention and changed my life. I wish to thank Katharine Liptak for her intelligent and perceptive guidance through many subtle editorial decisions. Paolo, my husband, as always, offered unmeasured help and stimulation, while accepting the demands of my writing a book. For the long Covid lockdown, as another gift, he became an even more impressive cook. Anna Podestà and Susan Tiberghien reading the first draft, with lightning insights, made me see where to go. My brother Alex read the final draft, adding helpful remarks.

Tobias Jones, a British journalist living in Parma, sent me various emails signaling other books with silence as a topic. I didn't read any then, but they made me aware that the topic is crucial to our time. Now that I have read several, I am certain that the topic is inexhaustible.

In the months in which we were quarantined in Italy, I finished my final draft. Being confined was an unexpected solution to experiencing many kinds of silence and solitudes. In those months, two were painful limits. A friend in Florence, with whom I have shared experiences over half a century, was losing her husband. It was an extraordinary last chapter for a man who had already faced death, starting from being born a Jewish child in Budapest in World War II to leaving his family and becoming a refugee at sixteen when Russia invaded Hungary. Largely confined to bed for seven months, having refused further treatment, he faced death this time as a card he held, and as in bridge, his passion, he played his hand magnificently, with daring, imagination, and grace. The closed frontier blocked us in his last month.

Equally painful was realizing that the distance between my daughter, her husband, and our granddaughters might become a permanent challenge. We had grown used to crossing the ocean as if it were normal. Always on the lookout for the next bargain ticket or teaching opportunity, we had never fully appreciated how we could share our lives with our eyes, our arms, our tears and shouts. The experience of screens, indeed another human miracle, tested the limits of virtual contact, especially with the children. A screen conditions; awareness of it sets up something that is more performance than sharing. A kind of involuntary censorship of the real and the deep leaves vague sensations of frustration and alienation.

I feel the barrier as if we are birds hitting closed windows. The resistance may well grow. I hope my daughter's family will welcome letters, allowing me to return to the hand where I can speak silently face-to-face. That releases energies in thought and love, slowing down time, making me feel closer and the distance bearable.